"*Tough Topics* offers every questioning person an opportunity to press thoughtfully into the Bible's answers. Sam Storms is that rare guide we all are looking for—fair-minded, with no axe to grind. I cheerfully commend *Tough Topics* for your tough questions!"

Ray Ortlund, Lead Pastor, Immanuel Church, Nashville, Tennessee

"Let's face it, the church has not always done the best possible job at fielding the hard questions posed to it by both skeptics and members. In the case of the first group, skeptics end up discounting Christianity, dismissing it as irrational, head-in-the-sand religious fanaticism. In the case of the second group, members become frustrated with the Christian faith and often drift away from what they have found to be a shallow, inconsistent, and quite unsatisfying worldview. Sam Storms is a leader whom the Lord has wonderfully gifted not only to answer the tough questions, but also to provide an accessible resource for Christian leaders to be better prepared to engage skeptics and church members who wrestle with these issues rather than to rebuff them and discount their difficulties. Sam's passion is to deal with twenty-five of the most challenging questions you will ever face, and to do it in such a way that you become convinced of the answers and are prepared to offer help to others who face them as well. He accomplishes this goal, not by offering his own good ideas and the best of human counsel, but by relying on the wisdom of God as found in Scripture."

Gregg R. Allison, Professor of Christian Theology, The Southern Baptist Theological Seminary; author, *Historical Theology: An Introduction to Christian Doctrine* and *Sojourners and Strangers: The Doctrine of the Church*

"Sam Storms's *Tough Topics* is equally the work of a deeply concerned and caring pastor and that of a thoughtful, seasoned, and biblically saturated theologian. As I read this book, specific people kept coming to mind who would be helped greatly by one or more of its chapters—such wisdom, balance, and biblical clarity. Readers will likely differ at points with their pastor-theologian guide, but they will rise up and thank him for offering such wise counsel on a wide array of difficult and important questions. There's something here for everyone. Pick up and read, and see how faithful pastoral theology really does bless the church."

Bruce A. Ware, Professor of Christian Theology, The Southern Baptist Theological Seminary

"Some questions about God and the Bible intrigue us. Others get completely under our skin and frustrate us. The chances are good that if a question is bothering you, you are not the first to ask it! Sam Storms draws on all his pastoral experience in this helpful book as he honestly answers questions some people like to avoid."

Adrian Warnock, author, *Raised with Christ*; blogger

"People are inquisitive by nature. It is the way God made us. We have all kinds of questions about him. When people learn that I teach theology for a living, the first thing they do is begin to ask questions—*tough questions*. Sam Storms has given us an incredibly useful resource in his book *Tough Topics*. He has braved the minefield of some of the most difficult questions people have concerning God, the Bible, the church, and Christianity in general. What I like about this work is not simply its accessibility, but also Sam's gentle and balanced scholarship. When we have questions about God, that is no casual thing requiring the opinions of sages on street corners. These are serious questions requiring someone who is well versed in the Bible. Sam has always been one to whom I go when I have questions. Now I have the book! And, as Sam says, the answers to these questions do not drive us to be puffed up in knowledge—they drive us to worship."

C. Michael Patton, President, Credo House Ministries; author, *Increase My Faith* and *Now That I'm a Christian*; blogger, Parchment and Pen

"Sam Storms is an ideal guide to help us navigate through difficult theological questions. He brings a pastor's heart and four decades of caring for souls to the journey. Along with that, he brings the brilliant mind of a trained theologian. He writes because he cares deeply about the truth and because he loves people. The answers in this book bring clarity instead of confusion. The stated goal of the book is knowledge that leads to worship. Mission accomplished!"

Erik Thoennes, Professor of Biblical Studies and Theology, Talbot School of Theology, Biola University; Pastor, Grace Evangelical Free Church, La Mirada, California; author, *Life's Biggest Questions*

Tough Topics

Other Books in the Re:Lit Series

Everyday Church: Gospel Communities on Mission,
Tim Chester and Steve Timmis (2012)

Mistakes Leaders Make, Dave Kraft (2012)

The Explicit Gospel, Matt Chandler with Jared Wilson (2012)

Gospel-Centered Discipleship, Jonathan K. Dodson (2012)

Rid of My Disgrace: Hope and Healing for Victims of Sexual Assault,
Justin S. Holcomb and Lindsey A. Holcomb (2011)

*Redemption: Freed by Jesus from the Idols We Worship and
the Wounds We Carry*, Mike Wilkerson (2011)

*A Meal with Jesus: Discovering Grace, Community, and
Mission around the Table*, Tim Chester (2011)

Note to Self: The Discipline of Preaching to Yourself, Joe Thorn (2011)

Community: Taking Your Small Group off Life Support, Brad House (2011)

Disciple: Getting Your Identity from Jesus, Bill Clem (2011)

Church Planter: The Man, the Message, the Mission, Darrin Patrick (2010)

Doctrine: What Christians Should Believe, Mark Driscoll
and Gerry Breshears (2010)

Scandalous: The Cross and Resurrection of Jesus, D. A. Carson (2010)

Leaders Who Last, Dave Kraft (2010)

Vintage Church: Timeless Truths and Timely Methods,
Mark Driscoll and Gerry Breshears (2009)

Religion Saves: And Nine Other Misconceptions, Mark Driscoll (2009)

Total Church: A Radical Reshaping around Gospel and Community,
Tim Chester and Steve Timmis (2008)

*Practical Theology for Women: How Knowing God Makes a Difference
in Our Daily Lives*, Wendy Horger Alsup (2008)

Vintage Jesus: Timeless Answers to Timely Questions,
Mark Driscoll and Gerry Breshears (2008)

Death by Love: Letters from the Cross, Mark Driscoll
and Gerry Breshears (2008)

R | RE:LIT

Tough Topics

Biblical Answers to 25 Challenging Questions

Sam Storms

:: CROSSWAY

WHEATON, ILLINOIS

Library of Congress Cataloging-in-Publication Data

Storms, C. Samuel, 1951–
   Tough topics : Biblical answers to 25 challenging ques-
tions / Sam Storms.
      p. cm.— (Re:Lit)
   Includes bibliographical references and index.
   ISBN 978-1-4335-3493-5
   1. Theology, Doctrinal—Popular works. I. Title.
BT77.S735   2013
230—dc23   2012046023

Affectionately dedicated to
my two sons-in-law
Brad and Brett

May your love for God's Word, even its "tough topics,"
deepen and intensify

Contents

Preface

Lucy and Linus are gazing out the window at a staggering downpour.

"Boy, look at it rain," Lucy says, fear etched on her face. "What if it floods the whole world?"

"It will never do that," Linus responds confidently. "In the ninth chapter of Genesis, God promised Noah that would never happen again, and the sign of the promise is the rainbow."

"You've taken a great load off my mind," Lucy says with a sigh of relief.

Linus replies, "Sound theology has a way of doing that!"

That is my aim in this book: to articulate good theology in order to put worried minds at rest. All of us are familiar with the sorts of problems and questions and doctrinal conundrums that plague the human mind and agitate the human heart, questions like the one lingering in the thinking of Lucy: Will God ever flood the entire earth again?

In my experience these nearly forty years of Christian ministry, I've seen countless people worried and angry and fearful and just plain confused when it comes to some of the more perplexing issues that life poses and the Bible provokes, such as:

- Sam, is my baby in heaven?
- Is it ever okay to divorce your spouse, and if it is, can I get remarried?

- What about the heathen in Africa who've never heard the gospel?
- My neighbor said I have to be baptized to be saved. Is she right?
- If my friend goes to hell, how can I possibly enjoy heaven?
- I'm so angry with my father. People tell me I should forgive him. What does that mean?
- I'm afraid I've committed blasphemy against the Holy Spirit. Have I?
- Do demons exist? What can they do to me? What can I do to them?
- Is it ever okay to lie?
- Will there be sex in heaven?

These aren't ordinary questions that yield to an easy or simplistic answer. These are among the most challenging subjects people face. The failure to provide a good and biblical answer often leaves Christians in fear or guilt or confusion and can occasionally erode their confidence in the sufficiency of Scripture to say something meaningful and satisfying. *Tough Topics* makes no claim to answer every question Christians ask. But it does propose to provide solid and scriptural answers to twenty-five of them. Sadly, many believers walk away from church or from a friend or even from a pastor, frustrated that such issues are either answered badly or met with an "I don't know," or perhaps even ignored altogether. My aim in this book is to overcome that frustration by looking deeply, not superficially, at what Scripture says and deriving clear and persuasive explanations for these thorny matters.

The chapters vary in length, often in direct proportion to the difficulty of the questions they seek to answer. All are written with the educated Christian layperson in mind. In only a few places do I appeal to the original Greek text, and when I do, it is done in such a way that the person who reads only English can follow the argument.

My hope is that in providing the body of Christ with a resource of this length and depth, much confusion will be removed, and hours of unproductive research can be reduced. In none of the chapters do I respond with a short or simplistic answer. My desire is that by looking deeply into the biblical text and by stretching our minds to explore every possible option, we will walk away not only more informed about what the Bible teaches but also, and even more importantly, more in awe of the greatness and goodness of God. In other words, *the ultimate aim of this book isn't knowledge; it's worship.* By seeing more clearly how God acts and what he meant and why he responds the way he does, I trust that we all will love him more passionately and praise him more fervently.

I suppose some might be tempted to conclude that the easy thing to do would simply be to say "yes" or "no" or "sometimes" to the twenty-five questions posed in this book, and leave it at that. But that wouldn't be of much help to you when it comes to knowing *why* the Bible provides the answer it does. If you never move beyond the shallow one-word response to the most puzzling and pressing questions in life, you will forever remain spiritually stunted and immature. And you will be of little to no benefit to others who approach you with their curiosity about these matters. Your grasp of who God is and how and why he does what he does would not be very deep or substantive. The bottom line is this: we need to wrestle with the hard texts and the tough topics in Scripture. Only then will our thinking skills be honed, our minds expanded, our spirits enriched, and our hearts filled with joy and delight to understand the mysterious ways of our great God and Savior.

Some of these chapters may well leave you hungry for more. For that reason I've included a brief list of recommended reading to help you continue your pursuit of a more comprehensive explanation in each case.

Most of these chapters stand independent of each other. In other words, you may want to scan the table of contents and read first (or perhaps only) those chapters that intrigue you most. However, there are a few chapters that answer questions related to each other, which is to say they are concerned with the same general theme in Scripture. In those cases I recommend that you read them in order because they do build upon one another to some extent. But on the whole, I've written the book so that the person who wishes to read it more selectively can do so without significant loss.

1

Is the Bible Inerrant?

This book is entirely devoted to providing what I hope will be biblical answers to hard questions people ask. What you or I may *prefer* to be true or what may or may not make us *feel comfortable* or what appears to our *judgment* to be fair or unfair simply doesn't matter. When we say we believe in the inspiration, inerrancy, and authority of the Bible, we are making known that the only answers we will embrace to troublesome questions are those found in Scripture. It seems only appropriate, therefore, that we begin our journey together by asking: Is the Bible in fact inerrant? Are the answers that it gives us always true? Can we trust what the Word of God says on any subject on which it speaks? So let's get started!

By What Authority?

There is no more critical issue in life than that of authority. In other words, by what standard, or on what grounds, and from what source, and for what reasons do you believe something to be true and therefore binding on your conscience (beliefs) and conduct (behavior)?

Authority for the Christian is thought to come from one of three sources. For some, primarily Roman Catholics and those in the Eastern Orthodox tradition, the consensus of the *church* as expressed in its traditions and creedal formulations is the authoritative guide to God's will. Hence, as far as these folk are concerned, "What the church says, God says." A few would insist that the *individual* is the final authority, such that the Bible and the church are little more than resource materials to assist each person in making up his or her own mind on what is true and authoritative. Thus, they conclude, "What my own spirit says, God says."

I hope that you are among those who embrace the third option. According to this view, the *Bible* is the final authority for all matters of faith and life. Consider how this is stated in the Westminster Confession of Faith: "The supreme judge by which all controversies are to be determined, and all decrees of councils, opinions of ancient writers, doctrines of men, and private spirits, are to be examined, and in whose sentence we are to rest, can be no other but the Holy Spirit speaking in the Scripture."[1] Thus, "What Scripture says, God says."

It is for this third option that I will contend. The first paragraph in most local church doctrinal statements affirms belief in the inspiration and authority of the sixty-six books of the Bible. How could it be otherwise? For apart from a belief in the authority of Scripture, we would have no way of knowing with any certainty whether any of the remaining doctrinal affirmations is true or false. If the Bible is not the sole, sufficient revelation of God himself, how could we possibly know that God is a Trinity of coequal persons, or that the second person of that Trinity became a man in Jesus of Nazareth and died for sinners and was raised on the third day? Simply put, the inspiration and authority of the Bible is the *bedrock* upon which our faith is built. Without it, we are doomed to uncertainty, doubt, and a hopeless groping in the darkness of human speculation.

But do we have good reason to believe that this book, the Bible, is different from Plato's *Republic* or Shakespeare's *Hamlet* or any

---

[1] The Westminster Confession of Faith 1.10.

other human composition? Why do we believe that the sixty-six books of the Bible are divine revelation and authoritative for belief and life? There are any number of reasons, drawn from historical, archaeological, theological, and experiential resources and arguments (perhaps chief among which is that the Holy Spirit has borne witness in our hearts that Scripture is God's Word). But we must also take into consideration that *Jesus himself clearly believed in the inspiration and authority of Scripture.* Being a disciple of Jesus entails not only doing what Jesus did *but also believing what Jesus believed.* It is impossible to accept the authority of Christ without also accepting the authority of Scripture. To believe and receive Jesus as Lord and Savior is to believe and receive what he taught about Scripture.

Clearly, then, the question What do you think of the Bible? reduces to the question What do you think of Christ? To deny the authority of Scripture is to deny the lordship of Jesus. Consider the people and events of the Old Testament, for example, which Jesus frequently mentioned. He referred to Abel, Noah and the great flood, Abraham, Sodom and Gomorrah, Lot, Isaac and Jacob, the manna from heaven, the serpent in the desert, David eating the consecrated bread and his authorship of the Psalms, Solomon, Elijah, Elisha, and Zechariah, and so on. In each case he treated the Old Testament narrative as a straightforward record of historical fact.

But, critics respond, perhaps Jesus was simply *accommodating* himself to the mistaken beliefs of his contemporaries. That is to say, Jesus simply met his contemporaries on their own ground without necessarily committing himself to the correctness of their views. He chose graciously not to upset them by questioning the veracity of their belief in the truth and authority of the Bible.

I'm sorry, but that's not the Jesus about whom I read in the New Testament. The Jesus of the Gospels was not at all sensitive about undermining mistaken, though long-cherished, beliefs among the people of his day. He loudly and often denounced the traditions of the Pharisees and took on their distortion of the Old Testament law in the Sermon on the Mount. Jesus challenged nationalistic conceptions of the kingdom of God and the coming of the Messiah. He was even willing to face death on a cross for the truth of what he declared. In referring to the Old Testament, Jesus declared that "the Scripture cannot be broken" (John 10:35). Again, "It is easier for heaven and earth to pass away than for one dot of the law to become void" (Luke 16:17; see also Mark 7:6–13; Luke 16:29–31). He rebuked the Sadducees, saying, "You are wrong, because you know neither the Scriptures nor the power of God" (Matt. 22:29). When faced with Satan's temptations, it was to the truth and authority of the Old Testament that he appealed (Matt. 4:4–10). Note especially his words, "It is written." And Jesus didn't hesitate to deliberately offend the religious sensibilities of his contemporaries when he chose to eat and socialize with both publicans and prostitutes.

There is a tendency in some evangelical circles to drive a wedge between revelation (the transcendent Word of God) and the Bible (understood as man's written record of or witness to the Word). It is said that we cannot identify the words of Scripture with divine revelation. Rather, the words are the sacramental means or instrumentality by which divine revelation encounters or engages us experientially. The writings of Scripture are said to *mediate* the revelatory Word to us. But the former are not identical with the latter.

I believe, on the other hand, what Augustine meant when he envisioned God saying, "O man, true it is that *what My Scripture says I myself say.*"[2] Scripture is thus the "transcript of divine speech."[3] In his article "Inspiration," J. I. Packer unpacks the significance of this principle:

> Christ and his apostles quote Old Testament texts not merely as what, e.g., Moses, David or Isaiah said (see Mk. 7:10, 12:36, 7:6; Rom. 10:5, 11:9, 10:20, etc.), but also as what God said through these men (see Acts 4:25, 28:25, etc.), or sometimes simply what "he" (God) says (e.g., 2 Cor. 6:16; Heb. 8:5, 8), or what the Holy Ghost says (Heb. 3:7, 10:15). Furthermore, Old Testament statements, not made by God in their contexts, are quoted as utterances of God (Mt. 19:4f.; Heb. 3:7; Acts 13:34f.; citing Gen. 2:24; Ps. 95:7;

---

[2] *The Confessions of St. Augustine*, trans. John K. Ryan (New York: Doubleday, 1960), 13.29 (emphasis mine).

[3] J. I. Packer, *God Has Spoken: Revelation and the Bible*, 3rd ed. (Grand Rapids: Baker, 1998), 28.

Is. 55:3 respectively). Also, Paul refers to God's promise to Abraham and his threat to Pharaoh, both spoken long before the biblical record of them was written, as words which *Scripture* spoke to these two men (Gal. 3:8; Rom. 9:17); which shows how completely he equated the statements of Scripture with the utterance of God.[4]

Let's begin by defining two critical terms: *revelation* and *inspiration*. Revelation is the activity of God by which he unveils or discloses or makes known what is otherwise unknowable to humanity. It is God making himself known to those shaped in his image. Revelation is what God does, not what mankind achieves. It is a divinely initiated disclosure, not an effort or endeavor or achievement on the part of mankind. Packer explains: "Revelation does not mean man finding God, but God finding man, God sharing His secrets with us, God showing us Himself. In revelation, God is the agent as well as the object."[5] The God of the Bible, notes Donald Bloesch, "is not a God who is discovered in the depths of nature or uncovered in human consciousness. Nor is he a God who is immediately discernible in the events of history. . . . For the living God to be known, he must make himself known, and he has done this in the acts and words recorded in Scripture."[6]

Much has been made of an alleged distinction between revelation as *propositional* and revelation as *personal*. Since God is himself a person, so some say, revelation cannot be propositional (or at least, not primarily so). Revelation is God making *himself* known, the event of disclosing his person to other persons. But Packer is certainly correct in pointing out that this distinction should not be pressed too far. He notes:

> Personal friendship between God and man, grows just as human friendships do—namely, through talking; and talking means making informative statements, and informative statements are propositions. . . . [Indeed] to say that revelation is non-propositional is actually to *depersonalize* it. . . . To maintain that we may know

---

[4] J. I. Packer, "Inspiration," in *The New Bible Dictionary*, ed. J. D. Douglas et al. (London: Inter-Varsity, 1962), 564.

[5] Packer, *God Has Spoken*, 47.

[6] Donald G. Bloesch, *A Theology of Word and Spirit: Authority and Method in Theology* (Downers Grove, IL: InterVarsity, 1992), 20.

God without God actually speaking to us in words is really to deny that God is personal, or at any rate that knowing Him is a truly personal relationship.[7]

In other words, special revelation is a *verbal* activity, in the sense that "God has communicated with man by means of significant utterances: statements, questions, and commands, spoken either in His own person or on His behalf by His own appointed messengers and instructors."[8] This does not mean that God is less active, less personal, as if he were nothing but a celestial lecturer. He discloses himself by powerful acts in history, encountering his people, showing himself gracious by redeeming them, kind by forgiving them, strong by delivering them, and so forth. The Bible "itself is essentially a recital of His doings, an explanatory narrative of the great drama of the bringing in of His kingdom, and the saving of the world."[9] Let us not forget that faith is often portrayed in Scripture as trusting, often against great odds, what God has *said* (see Rom. 4:3; Gal. 3:6; Heb. 6:13ff.; 11:8–13, 17, 33).

The fact that revelation is verbal does not mean that knowing God is simply a matter of memorizing texts or cataloging doctrines.

But what the claim that revelation is essentially verbal does imply is that no historical event, as such, can make God known to anyone unless God Himself discloses its meaning and place in His plan. Providential happenings may serve to remind us, more or less vividly, that God is at work (cf. Acts 14:17), but their link, if any, with His saving purpose cannot be known until He Himself informs us of it. No event is self-interpreting at this level.[10]

Again,

All history is, in one sense, God's deed, but none of it reveals Him except in so far as He Himself talks to us about it. God's revelation is not through deeds without words (a dumb charade!) any more than it is through words without deeds; but it is through

---

[7] Packer, *God Has Spoken*, 52–53.
[8] Ibid., 63.
[9] Ibid., 71.
[10] Ibid., 72.

deeds which He speaks to interpret, or, putting it more biblically, through words which His deeds confirm and fulfill.[11]

Packer's point is simply this:

> No public historical happening, as such (an exodus, a conquest, a captivity, a crucifixion, an empty tomb), can reveal God apart from an accompanying word from God to explain it, or a prior promise which it is seen to confirm or fulfill. Revelation in its basic form is thus of necessity propositional; God reveals Himself by telling us about Himself, and what He is doing in His world.[12]

The notion of propositional revelation in no way denies the revelatory activity of God in events, in personal encounters, or in the dynamic and relational ways whereby he engages his people and makes himself immediately and experientially known to them (see Heb. 1:1). The "many ways" in which God revealed himself personally included theophanies, angelic visitations, an audible voice from heaven, visions, dreams, supernatural writing, inward impressions, natural phenomena, and more. But in each of these instances the divine disclosures introduced or confirmed by these means were propositional in substance and verbal in form. In other words, whereas not every statement or revelatory deed comes to us in strict propositional form, all do in fact *presuppose a proposition* on the basis of which a truth claim about the nature of reality is being made.

Another characteristic of revelation is that it is *progressive*, that is, cumulative. God has not revealed himself comprehensively at any one stage in history or in any one event. Revelation is a series of divine disclosures, each of which builds upon and unpacks or unfolds that which preceded it. Revelation moves from what is piecemeal and partial and incomplete (but always accurate) to what is comprehensive and final and unified. This contrast between the incomplete and complete, between the partial and the full, is not a contrast between false and true, inaccurate and accu-

---

[11] Ibid., 73.
[12] Ibid., 76–77.

rate, but a contrast between shadow and substance, between type and antitype, between promise and fulfillment.

Inspiration, on the other hand, was the related process whereby God preserved the biblical authors from error when communicating, whether by his voice or in writing, that which he had shown them. The Holy Spirit *superintended* the writing of Scripture, that is to say, he acted to insure that what the human authors intended by their words is equivalent to what God intended (a process also referred to as *concursive inspiration*). Thus "each resultant oracle was as truly a divine utterance as a human, as direct a disclosure of what was in God's mind as of what was in the prophet's."[13] The Spirit thus brought the free and spontaneous thoughts of the human author into coincidence with the thoughts of God.

Many question how this can be done. They contend that if God's control over what the biblical authors said was exhaustive, they must have written as mindless automatons. On the other hand, if their minds operated freely according to their own volitional creativity, then God cannot have kept them free from error. But this dilemma "rests on the assumption that full psychological freedom of thought and action, and full subjection to divine control, are incompatible."[14]

The doctrine of *verbal, plenary* (i.e., complete, total) *inspiration* means that *the words of the Bible are the words of God*. This doesn't mean that God spoke every word himself, but that the words spoken by the authors of Scripture are the words that God desired them to speak in the revelation of himself. Thus there is no significant difference between the ultimate authority of God and the immediate authority of Scripture. "The authority of Scripture is the divine authority of God Himself speaking."[15] Some argue that one cannot stand under the authority of the living Word, Jesus Christ, and at the same time stand under the authority of the written Word, the Bible. This is a false antithesis. Jesus Christ is the Lord of the Scriptures and in the latter the former is revealed and

---

[13] Ibid., 91.
[14] Ibid., 93.
[15] Ibid., 96.

made known, and his will unfolded. To obey the latter is to obey the former. To disobey the latter is to disobey the former.

Inerrancy

The debate over whether Scripture is inerrant shows no signs of slowing down, much less going away. Among evangelicals, two views have dominated the landscape. Some embrace what has been called "limited inerrancy." One of the more able and articulate defenders of this view is Daniel Fuller.[16] According to Fuller and those who follow his lead, the inerrancy of a book or piece of literature can be evaluated solely in light of the author's intention or purpose. Does the author fulfill his or her purpose in writing? If so, the work is inerrant. If not, it is not. The purpose of the Bible, they say, is to make us "wise unto salvation" (2 Tim. 3:15). The purpose of the Bible is not to make us wise unto botany or geology or astronomy or history. Rather, according to Fuller, the biblical writers declare that their purpose is to report the events and meaning of the redemptive acts of God in history so that men might be made wise unto salvation. By this criterion, says Fuller, the Bible is inerrant. It perfectly lives up to its purpose. It never fails to fulfill its purpose or intent of making the reader wise unto salvation.

Since, in this view, inerrancy should be expected only in the case of those biblical assertions which teach or rightly imply knowledge that makes man wise unto salvation, Scripture can and does err in other matters. That is to say, there are passages in the Bible that are but incidentally related or entirely unrelated to its primary purpose. Fuller calls these incidents or texts *nonrevelational* matters—biblical statements on such topics as geology, meteorology, cosmology, botany, astronomy, geography, history, and the like. Since the *principal aim* or *authorial intent* of Scripture is *not* to teach truths on such matters as these, such statements may err while the statements in keeping with its primary purpose remain

---

[16] See his two articles, "The Nature of Biblical Inerrancy," *Journal of the American Scientific Affiliation* 24, no. 2 (June 1972); and "Benjamin B. Warfield's View of Faith and History," *Bulletin of the Evangelical Theological Society* 11, no. 2 (Spring 1968).

inerrant. The Bible is inerrant on those matters it intends to teach, matters essential to making us wise unto salvation. These, and these alone, are revelatory.

Fuller is not saying that the Bible *cannot* err on revelational matters. He is saying that on nonrevelational matters there may indeed be errors in Scripture (he believes there are), but that on revelational matters he has discovered none yet and hopes he never will. "I sincerely hope," writes Fuller, "that as I continue my historical-grammatical exegesis of Scripture, I shall find no error in its teachings. But I can only affirm inerrancy with high probability."[17]

Contrary to the above perspective, the Bible makes no distinction between inspired and uninspired texts or topics, nor does it place any restrictions on the kinds of subjects on which it speaks truthfully (see esp. Luke 24:25; Acts 24:14; Rom. 15:4; 1 Cor. 10:11). Thus I embrace and want to argue for what I'll call the doctrine of "complete inerrancy." Some prefer that we use the word *infallibility*, which comes from the Latin *infallibilitas*, meaning the quality of neither deceiving nor being deceived. *Inerrancy* comes from the Latin *inerrantia* and simply means freedom from error. This means that Scripture does not affirm anything contrary to fact. Together both ideas express the idea that all Scripture comes to us as the very words of God and is thus reliable and true and free of error. Consider these definitions of inerrancy, each of which makes an excellent contribution to our understanding of what is at stake:

> Inerrancy will then mean that at no point in what was originally given were the biblical writers allowed to make statements or endorse viewpoints which are not in conformity with objective truth. This applies at any level at which they make pronouncements.[18]

> Inerrancy means that when all facts are known, the Scriptures in their original autographs and properly interpreted will be shown

---

[17] Daniel Fuller, "On Revelation and Biblical Authority," *Journal of the Evangelical Theological Society* 16, no. 2 (Spring 1973): 67–69.

[18] Roger R. Nicole, "The Nature of Inerrancy," in *Inerrancy and Common Sense*, ed. Roger R. Nicole and J. Ramsey Michaels (Grand Rapids: Baker, 1980), 88.

to be wholly true in everything that they affirm, whether that has to do with doctrine or morality or with the social, physical, or life sciences.[19]

When all the facts are known, the Bible (in its original writings) properly interpreted in light of which culture and communication means had developed by the time of its composition will be shown to be completely true (and therefore not false) in all that it affirms, to the degree of precision intended by the author, in all matters relating to God and his creation.[20]

Except for the types of textual corruption that can arise in the course of repeated copying, the Bible offers an accurate, though not comprehensive, description and interpretation of the world and human history from the creation to the rise of the Christian church, as well as a reliable record of divinely revealed truths about God and his plans for humanity, which careful exegesis can demonstrate to be internally consistent and concerning which, through fair and informed analysis, plausible solutions for apparently fundamental conflicts between it and objective extra-biblical data can be suggested.[21]

2 Timothy 3:16–17

Anytime the concepts of inspiration and inerrancy are mentioned, 2 Timothy 3:16–17 soon becomes the focus of discussion. "All Scripture," writes the apostle Paul, "is breathed out by God and profitable for teaching, for reproof, for correction, and for training in righteousness, that the man of God may be complete, equipped for every good work." It will do us well to make a few observations on what Paul meant.

The word "all" (in "all Scripture") has a collective sense and means the whole of Scripture: the entirety of the Bible, inclusive of all its parts. Some translations employ the term "every," which has a distributive sense and means each Scripture individually, the

---

[19] Paul Feinberg, "The Meaning of Inerrancy," in *Inerrancy*, ed. Norman L. Geisler (Grand Rapids: Zondervan, 1979), 294.

[20] David S. Dockery, *Christian Scripture: An Evangelical Perspective on Inspiration, Authority and Interpretation* (Nashville: Broadman & Holman, 1995), 64.

[21] Richard Shultz, "The Crisis of Knowledge: Biblical Authority and Interpretation" (unpublished essay, March 2004), 13.

various parts of the Bible comprised in the whole. Whether it is translated "all" Scripture or "every" Scripture, Paul is saying that *whatever* is Scripture is God-breathed.

But what does Paul have in mind when he refers to "Scripture"? In verse 15 the words "sacred writings" refer solely to the Old Testament. On what grounds, then, do we extend the affirmation of inspiration to the New Testament writings? First of all, Peter refers to Paul's writings as "Scriptures" in 2 Peter 3:14–16. We also know that Paul directs that his epistles be read publicly for instruction in the church, presumably along with the Old Testament (Col. 4:16; 1 Thess. 5:27). Paul also calls his message "the word of God" in 1 Thessalonians 2:13. In 1 Corinthians 2:13 he refers to what God has revealed to him as "words not taught by human wisdom but taught by the Spirit." And in 1 Timothy 5:18 Paul indicates that there is more to Scripture than the Old Testament: he places Luke's Gospel (or at least the materials from which Luke's Gospel was to be composed) on a par with Deuteronomy.

But should we translate the text "all God-breathed Scripture is also profitable" (or "all Scripture that is God-breathed is also profitable") or "all Scripture is breathed out by God and profitable"? The former might (but need not) suggest that only some of Scripture is God-breathed, not all, and hence only some Scripture is profitable. The latter, however, is more likely. It is a double predicate adjective connected by *kai* ("and").

Most important of all is the meaning of the word translated "breathed out by God" (*theopneustos*). The translation "inspired" can be misleading, for it might suggest to some an already existent text into which God breathed or to which he imparted some special spiritual or divine quality. The Greek word actually means "breathed out from God" not "breathed into by God." The Scriptures are a product of the divine breath (origin). The Scriptures find their origin in God, not in the creative genius of humans. In the Old Testament the "breath" of God is his creative power (cf. Job 32:8; 33:4; 34:14; see also Gen. 2:7; Ps. 33:6).

Lastly, it is difficult to see how error can be "profitable" and contribute to our "teaching" and "correction" and "training" in righteousness. According to Packer, "authority belongs to truth and truth only. . . . I can make no sense—no reverent sense, anyway—of the idea, sometimes met, that God speaks his truth to us in and through false statements by biblical writers."[22]

Clarifying Misconceptions of Biblical Inerrancy

People often reject the concept of biblical inerrancy because they misunderstand what is being affirmed by our use of this term. So let me address several misunderstandings about what inerrancy does and does not entail.

First off, it is no objection to inerrancy that God used sinful, error-prone human beings in the process of inscripturation. It is one thing to say that because we are human we *can* make mistakes. It is another thing to say we *must* (see esp. 2 Pet. 1:20–21). The doctrine of inerrancy, therefore, does not diminish the humanity of Scripture any more than the deity of Christ diminishes the reality of his human flesh.

It is no objection to inerrancy that sometimes the Bible describes things as they *appear*, that is, phenomenologically, rather than as they really are. We would be compelled to acknowledge an error only if the Bible explicitly taught that things *appeared* one way when in fact they did not, or if the Bible explicitly taught that things *were* one way when in actual fact they were altogether other. But when the Bible says that an event appears in a particular way, that is to say, it seems to the naked eye and from the vantage point of human observation to be a particular way when in fact it actually is another way, it is not an error.

It is no objection to inerrancy that God often accommodates himself to human language and experience when making known his will and ways in Scripture. Similarly, it is no objection to inerrancy that the Bible contains figures of speech. Some erroneously believe that inerrancy requires that everything in the Bible be taken literally, as if to suggest that God literally has wings and

---

[22] J. I. Packer, *Truth and Power: The Place of Scripture in the Christian Life* (Wheaton, IL: Shaw, 1996), 46.

that mountains literally leap for joy. But truth is often expressed in nonliteral or figurative and symbolic language.

Inerrancy is perfectly compatible with the fact that the Bible emphasizes certain concepts or doctrines more than others. Some have drawn the unwarranted conclusion that since the Bible does not emphasize, say, geology, anything it does say concerning geology is in error. It is true that the declaration "Jesus Christ [is] risen from the dead" (2 Tim. 2:8) is more important than "Erastus remained at Corinth" (2 Tim. 4:20). But the comparative unimportance of the latter does not imply its falsity.

It is no objection to inerrancy that the authors of Scripture occasionally sidestep conventions of grammar. A statement can be ungrammatical in its style while entirely true in its content. As John Frame points out, "'I ain't goin'' is considered less proper than 'I am not going.' But the meaning of both phrases is clear. They say the same thing, and they can both express truth."[23]

It is no objection to inerrancy that our interpretations of the Bible are less than uniform. The explanation for disparate interpretations must rest with the interpreter, not with the text. The fact that I am a credo-baptist (only believers should be baptized) and one of my close friends is a paedo-baptist (he practices infant baptism) means that one of us is wrong, but not that Scripture is.

It is no objection to inerrancy that the Bible is not equally clear in every place. In other words, the inerrancy of Scripture does not guarantee its complete lucidity. Even the apostle Peter acknowledged that the apostle Paul wrote some things "that are hard to understand" (2 Pet. 3:16). But the complexity and difficulty of what Paul wrote doesn't mean it is less true or less accurate than anything Peter or Luke or John may have written.

It is no objection to inerrancy that the Bible records lies and unethical actions. We must distinguish between what the Bible merely *reports* and what it *approves*, between *descriptive* authority and *normative* authority.

It is no objection to inerrancy that authors of the New Testament cite or allude to the Old Testament with less than verbal pre-

---

[23] John M. Frame, *The Doctrine of the Word of God* (Phillipsburg, NJ: P&R, 2010), 175.

cision.[24] We must be careful not to artificially impose on authors in the first century the literary standards of the twenty-first century. Matthew, Mark, Luke, and John, for example, had never heard of Kate Turabian or *The Chicago Manual of Style*!

Likewise, it is no objection to inerrancy that the authors of Scripture round off or approximate numbers and measurements. Alleged "inaccuracies" must be judged by the accepted standards of the cultural-historical context in which the author wrote, not by the scientifically and computerized precision of twenty-first-century technology. "The limits of truthfulness," notes Wayne Grudem, "would depend on the degree of precision implied by the speaker and expected by his original hearers."[25] Frame agrees, reminding us that *"precision* and *truth* are not synonyms, though they do overlap in meaning. A certain amount of precision is often required for truth, but that amount varies from one context to another."[26] For example, if you asked me how old I was when I wrote this paragraph, I would say, "sixty." But that is not precise. I was literally 60 years, 7 months, 16 days, 7 hours, and 22 minutes old. Although I did not answer you *precisely*, I did answer you *truthfully*. Or if you wanted to know how far I live from my church office, I would be truthful in saying "ten miles," although the *precise* distance is 9.4. Thus, as Frame notes, inerrancy

> means that the Bible is true, not that it is maximally precise. To the extent that precision is necessary for truth, the Bible is sufficiently precise. But it does not always have the amount of precision that some readers demand of it. It has a level of precision sufficient for its own purposes, not for the purposes for which some readers might employ it.[27]

It is no objection to inerrancy that the recorded account of cer-

---

[24] Gregory K. Beale and D. A. Carson have provided a superb resource that addresses every instance in which a New Testament author cites, quotes, or even merely alludes to an Old Testament text. In each case they contend that the New Testament author reflects a proper reading of the Old Testament passage. See their *Commentary on the New Testament Use of the Old Testament* (Grand Rapids: Baker Academic, 2007).

[25] Wayne Grudem, *Systematic Theology: An Introduction to Biblical Doctrine* (Grand Rapids: Zondervan, 1994), 91.

[26] Frame, *The Doctrine of the Word of God*, 171.

[27] Ibid., 173.

tain events is not exhaustive in detail. That the description of an event is partial does not mean it is false. Inerrancy simply means that when Scripture does speak, however extensive or minimal it may be, it speaks accurately. Related to this are those instances when two authors record the same event from differing perspectives and for different purposes. Thus it is no error that Matthew mentions one angel at the tomb of Jesus (Matt. 28:2) while Luke mentions two (Luke 24:4). After all, if there were two, there was assuredly one. If Matthew had said there was "only" one angel and Luke had said there were two, we'd have a problem. But such is not the case.

It is no objection to inerrancy that the biblical authors used uninspired and errant material in composing Scripture. Inerrancy simply means that when they do quote or borrow from uninspired sources, they do so accurately. It is no objection to inerrancy that we cannot, at this time, harmonize all allegedly disparate events or data. This would make the authority of the Bible depend on the resourcefulness of humans. It would also indicate that we have learned little from history, for on countless occasions historical, archaeological, exegetical, and scientific discoveries have resolved what were apparent contradictions in the Bible.

Conclusion

So, why is this doctrine or concept of Scripture as verbally, plenarily, and inerrantly inspired so critical? First, because

> biblical *veracity* and biblical *authority* are bound up together. Only truth can have final authority to determine belief and behavior, and Scripture cannot have such authority further than it is true. A factually and theologically trustworthy Bible could still impress us as a presentation of religious experience and expertise, but clearly, if we cannot affirm its total truthfulness, we cannot claim that it is all God's testimony and teaching, given to control our convictions and conduct.[28]

Second, we should subject our souls to the infallibility and au-

---

[28] Packer, *Truth and Power*, 134.

thority of the Scriptures, immerse our minds in its truths, and bathe our spirits in its teachings because the inerrant special revelation of God in Scripture has the *power* to change human lives and to transform the experience of the church.

The Word of God is the means or instrument by which the Holy Spirit regenerates the human heart. That is to say, the proclamation or communication of the Word is the catalyst for the inception of spiritual life. When we look at 1 Peter 1:23–25, we discover that this "word" that brings life is a "preached" word! The Word of God is the power of God unto salvation (see esp. Rom. 1:16–17; 10:14–15; 1 Cor. 1:18–25). The Word of God is the spring from which the waters of faith arise. Paul says in Romans 10.17 that "faith comes from hearing" and that hearing comes "through the word of Christ."

It is from or through the Scriptures that the Spirit imparts perseverance and encouragement: "For whatever was written in former days was written for our instruction, that through *endurance and through the encouragement of the Scriptures* we might have hope" (Rom. 15:4). It is from or through the Scriptures that joy, peace, and hope arise. How so? Paul prays in Romans 15:13 that God would "fill you with all joy and peace in believing, that you may abound in hope by the power of the Holy Spirit." Both joy and peace are the fruit of *believing*, which in turn yields hope. But believe *what*? Belief is confidence placed in the truth of what God has revealed to us in Scripture about who he is and our relationship to him through Jesus. Belief does not hover in a contentless vacuum, but is rooted in the firm foundation of inspired, revelatory words inscripturated for us in the Bible.

It is the Word of God that accounts for the ongoing operation of the miraculous in the body of Christ. We read in Galatians 3:5, "Does he who supplies the Spirit to you and works miracles among you do so by works of the law, or by hearing with faith?" The instrument God uses is the faith that we experience *upon hearing the Word of God*! When we hear the Word of God (in preaching and teaching), our thoughts and hearts become God-centered; our focus is on his glory, and thus our faith in his greatness expands and deepens, all of which is the soil in which the seeds of the supernatural are sown. Apart from the truths of preached texts, there can be no genuine, long-lasting, Christ-exalting faith; and apart from such faith there can be no (or at best, few) miracles.

It is the Word of God, expounded and explained and applied, that yields the fruit of sanctification and holiness in daily life. Consider the following:

> And we also thank God constantly for this, that when you received the word of God, which you heard from us, you accepted it not as the word of men but as what it really is, the word of God, which is at work in you believers. (1 Thess. 2:13)

> If you put these things before the brothers, you will be a good servant of Christ Jesus, being trained in the words of the faith and of the good doctrine that you have followed. (1 Tim. 4:6)

> Like newborn infants, long for the pure spiritual milk, that by it you may grow up into salvation. (1 Pet. 2:2)

> For the word of God is living and active, sharper than any two-edged sword, piercing to the division of soul and spirit, of joints and of marrow, and discerning the thoughts and intentions of the heart. (Heb. 4:12)

So, is the Bible not only inspired or breathed out by God, but also inerrant? And does it matter? The answer to both questions is, "By all means, yes, and again, *yes!*"

Recommended Reading

Frame, John M. *The Doctrine of the Word of God*. Phillipsburg, NJ: P&R, 2010.

Nichols, Stephen J., and Eric T. Brandt. *Ancient Word, Changing Worlds: The Doctrine of Scripture in a Modern Age*. Wheaton, IL: Crossway, 2009.

Packer, J. I. *God Has Spoken: Revelation and the Bible*. 3rd ed. Grand Rapids: Baker, 1998.

Poythress, Vern Sheridan. *Inerrancy and Worldview: Answering Modern Challenges to the Bible*. Wheaton, IL: Crossway, 2012.

2

What Is Open Theism?

Has it ever occurred to you that nothing ever occurs to God? You may want to take a moment and reflect on that question. It reminds us that nothing takes God by surprise. Nothing suddenly *occurs* to him that he did not already know. Nothing takes place that he has not already planned. Nothing catches him off guard. At no time does some unforeseen event happen, such that God (figuratively speaking, of course) slaps himself upside the head and exclaims, "Wow, I never saw that coming!"

However, in recent years there has appeared a radical departure from this understanding of God that denies his exhaustive foreknowledge of all future events. According to what is commonly called the *openness of God* theory or *open theism*, God does not, indeed cannot, know with absolute certainty what will be the free choices of men or women. Although there are numerous components in this new view of God, its fundamental principles are as follows.

Components of Open Theism

First, proponents of the openness doctrine believe that the classical or traditional view of God in which he is portrayed as knowing all future events is derived not from Scripture but from Greek philosophical concepts that corrupted Christian theology in the first few centuries of the church's existence. They also reject both the classical doctrine of divine immutability and divine timelessness, insisting that these, too, reflect more the emphasis of Greek philosophy than Scripture.

Second, according to open theism God does not know in advance everything humans will do. He knows human decisions only as they occur. He *learns* from what happens. God's experience of the world is "open" in the sense that he becomes aware of developments in the world and responds to them as they unfold. He is "open" to new stimuli and new experiences. God is thus a risk taker, for he neither knows nor controls the decisions and actions of humans.[1]

Third, proponents of this doctrine insist this "open" view of God is the only way that he can engage in a both meaningful and loving interpersonal relationship with his creatures. For this sort of interaction to occur, the future must be utterly contingent (nonfixed, uncertain) both for God and for mankind. Open theists contend that if God knows the future in exhaustive detail, the future is certain. And if the future is certain, there can be no genuine, loving, caring involvement of God with us in a give-and-take relationship in which we respond to God, God responds to us, and so on.

Fourth, some have charged these men with embracing *process theology* (a charge that they would strongly deny). According to process theology, God is himself in process even as humans are. God is growing and developing and changing and adapting and becoming something he didn't used to be. God is *learning* new things every moment, of which he was ignorant before. God is constantly being *surprised* and is always *discovering* things heretofore unknown.

In other words, the best that God can do with the future is *guess* at what might happen based on his wisdom and his vast experience of the past and what he has gleaned from his interaction with human nature and human behavior. God is like a chess grandmaster who is playing against novices. His understanding of the game

---

[1] Thus, the title to John Sanders's book, *The God Who Risks* (Downers Grove, IL: InterVarsity, 1998).

and the possible moves enables him to win, but the outcome is not absolutely certain. According to this view, God is constantly changing his plans as well as his mind, is reevaluating his purposes, is altering his intentions, is always and ever adapting to human decisions that he could not foresee or anticipate. Openness advocates would deny that they are process theologians, but it is hard to see the difference. They would contend that, since they believe God's moral character (love, goodness, mercy, grace, holiness, etc.) never changes, they are in a different category from process thinkers.

Fifth, although all proponents of the openness theory are Arminians when it comes to the doctrines of election and salvation, they deviate significantly from the classical Arminian concept of God. James Arminius himself, as well as John Wesley and others who have stood in that tradition, have always affirmed divine knowledge of the future.[2]

Sixth, while explicitly denying exhaustive divine foreknowledge, the openness theorists continue to affirm divine omniscience. Their argument goes like this: To say that God is omniscient is to say he knows all "things," that is, God knows *whatever can be known*. But since the future has not yet happened, nothing in it is a "thing" that might be a proper object of knowledge. Therefore, the fact that God does not know the future does not mean he isn't omniscient, because the future is, by definition, unknowable (because uncertain). Or again, "the reason God does not know the future is because it is not yet there to be known. . . . It is less like a rug that is unrolled as time goes by than it is like a rug that is being woven."[3] This is how they affirm divine omniscience (and

---

[2] Observe the following explanation of divine election given by Arminius: "To these succeeds the fourth decree, by which God decreed to save and damn certain particular persons. This decree has its foundation in the foreknowledge of God, by which he knew from all eternity those individuals who would, through his preventing grace, believe, and, through his subsequent grace would persevere, according to the before described administration of those means which are suitable and proper for conversion and faith; and, by which foreknowledge he likewise knew those who would not believe and persevere" (James Arminius, *The Writings of James Arminius*, trans. James Nichols [Grand Rapids: Baker, 1977], 1:248). Thus, Arminianism insists that God's election of men and women to salvation is conditional, being based on his foreknowledge of how each person will exercise free will in response to the gospel of Jesus Christ.

[3] Millard J. Erickson, *God the Father Almighty: A Contemporary Exploration of the Divine Attributes* (Grand Rapids: Baker, 1998), 73. Erickson, it should be noted, is not himself an open theist. See his book *What Does God Know and When Does He Know It? The Current Controversy over Divine Foreknowledge* (Grand Rapids: Zondervan, 2003).

thus retain the appearance of orthodoxy) while denying that God has foreknowledge. Clark Pinnock puts it this way:

> The future does not yet exist and therefore cannot be infallibly anticipated, even by God. Future decisions cannot in every way be foreknown, because they have not yet been made. God knows everything that can be known [and hence is "omniscient," so he says]—but God's foreknowledge does not include the undecided.[4]

The reason open theists deny that the future (or events and decisions in it) is a "thing" that can be known is traceable to two arguments. First, openness theorists deny that God is timeless, that he in some way transcends the events and processes of temporal reality and thus is able to see all events in one eternal "now." They argue, on the other hand, that God is both present in and a part of time and that he therefore sees and knows events only as they occur. Second, they deny foreknowledge because it requires foreordination. That is to say, God knows the future precisely because he has foreordained what will occur in it. But this they deny, for if future events are foreordained, they are certain to occur, and if they are certain to occur, man has lost his freedom. For man to be truly free, the future must be truly "open."[5]

The evidence open theists cite in defense of their view is primarily twofold. They appeal to biblical statements that appear to affirm in one way or another that God is responsive to what happens in the world, that such events evoke emotions in him such as grief, sorrow, regret, anger, surprise, and even a change in his attitude, intentions, or plans (see, e.g., Gen. 6:5–7; 22:12; Jer. 26:2–3; Ezek. 12:1–3).

They also appeal to statements that assert human freedom. If God knows what I am going to do, it is certain that I will do it and not something else. If I were to do otherwise, then God's knowledge would be in error. Thus if God has infallible knowledge of all my future decisions, I am not truly free for all my future actions must

---

[4] Clark Pinnock et al., *The Openness of God: A Biblical Challenge to the Traditional Understanding of God* (Downers Grove, IL: InterVarsity, 1994), 123.

[5] Generally speaking, Arminians have affirmed divine foreknowledge based on divine timelessness, whereas Calvinists have affirmed it based on divine foreordination.

already be certain to occur. But if I am truly free, nothing about my future is certain, for there is always the possibility that I will choose to do other than what I planned or what one might expect. Therefore, *God cannot know what my future choices will be, since I don't know what they will be.* Even though I might "intend" or "plan" to do something, the possibility always exists that I will change my mind and choose another option. Thus God does not, indeed cannot, know the future.

There may yet be two additional reasons for the emergence of this view of God, both of which openness proponents would no doubt deny. First, the majority of those who advocate open theism are professional philosophers. Why is this significant? Because, as Donald Bloesch has pointed out, "the predilection of philosophy is to overcome the polarities and ambiguities of life by arriving at a synthesis that perfects and crowns human reasoning. It cannot tolerate anything that defies rational comprehension, for this is to acknowledge a surd in human existence."[6] The mystery of *compatibilism*, according to which exhaustive divine foreknowledge (and therefore certainty) of the future and genuine human freedom coexist, is simply unacceptable to many philosophers.

Others have suggested that the theory is driven in some measure by a desire to maintain human autonomy in the presence of a sovereign God. Their solution is to eliminate, or at least greatly reduce, God's sovereignty so that it no longer poses a threat to unfettered human liberty. Open theists simply cannot conceive how God can know the future and exercise providential control over it even while humans retain moral responsibility for their actions (the doctrine known as *compatibilism*). Stephen Charnock would ask this question of the openness folk: "But what if the foreknowledge of God, and the liberty of the will, cannot be fully reconciled by man? Shall we therefore deny a perfection in God to support a liberty in ourselves? Shall we rather fasten ignorance upon God, and accuse him of blindness, to maintain our liberty?"[7]

---

[6] Donald G. Bloesch, *A Theology of Word and Spirit: Authority and Method in Theology* (Downers Grove, IL: InterVarsity, 1992), 80.
[7] Stephen Charnock, *The Existence and Attributes of God*, vol. 2 (1853; repr., Grand Rapids: Baker, 1996), 450.

A Brief Response to Open Theism

Space does not allow a thorough response to open theism, so I will restrict myself to the explicit refutation of it found in Isaiah 41–48. These chapters are, in a manner of speaking, a challenge by God to the pagan deities: *put up or shut up!* That is to say, God proves his deity, that he and he alone is God, by appealing to his exhaustive foreknowledge of the future and his ability to predict to the smallest of details everything that is coming to pass. He calls on all so-called "gods" and idols to do the same. In the final analysis, if God does not have knowledge of the future, he is no better than the stone and wood idols before which misguided men and women bow down in futile allegiance.[8] Let's look closely at several of these passages from Isaiah the prophet. We begin with Isaiah 41:21–26.

> Set forth your case, says the LORD;
> > bring your proofs, says the King of Jacob.
> Let them bring them, and tell us
> > what is to happen.
> Tell us the former things, what they are,
> > that we may consider them,
> that we may know their outcome;
> > or declare to us the things to come.
> Tell us what is to come hereafter,
> > that we may know that you are gods;
> do good, or do harm,
> > that we may be dismayed and terrified.
> Behold, you are nothing,
> > and your work is less than nothing;
> > an abomination is he who chooses you.
>
> I stirred up one from the north, and he has come,
> > from the rising of the sun, and he shall call upon my name;
> he shall trample on rulers as on mortar,
> > as the potter treads clay.

---

[8] Open theists have insisted that the texts you are about to read refer only to those actions or plans that God himself intends to pursue. In other words, God may indeed have foreknowledge of his own actions, plans, and purposes. But he can have no such advance knowledge of the actions, plans, and purposes of other beings. As you read these texts, ask yourself, Does Isaiah portray God as knowing only what he, God, will do, or does Isaiah also portray God as knowing exhaustively and infallibly all that we, his people, will do?

Who declared it from the beginning, that we might know,
and beforehand, that we might say, "He is right"?
There was none who declared it, none who proclaimed,
none who heard your words.

Here the pagan deities are called to account: "Set forth your case," amass your evidence; this is the opportunity for you to establish empirical proof that you are worthy of allegiance. All the "gods" need to do is "tell us what is to happen" and "declare to us the things to come." Simply "tell us what is to come hereafter, that we may know that you are gods." It is precisely the failure to know and predict the future that exposes any and all self-proclaimed "deities" or "gods" as frauds. *The unavoidable sign of not being God is the absence of foreknowledge!* In verse 26 Yahweh issues a challenge, saying in effect: "Which of you predicted Cyrus's coming? I and I alone have done this." John Oswalt explains: "The gods are being asked to explain the past in such a way as to make sense of the present, and to foretell the future in such a way as to make its developments intelligible. This is exactly what God had done for his people throughout their history. Can the gods do that?"[9]

We look next at Isaiah 42:8–9.

I am the LORD; that is my name;
my glory I give to no other,
nor my praise to carved idols.
Behold, the former things have come to pass,
and new things I now declare;
before they spring forth
I tell you of them.

Here again God's "glory" lies in his capacity to do what the idols cannot: before new things come to pass, God alone declares what they shall be and proclaims them to the people. There is no guesswork involved. This is not "might be" or "hope to be" or "odds look good that," but rather specific declaration in advance of what will come to pass.

---

[9] John N. Oswalt, *The Book of Isaiah: Chapters 40–66*, New International Commentary on the Old Testament (Grand Rapids: Eerdmans, 1998), 101.

Isaiah 43:8–13 reads as follows:

Bring out the people who are blind, yet have eyes,
     who are deaf, yet have ears!
All the nations gather together,
     and the peoples assemble.
Who among them can declare this,
     and show us the former things?
Let them bring their witnesses to prove them right,
     and let them hear and say, It is true.
"You are my witnesses," declares the LORD,
     "and my servant whom I have chosen,
that you may know and believe me
     and understand that I am he.
Before me no god was formed,
     nor shall there be any after me.
I, I am the LORD,
     and besides me there is no savior.
I declared and saved and proclaimed,
     when there was no strange god among you;
     and you are my witnesses," declares the LORD, "and I am God.
Also henceforth I am he;
     there is none who can deliver from my hand;
I work, and who can turn it back?"

Oswalt's comments on verse 9 are direct and to the point:

Each of the nations and peoples has its god, but *Who among them* (the gods) *can declare* (foretell) a future like *this*? The indefiniteness of *this* has given rise to a number of interpretations. The most common one is that it refers to the destruction of Babylon and the release of the captives by Cyrus (41:2–4, 25–26). While this view seems likely, we should also ask why the author chose the ambiguous demonstrative. Perhaps he had in mind the entire situation of sin and exile and return and reestablishment. In that case, we would do a disservice to the text to limit it too narrowly.[10]

Remember also that the destruction of Babylon was an event that encompassed hundreds of thousands, perhaps hundreds of mil-

---

[10] Ibid., 145.

lions (who can calculate?) of human decisions and actions, and count-less consequences to each. In order for the captives to be released by Cyrus, there must have been a mother and father who decided to give birth to a child whose life would be filled with thousands of decisions that would culminate in his being at the right place at the right time (all of which must itself have been brought to pass by thousands of decisions and actions of perhaps thousands of other people). Furthermore, for the Jews to be released from captivity they first had to be taken captive. For this to occur, the Babylonians had to have decided to invade Jerusalem. Countless military decisions and maneuvers were involved on both sides of the battle lines.

The point is this: for God to foreknow and predict the fall of Babylon and the release of the people through Cyrus, God must have foreknown countless thousands, perhaps millions, of other events and choices on which the fall and release depended. No event ever occurs in a vacuum or stands in isolation from other events. Any single event in history is itself both the product of and the precursor to a complex web of countless millions of other events. How could one foreknow infallibly the certainty of any one event apart from infallible foreknowledge of every preceding event that in its own way would contribute to that one event coming to pass and apart from which that one event would *not* come to pass?

Isaiah 44:6–8 affirms yet again what we've already seen.

> Thus says the LORD, the King of Israel
> 　and his Redeemer, the LORD of hosts:
> "I am the first and I am the last;
> 　besides me there is no god.
> Who is like me? Let him proclaim it.
> 　Let him declare and set it before me,
> since I appointed an ancient people.
> 　Let them declare what is to come, and what will happen.
> Fear not, nor be afraid;
> 　have I not told you from of old and declared it?
> 　And you are my witnesses!
> Is there a God besides me?
> 　There is no Rock; I know not any."

Once more, the fundamental proof of God's uniqueness, that which sets him apart from all "gods" and idols, is his ability to predict what seems impossible to foreknow, declare that it will be, and then bring it to pass. Verse 7 is emphatic, saying in essence, "If you claim to be like me, proclaim and declare the future as I do!" Note well the object of God's knowledge: the things that are coming and the events that are going to take place, all of which encompass the lives, decisions, thoughts, reactions, feelings, and destinies of men and women and children, and not simply the actions that God himself, in isolation from others, intends to accomplish. The fruit of divine foreknowledge is fearlessness on the part of his people. According to verse 8, history is in God's hands. Therefore, "fear not, nor be afraid." Says Oswalt:

> Their faith will not be shown to have been misguided; God will not abandon them; Babylon will not devour them; the ancient promises will not fall to the ground. Isaiah's own ministry was all to that end. When all the promises of the exile had come horrifyingly true, alongside them stood these detailed promises, equally old, that the exile would not be the end: *have I not made you hear from of old?* Before all the world Israel will be a living witness to the fact that God had predicted all of this far in advance, and that he had the power to make his promises come true.[11]

Isaiah's polemic continues in 44:24–28.

Thus says the LORD, your Redeemer,
  who formed you from the womb:
"I am the LORD, who made all things,
  who alone stretched out the heavens,
  who spread out the earth by myself,
who frustrates the signs of liars
  and makes fools of diviners,
who turns wise men back
  and makes their knowledge foolish,
who confirms the word of his servant
  and fulfills the counsel of his messengers,
who says of Jerusalem, 'She shall be inhabited,'

---

[11] Ibid., 172–73.

and of the cities of Judah, 'They shall be built,
and I will raise up their ruins';
who says to the deep, 'Be dry;
I will dry up your rivers';
who says of Cyrus, 'He is my shepherd,
and he shall fulfill all my purpose';
saying of Jerusalem, 'She shall be built,'
and of the temple, 'Your foundation shall be laid.'"

God foreknows and foretells that Jerusalem will be "inhabited" once again. But for this to happen, people have to make decisions: they must deliberate, they must weigh evidence, they must wrestle in their souls and among their families with a variety of options and the consequences that come with each, and they must choose to live there. All these voluntary, free choices on the part of the people are entailed in the repopulation of the city. Apart from these voluntary, free choices of the people there will *not be* a repopulating of the city. Yet God *knows* the city will be inhabited again. Therefore, *God foreknows the voluntary, free choices made by the people* and knows them in such a way that they remain *both voluntary and free*, on the one hand, and *absolutely certain to occur*, on the other![12]

Yet again, Isaiah 45:1–13 confirms what we've seen repeatedly.

Thus says the LORD to his anointed, to Cyrus,
    whose right hand I have grasped,
to subdue nations before him
    and to loose the belts of kings,
to open doors before him
    that gates may not be closed:
"I will go before you
    and level the exalted places,
I will break in pieces the doors of bronze
    and cut through the bars of iron,
I will give you the treasures of darkness
    and the hoards in secret places,

---

[12] The naming of Cyrus was surely a free and voluntary decision by his parents. Yet God knew infallibly and certainly that this was to be his name. So much for the "doctrine" that God's infallible foreknowledge of human decisions eliminates human freedom.

that you may know that it is I, the Lord,
    the God of Israel, who call you by your name.
For the sake of my servant Jacob,
    and Israel my chosen,
I call you by your name,
    I name you, though you do not know me.
I am the Lord, and there is no other,
    besides me there is no God;
    I equip you, though you do not know me,
that people may know, from the rising of the sun
    and from the west, that there is none besides me;
    I am the Lord, and there is no other.
I form light and create darkness,
    I make well-being and create calamity,
    I am the Lord, who does all these things.

"Shower, O heavens, from above,
    and let the clouds rain down righteousness;
let the earth open, that salvation and righteousness may
      bear fruit;
    let the earth cause them both to sprout;
    I the Lord have created it.

"Woe to him who strives with him who formed him,
    a pot among earthen pots!
Does the clay say to him who forms it, 'What are you making?'
    or 'Your work has no handles'?
Woe to him who says to a father, 'What are you begetting?'
    or to a woman, 'With what are you in labor?'"

Thus says the Lord,
    the Holy One of Israel, and the one who formed him:
"Ask me of things to come;
    will you command me concerning my children and the work
      of my hands?
I made the earth
    and created man on it;
it was my hands that stretched out the heavens,
    and I commanded all their host.
I have stirred him up in righteousness,
    and I will make all his ways level;

> he shall build my city
> > and set my exiles free,
> not for price or reward,"
> > says the Lord of hosts.

Amazingly, Cyrus functions in this unusual capacity as God's "anointed" without coming to saving faith in God (cf. v. 4)! "Thus," says Oswalt,

> just as the pharaoh [in Moses's day] came to recognize that the God of Israel is the Lord without ever coming to faith in him, so Cyrus could well acknowledge that he had been commissioned by the God of Israel (as, according to Ezra 1:2–4, he did), without surrendering himself to the exclusive worship of the Lord.[13]

Notice that according to verse 1 of Isaiah 45, God even predicts the *emotional reactions* ("to loose the loins of kings," NASB) of Cyrus's enemies. Concerning verse 4, Oswalt writes:

> Effortless sovereignty is apparent in the statement that God has given Cyrus his honorific titles of "shepherd" ([Isa.] 44:28) and "anointed" (45:1), when Cyrus knew nothing of the Lord. It is not necessary for the Creator to have the permission of someone's faith before that person can be given a front-rank position in God's plans. He is the Lord, and we will serve him, either with our glad comprehension (cf. 44:5 where the persons joyously title themselves), or in spite of our sullen rebellion or placid ignorance.[14]

Isaiah 45:4–6 must be seen in its collective force.

> How can the prophet make such sweeping assertions in the name of God? Because there *is* no other God! Everything that happens is a result of the plans and purposes of the one divine, transcendent being. Therefore it does not matter whether Cyrus knew about the Lord beforehand, or whether he acknowledges him now. All events have one cause whether the persons participating in them know that or not.[15]

---

[13] Oswalt, *The Book of Isaiah*, 202.
[14] Ibid.
[15] Ibid.

The word translated "evil" in the KJV (Heb. *ra*, v. 7) is often used in the Old Testament to encompass every conceivable sort of "badness," from natural disasters to divine judgments to moral evil on the part of people. Here the ESV term "calamity" captures the sense of "painful circumstances" because of its contrast with *shalom*, which encompasses health, well-being, peace, good fortune. Thus the "darkness" and "calamity" of Israel here is probably a reference to the troubles and pains and harsh circumstances of the exile in Babylon.

In verses 9–13 the issue is stated in terms of the right of the Creator to develop his creation in the way he chooses. "The creation," notes Oswalt, "is in no position to dictate the terms or conditions of its development. So long as God does what is consistent with his own character and his stated purposes for creation, no successful challenge to his dominion can be mounted."[16] Verse 9 is quite explicit: to challenge the way God has fashioned one's life in particular or the world in general "is not merely a matter of preference or outlook. At bottom, it is a refusal to let God be God, a reversal of roles, in which the creature tries to make the Creator a servant to carry out the creature's plan."[17]

> Verse 13 again focuses on Cyrus. This Persian king did not arise by accident, nor by his own choice. He rose up because *I* [God] called him. . . . History is solely in the hands of the Creator. The great Persian emperor, like the earth and the stars, exists and comes forth at the command of God alone. . . . Whether Cyrus knows it or not, he is not undertaking his conquests for personal aggrandizement, or because of human inducements, but in order to accomplish the particular projects of Israel's God (*build my city, free my captives*), who happens to be the sole Master of the universe.[18]

We look next to Isaiah 45:20–24.

"Assemble yourselves and come;
   draw near together,

---

[16] Ibid., 208.
[17] Ibid.
[18] Ibid., 210–11.

you survivors of the nations!
They have no knowledge
    who carry about their wooden idols,
and keep on praying to a god
    that cannot save.
Declare and present your case;
    let them take counsel together!
Who told this long ago?
    Who declared it of old?
Was it not I, the Lord?
    And there is no other god besides me,
a righteous God and a Savior;
    there is none besides me.

"Turn to me and be saved,
    all the ends of the earth!
For I am God, and there is no other.
By myself I have sworn;
    from my mouth has gone out in righteousness
    a word that shall not return:
'To me every knee shall bow,
    every tongue shall swear allegiance.'

"Only in the Lord, it shall be said of me,
    are righteousness and strength;
to him shall come and be ashamed
    all who were incensed against him."

The challenge is once again issued: "I alone," says the Lord in effect, "have announced these events and declared them long before they occurred. If another 'god' can do this, step up to the microphone and make your case!" The evidence for Yahweh's exclusive claim to deity is his ability to predict the future with absolute certainty and specificity. If Yahweh cannot do this, he has no more right to be called God than do the lifeless and powerless idols before whom people stupidly bow.

Note again verses 23–24:

By myself I have sworn;
    from my mouth has gone out in righteousness

a word that shall not return:
"To me every knee shall bow,
    every tongue shall swear allegiance."

Only in the LORD, it shall be said of me,
    are righteousness and strength;
to him shall come and be ashamed
    all who were incensed against him.

Observe yet once more what it is that God infallibly knows. He knows that "every knee shall bow" to him. This probably entails both willing faith and unwilling subjection to the lordship of Yahweh. In any case, it entails human willing, human decision making, the very "things" that open theists insist cannot possibly be known in advance because they are not yet existent "things," having not yet been decided by free moral agents. Yet God knows them! God also knows what free moral agents will "say" of him, namely, that "only in the LORD . . . are righteousness and strength."

But how can God know this if open theism is correct? According to that view, everyone may well choose at any time or on the final day *not* to acknowledge God. For all God knows (and according to open theism, he knows very little for sure), there may well be no one to willingly bow the knee in his presence and happily acknowledge him as Lord. Yet Isaiah declared otherwise. God *does* know, and what he infallibly knows are the free moral decisions of people created in his image who are acting or deciding not in some mindless, mechanical way, but in a morally accountable way.

Isaiah's onslaught continues in 46:8–11!

Remember this and stand firm,
    recall it to mind, you transgressors,
    remember the former things of old;
for I am God, and there is no other;
    I am God, and there is none like me,
declaring the end from the beginning
    and from ancient times things not yet done,
saying, "My counsel shall stand,

and I will accomplish all my purpose,"
calling a bird of prey from the east,
   the man of my counsel from a far country.
I have spoken, and I will bring it to pass;
   I have purposed, and I will do it.

God calls on his people to recall "the former things," that is, creation, the flood, the calling and covenant with Abraham, the experience of Moses, the exodus, the giving of the law, the conquest, the judges, David and Solomon and the temple, and on and on and on. All these were part of the foreknown and declared purpose and good pleasure of God. All of these things were part of a divinely ordained plan that none could thwart. Only the Being who has done all this has the right to be called God, and say, "there is no other . . . and there is none like me." God's right to be called God and worshiped as such is due to the fact that all events of the past ("former things of old") and all events of the future ("things not yet done") are encompassed in the divine plan that God and God alone has "declared" and "purposed." He is God because he declares "the end from the beginning," that is, he declares what the outcome will be right from the start!

Note also that part of God's foreknown purpose is the calling of a "man" from a far country. All agree that such a "man" will be morally accountable to God and make a meaningful and significant contribution to the divine purpose. Yet, his morally significant decisions are infallibly known by God before they are made and are therefore certain to occur. The certainty of divine foreknowledge and the morally significant freedom of human decision making are therefore *compatible*.

Finally, in Isaiah 48:1–11 God declares:

Hear this, O house of Jacob,
   who are called by the name of Israel,
   and who came from the waters of Judah,
who swear by the name of the Lord
   and confess the God of Israel,
   but not in truth or right.
For they call themselves after the holy city,

and stay themselves on the God of Israel;
    the LORD of hosts is his name.

The former things I declared of old;
    they went out from my mouth, and I announced them;
    then suddenly I did them, and they came to pass.
Because I know that you are obstinate,
    and your neck is an iron sinew
    and your forehead brass,
I declared them to you from of old,
    before they came to pass I announced them to you,
lest you should say, "My idol did them,
    my carved image and my metal image commanded them."

You have heard; now see all this;
    and will you not declare it?
From this time forth I announce to you new things,
    hidden things that you have not known.
They are created now, not long ago;
    before today you have never heard of them,
    lest you should say, "Behold, I knew them."
You have never heard, you have never known,
    from of old your ear has not been opened.
For I knew that you would surely deal treacherously,
    and that from before birth you were called a rebel.

For my name's sake I defer my anger,
    for the sake of my praise I restrain it for you,
    that I may not cut you off.
Behold, I have refined you, but not as silver;
    I have tried you in the furnace of affliction.
For my own sake, for my own sake, I do it,
    for how should my name be profaned?
    My glory I will not give to another.

The central crisis being faced by the people of Israel was: Who is God? Is history governed by the "gods" of the Assyrians and the Babylonians and the Persians? Or is Yahweh God? Isaiah's principal strategy in chapters 40–48 is to demonstrate through an appeal to predictive prophecy that these "carved" gods, the products of mere human handiwork, are no gods at all. Isaiah makes it clear that God foreknew and foretold the events of the past in all their intricate complexity, with all their countless details, as well as those events yet to transpire, precisely to undermine any claim on the part of some other "god" to have been responsible for it.

But there is yet another, more important reason why God has foreknown and foretold all these events. Oswalt's explanation is masterful and deserves a careful and complete reading:

> Why did God tell in advance what he was going to do? . . . He did it because of the fallen human nature. If some wonderful thing were to occur in our lives, whom would we tend to thank? God, the transcendent creator? No, *my idol . . . my handcrafted image!* . . . The imagery the author uses here . . . is that of a *stubborn* animal that digs in its heels, stiffens its *neck*, and refuses to be led in a way it does not want to go (Exod. 32:9; Deut. 9:6, 13; Ps. 75:6 [Eng. 5]). All too often, the only reason it does not want to go in that direction is just that that is the way the master wants it to go. Along with the image of the neck as stiff as *iron* is *a forehead of brass*. . . . It may refer to male animals butting heads. But it may also refer to humans thrusting their faces forward in obstinate and impudent insistence on their own way. . . . This perversity of heart means that we refuse to see the normal signs that point to the existence of a God beyond time and space who is not subject to our control. To admit his existence would be to admit his right to rule our lives, an intolerable conclusion. Therefore we, even after we have experienced his intervention for good in our lives, like Israel, would still rather thank the works of our hands, indeed, ourselves, for whatever has been accomplished in our lives. . . . What can God do to counteract this tendency to idolatry? The answer is predictive prophecy. If he can inspire prophets with specific predictions of coming events; if the prophets will clearly attribute them to God; and if the events will come true as predicted, this will be strong evidence that God is who he says he is. Furthermore, if the Lord had long ago predicted the event that has just occurred, it is difficult for people to ascribe it to some other deity, especially one that they just made with their own hands.[19]

---

[19] Ibid., 262–63.

Look now at Isaiah 48:7–8. Here, says Oswalt, we see that

> just as prophecy was given so as to refute the claims of idols (v. 5),
> so not all prophecy was given at once in order to refute the claims
> of human omniscience. All our attempts to be independent are
> frustrated by our lack of knowledge. If we could just know the
> future, then we would not need to live in this state of helpless-
> ness—or so we think.[20]

Here again Isaiah tells us one of the purposes of predictive prophecy. It isn't primarily that we might know the future, but in order
to demonstrate that we must trust in God. Verse 8 expands on this
point. Why is God only now revealing these yet-to-occur events?

> So that it will be plain that it was God at work and not one of the
> idols. Thus the principle of prophecy being enunciated here is:
> Enough information in enough time so that it will be unmistak-
> ably clear that God is in control of history, but not enough so that
> people can become secure in their own foreknowledge and not
> need to live in dependence on God.[21]

Conclusion

Remember, the contention of those who embrace the openness doctrine is that God cannot foreknow the free choices or feelings or
actions of people. If such events are foreknown, they are certain
to occur. And if they are certain to occur, they are not truly free.
Isaiah begs to differ! He has made it repeatedly clear that God
does infallibly foreknow and predict the future choices of people
and that such knowledge in no way eliminates or diminishes the
voluntary nature of their choices or the moral accountability that
such choices demand (hence, the doctrine of *compatibilism*).

Not only did God foreknow and predict in advance that Cyrus
would help rebuild Jerusalem (Isa. 44:28); he also foreknew that
Josiah would destroy Jeroboam's altar (1 Kings 13:2). As noted
before, it is stunning that God would foreknow the free choices of

---

[20] Ibid., 268.
[21] Ibid.

Cyrus's and Josiah's parents in their choosing those precise names for their sons. Furthermore,

> God predicted Pharaoh's choice to honor the butler and hang the baker (Gen. 40:13, 19). He predicted the decisions of sinful men to pierce Jesus and not break a bone (Ps. 34:20; Zech. 12:10; John 19:36–37) and the decisions to divide his garments (Ps. 22:18; John 19:24). He foreknew the decision of the Egyptians to oppress Israel (Gen. 15:13); and the decision of Pharaoh to harden his heart (Ex. 3:19); and the decision of Isaiah's hearers to refuse to hear his message (Isa. 6:9); and the decision of the Israelites to rebel after Moses' death (Deut. 31:16); and the decision of Judas to betray Jesus (John 6:64).[22]

These are but a few of countless examples where God foreknew the decisions of men and women, thereby rendering those choices *certain*, yet without diminishing the *freedom* or moral significance with which they were made.

Recommended Reading

Frame, John M. *No Other God: A Response to Open Theism*. Phillipsburg, NJ: P&R, 2001.

Piper, John, Justin Taylor, and Paul Kjoss Helseth, eds. *Beyond the Bounds: Open Theism and the Undermining of Biblical Christianity*. Wheaton, IL: Crossway, 2003.

Ware, Bruce A. *God's Lesser Glory: The Diminished God of Open Theism*. Wheaton, IL: Crossway, 2000.

---

[22] John Piper, *The Pleasures of God: Meditations on God's Delight in Being God* (Portland, OR: Multnomah, 1991), 72–73.

3

Does God Ever
Change His Mind?

All people are fickle, in varying degrees. I suspect we'd be shocked to learn how many times in the course of a normal day we change our plans, reverse course, or pull out an eraser to delete an appointment or a task we had set for the week. Changing our minds feels so natural to us as humans, it's hard to envision life without it. In most instances the changes are harmless and typically result from unforeseeable circumstances, as well as the alterations that other people make that directly affect us. But what would it mean for God to change *his* mind? Does he? Could he? Or are all his plans and purposes *immutable*?

The importance of defining our theological terms with precision is most evident in the case of divine *immutability*. Here is a word that in contemporary evangelical circles evokes either protest or praise. Some see it as a threat to the biblical portrait of a God who does indeed change: he changes his mind ("repents") and he changes his mode of being ("the Word became flesh"). Others are equally concerned that a careless tampering with this attribute of God will reduce him to a fickle, unfaithful, and ultimately unworthy object of our affection and worship. It is imperative, therefore, that we proceed cautiously, and yet with conviction, in the explanation of the sense in which God both can and cannot change.

Immutability as Consistency of Character

The immutability of God is related to, but clearly distinct from, his eternity. In saying that God is eternal, in the sense of everlasting, we mean that he always has existed and always will exist. He was preceded by nothing and shall be succeeded by nothing. In saying that God is immutable we mean that he is consistently the same in his eternal being. The Being, who eternally is, never changes. This affirmation of unchangeableness, however, is not designed to deny that change and development take place in God's *relations* to his creatures. Consider the following:

- We who were once his enemies are now by the grace of Christ his friends (Rom. 5:6–11).
- The God who declared his intention to destroy Nineveh for its sin "changed" his mind upon its repentance (more on this below).
- Furthermore, this affirmation of immutability must not be interpreted in such a way that "the Word became flesh" is threatened (John 1:14). We must acknowledge (our salvation depends upon it!) that he who is in his eternal being very God became, in space-time history, very man. Yet the Word who became flesh did not cease to be the Word (no transubstantiation here!). The second person of the Trinity has taken unto himself or assumed a human nature, yet without alteration or reduction of his essential deity. He is now what he has always been: very God. He is now what he once was not: very man. He is now and forever will be both: the God-man. It is a simplistic and ill-conceived doctrine of immutability that denies any part of this essential biblical truth.

Thus, to say without qualification that God cannot change or that he can and often does change is at best unwise and at worst misleading. Our concept of immutability must be formulated in such a way that we do justice to every biblical assertion concerning both the "being" and "becoming" of God.

Clearly, then, to say that God is immutable is not to say that he is immobile or static, for whereas all change is activity, not all activity is change. It is simply to affirm that God always is and acts in perfect harmony with the revelation of himself and his will in Scripture. For example, Scripture tells us that God is good, just, and loving. Immutability, or constancy, simply asserts that when the circumstances in any situation call for goodness, justice, or love as the appropriate response on the part of the Deity, that is precisely what God will be (or do, as the case may be). To say the same thing, but negatively: if God ought to be good, just, or loving as the circumstances may demand, or as his promises would require, he will by no means ever be evil, unfair, or hateful.

Immutability means that the God who in Scripture is said to be omnipresent, omniscient, and omnipotent has not been, is not, and never will be—under any and all imaginable circumstances—localized, ignorant, or impotent. What he is, he always is. To be more specific, God is immutable in respect to (1) his *essential being* (which is to say that God can neither gain nor lose attributes); (2) his *life* (God neither became nor is becoming; his life never began, nor will it ever end); (3) his *moral character* (God can become neither better nor worse); and (4) his *purpose or plan* (God's decree is unalterable). Let's look briefly at each of these in turn.

Constancy of Being, Life, Character, and Plan

Immutability is a property that belongs to the divine essence in the sense that God can neither gain new attributes, which he didn't have before, nor lose those already his. To put it crudely, *God doesn't grow*. There is no increase or decrease in the divine Being. If God would increase (either quantitatively or qualitatively), he would necessarily have been incomplete prior to the change. If God were to decrease, he would be, necessarily, incomplete after the change. The Deity, then, is incapable of development either positively or negatively. He neither evolves nor devolves. His attributes, considered individually, can never be greater or less than what they are and have always been. God will never be wiser, more loving, more powerful, or holier than he ever has been and ever must be.

This is at least implied in God's declaration to Moses, "I AM WHO I AM" (Ex. 3:14), and is explicit in other texts:

> Every good gift and every perfect gift is from above, coming down from the Father of lights, with whom there is no variation or shadow due to change. (James 1:17)

> I the LORD do not change; therefore you, O children of Jacob, are not consumed. (Mal. 3:6)

> Jesus Christ is the same yesterday and today and forever. (Heb. 13:8)

When we talk about the immutability of God's life, we are very close to the notion of eternality or everlastingness. We are saying that God never began to be and will never cease to be. His life simply is. He did not come into existence (for to become existent is a change from nothing to something), nor will he go out of existence (for to cease existing is a change from something to nothing). God is not young or old: he simply is. Thus, we read:

> Of old you laid the foundation of the earth,
>   and the heavens are the work of your hands.
> They will perish, but you will remain;
>   they will all wear out like a garment.
> You will change them like a robe, and they will pass away,
>   but you are the same, and your years have no end.
>   (Ps. 102:25–27)

> Before the mountains were brought forth,
>   or ever you had formed the earth and the world,
>   from everlasting to everlasting you are God.
>   (Ps. 90:2; cf. 93:2)

Immutability may also be predicated of God's moral character. He can become neither better (morally) nor worse than what he is. If God could change (or become) in respect to his moral character, it would be either for the better or the worse. If for the better, it would indicate that he was morally imperfect or incomplete antecedent to the time of change, and hence never God. If for the worse, it would indicate that he is now morally less perfect or complete than before, and hence no longer God. It will not do to say that God might conceivably change from one perfect Being into another equally perfect Being. For one must then specify in what sense he has changed. What constitutes God as different in the second mode of being from what he was in the first? Does he have more attributes, fewer attributes, better or worse attributes? If God in the second mode of being had the same attributes (both quantitatively and qualitatively), in what sense would he be different from what he was in the first mode of being?

To deny immutability to God's purpose or plan would be no less an affront to the Deity than to predicate change of his being, life, and character. There are, as I understand, only two reasons why God would ever be forced or need to alter his purpose: (1) if he lacked the necessary foresight or knowledge to anticipate any and all contingencies (in which case he would not be omniscient, contrary to the claims of open theism); or (2) if, assuming he had the needed foresight, he lacked the power or ability to effect what he had planned (in which case he would not be omnipotent). But since God is infinite in wisdom and knowledge, there can be no error or oversight in the conception of his purpose. Also, since he is infinite in power (omnipotent), there can be no failure or frustration in the accomplishment of his purpose.

The many and varied changes in the relationship that God sustains to his creatures, as well as the more conspicuous events of redemptive history, are not to be thought of as indicating a change in God's being or purpose. They are, rather, the execution in time of purposes eternally existing in the mind of God. For example, the abolition of the Mosaic covenant was no change in God's will; it was, in fact, the fulfillment of his will, *an eternal will that decreed change* (from the Mosaic to the new covenant). Christ's coming and work were no makeshift action to remedy unforeseen defects in the Old Testament scheme. They were but the realization (historical and concrete) of what God had from eternity decreed.

The Lord brings the counsel of the nations to nothing;
    he frustrates the plans of the peoples.
The counsel of the Lord stands forever,
    the plans of his heart to all generations.
       (Ps. 33:10–11; cf. 110:4)

The Lord of hosts has sworn:
"As I have planned,
    so shall it be,
and as I have purposed,
    so shall it stand." (Isa. 14:24)

I am God, and there is no other;
    I am God, and there is none like me,
declaring the end from the beginning
    and from ancient times things not yet done,
saying, "My counsel shall stand,
    and I will accomplish all my purpose,"
calling a bird of prey from the east,
    the man of my counsel from a far country.
I have spoken, and I will bring it to pass;
    I have purposed, and I will do it. (Isa. 46:9–11)

Many are the plans in the mind of a man,
    but it is the purpose of the Lord that will stand.
       (Prov. 19:21)

But he is unchangeable, and who can turn him back?
    What he desires, that he does. (Job 23:13)

I know that you can do all things,
    and that no purpose of yours can be thwarted. (Job 42:2)

So when God desired to show more convincingly to the heirs of
the promise the unchangeable character of his purpose, he guaranteed it with an oath. (Heb. 6:17)

Can God Change His Mind?

No treatment of the doctrine of immutability would be complete
without a discussion of the problem posed by God's alleged "repen-

tance." If God's plan is unalterable and he is immutable, in what sense can it be said that he "changed his mind"?

The Hebrew word typically translated "change his mind" or "repent" is *nacham*. This word actually has a rather wide range of meanings, including everything from experiencing emotional pain such as grief or sorrow (cf. Gen. 6:6–7; Ex. 13:17; Judg. 21:6, 15; 1 Sam. 15:11, 35; Job 42:6; Jer. 31:19), to the experience of being comforted (cf. Gen. 24:67; 27:42; 37:35; 38:12; 2 Sam. 13:39; Pss. 77:3; 119:52; Isa. 1:24; Jer. 31:15; Ezek. 5:13; 14:22; 31:16; 32:31), to the more extreme notion of relenting from or repudiating a course of action previously embraced (cf. Deut. 32:36 = Ps. 135:14; Judg. 2:18; 2 Sam. 24:16 = 1 Chron. 21:15; Pss. 90:13; 106:45; Jer. 8:6; 20:16; 42:10), as well as retracting a statement or changing one's mind regarding a course of action (cf. Ex. 32:12, 14; Num. 23:19; 1 Sam. 15:29; Ps. 110:4; Isa. 57:6; Jer. 4:28; 15:6; 18:8, 10; 26:3, 13, 19; Ezek. 24:14; Joel 2:13–14; Amos 7:3, 6; Jonah 3:9–10; 4:2; Zech. 8:14).

This compels us to acknowledge the ambiguity of the English word *repent* and cautions us to be careful in ascribing it to God. Human beings repent of *moral evil*. We transgress God's law and acknowledge our sorrow for having done so and our determination to change how we behave. Obviously, whatever else God's "repenting" might mean, it does not mean he has sinned and is changing his ways. If that were the case, he would hardly be worthy of the title God; still less would he be worthy of anyone's worship. This is why most English versions (except the KJV) use the word "relent" or "retract" or something similar.

Let's look specifically at two passages, both of which use the word *nacham*.

> God is not man, that he should lie,
> or a son of man, that he should change his mind.
> Has he said, and will he not do it?
> Or has he spoken, and will he not fulfill it? (Num. 23:19)

> And Samuel said to him, "The LORD has torn the kingdom of Israel from you this day and has given it to a neighbor of yours, who is

better than you. And also the Glory of Israel will not lie or have regret, for he is not a man, that he should have regret." (1 Sam. 15:28–29)

Note well that 1 Samuel 15:11 and 35 say that God "regretted" making Saul king. Yet here in 1 Samuel 15:29 and Numbers 23:19 it says that God cannot repent, "change his mind," or "regret" an action he has taken. Scholars have generally said that there are four possible ways of responding to these texts:

- The statements in 1 Samuel 15:11, 35 and 1 Samuel 15:29 (as well as Num. 23:19) are contradictory.
- The statement in 1 Samuel 15:29 (and Num. 23:19) must be interpreted in light of 1 Samuel 15:11, 35.
- The statements in 1 Samuel 15:11, 35 must be interpreted in light of 1 Samuel 15:29 (and Num. 23:19).
- The statements in 1 Samuel 15:11, 35 use the word *nacham* to mean "regret" or "feel emotional sorrow," whereas in 1 Samuel 15:29 it means "deviate" from or "change one's mind" concerning a stated course of action; thus, in point of fact, there is no inconsistency between verses 11, 35, and verse 29.

Open theists contend that Numbers 23:19 means that whereas God generally can repent, in this particular case he chooses not to. However, were that true, Bruce Ware asks, "does it not follow from this text [Num. 23:19] that, while it is *generally* true that God *can lie*, in this *particular* case he chooses not to? That is, the parallelism of lying and repenting indicates that just as God cannot lie, he cannot repent. The question becomes, then, can God *ever* lie?"[1] Assuming that all would answer the latter question no (cf. 2 Tim. 2:13; Titus 1:2; Heb. 6:18), it would appear that "the parallel relation of God's repentance with lying would lead one to conclude that this passage is teaching more than simply that in this particular historical situation God chooses not to lie or repent. Rather, just as God *can never* lie, so He *can never* repent."[2]

One should also take note of the contrast made between God

---

[1] Bruce A. Ware, *God's Lesser Glory: The Diminished God of Open Theism* (Wheaton, IL: Crossway, 2000), 87.
[2] Ibid.

and man. God is said *not* to be like humans, who both lie and repent. Ware observes:

> Does not the force of this claim evaporate the instant one reads
> it to say, *in this particular situation* God is not like a man and
> so does not repent? Do men (i.e., human beings) *always* repent
> of what they say they will do? If so, the contrast can be main-
> tained. But if human beings *sometimes* carry out what they say
> and *sometimes* repent and do otherwise, and if God, likewise
> *sometimes* carries out what he says and *sometimes* repents and
> does otherwise, then how is God different from humans? The
> only way the contrast works is if God, unlike men, *never* repents.
> It is generally true, not merely situationally true, that God does
> not repent.[3]

This applies as well to the texts in 1 Samuel 15. In other words, "to
say that God sometimes repents (e.g., 1 Sam. 15:11, 35) and sometimes doesn't (1 Sam. 15:29) would be to argue that he sometimes
lies and, in the same sense as with 'repent,' sometimes doesn't. But
the truth is that God never lies, and so this text requires also that
he never repents."[4]

Two additional observations are in order. First, many have appealed to a common figure of speech known as *anthropopatheia* or
anthropopathism (from the Greek *anthropos*, "man," plus *pathos*,
"affection, feeling"). Thus, an anthropopathism is a figure of speech
in which certain human passions, feelings, mental activities, and
so on are predicated of God. This, of course, is related to the more
well-known figure of speech called *anthropomorphism* (again, from
the Greek for "man" plus *morphē*, "form"), in which there are ascribed to God human body parts (e.g., eyes, mouth, nostrils, hands).
Ware defines *anthropomorphism* as follows: "A given ascription to
God may rightly be understood as anthropomorphic when Scripture clearly presents God as transcending the very human or finite
features it elsewhere attributes to him."[5] Thus, God is *figuratively*
portrayed as "relenting" from a course of action or "changing his

---

[3] Ibid., 88.
[4] Ibid.
[5] Bruce A. Ware, "An Evangelical Reformulation of the Doctrine of the Immutability of God," *Journal of the Evangelical Theological Society* 29, no. 4 (1986): 442.

mind," but in *literal fact* he does not. Open theists often contend that we adopt this approach to the problem because of an extra-biblical presupposition concerning the nature of God derived from the Greek ideal of perfection. This alien, philosophical criterion is imposed on Scripture rather than allowing God's Word to shape our concept of God himself.

However, contrary to this assertion, most evangelicals appeal to anthropopathism because of what they believe Scripture explicitly teaches concerning the omniscience and immutability of God. It is the "analogy of faith," Scripture's harmonious interpretation of itself, not Greek philosophical presuppositions, that governs their treatment of such problem texts. Passages such as Numbers 23:19 and the others cited earlier are unequivocal: God is not a man. Therefore, he does not lie. He does not change his mind the way people do. He does not promise and then fail to fulfill. Those who appeal to anthropopathism insist that we are justified in interpreting the unclear in the light of the clear and utilizing a figure of speech generally acknowledged as entirely legitimate.

Second, and even more importantly, we must recognize the difference between unconditional divine decrees and conditional divine announcements (or warnings).[6] The former *will* occur irrespective of other factors. The latter *may* occur dependent on the response of the person or persons to whom they apply. Occasionally something explicit in the context will indicate which of the two is in view. Most often, however, statements of divine intent are ambiguous. That is to say, one must determine from other data whether the declaration or determination of God is unconditional or conditional. For example, what we find in the case of Jonah and the Ninevites is most likely *not* an unqualified and unconditional declaration of purpose. Consider carefully the nature of this passage from Jeremiah (18:5–12):

> Then the word of the LORD came to me: O house of Israel, can I not
> do with you as this potter has done? declares the LORD. Behold,

---

[6] Examples of an unconditional decree would be Num. 23:19; 1 Sam. 15:29; Ps. 110:4; Jer. 4:28; Ezek. 24:14; Zech. 8:14. Examples of conditional announcements or warnings would be Ex. 32:12, 14; Jer. 15:6; 18:8, 10; 26:3, 13, 19; Joel 2:13–14; Amos 7:3, 6; Jonah 3:9–10; 4:2.

like the clay in the potter's hand, so are you in my hand, O house of Israel. If at any time I declare concerning a nation or a kingdom, that I will pluck up and break down and destroy it, and if that nation, concerning which I have spoken, turns from its evil, I will relent of the disaster that I intended to do to it. And if at any time I declare concerning a nation or a kingdom that I will build and plant it, and if it does evil in my sight, not listening to my voice, then I will relent of the good that I had intended to do to it. Now, therefore, say to the men of Judah and the inhabitants of Jerusalem: "Thus says the LORD, Behold, I am shaping disaster against you and devising a plan against you. Return, every one from his evil way, and amend your ways and your deeds."

But they say, "That is in vain! We will follow our own plans, and will every one act according to the stubbornness of his evil heart."

That God declared his intention to destroy Nineveh, only to withhold his hand when they repented, is thus no threat to the doctrine of immutability. On the contrary, had God destroyed Nineveh notwithstanding its repentance, he would have shown himself mutable. William Shedd explains:

> If God had treated the Ninevites after their repentance, as he had threatened to treat them before their repentance, this would have proved him to be mutable. It would have showed him to be at one time displeased with impenitence, and at another with penitence. Charnock . . . remarks that "the unchangeableness of God, when considered in relation to the exercise of his attributes in the government of the world, consists not in always acting in the same manner, however cases and circumstances may alter; but *in always doing what is right, and in adapting his treatment of his intelligent creatures to the variation of their actions and characters.* When the devils, now fallen, stood as glorious angels, they were the objects of God's love, necessarily; when they fell, they were the objects of God's hatred, because impure. The same reason which made him love them while they were pure, made him hate them when they were criminal." It is one thing for God to will a change in created things external to himself and another thing for him to change in his own nature and character.[7]

---

[7] William G. T. Shedd, *Dogmatic Theology*, vol. 1 (1889; repr., Minneapolis: Klock & Klock, 1979), 352–53 (emphasis mine).

All this is simply to say that God's immutability requires him to treat the wicked differently from the righteous. When the wicked repent, his treatment of them must change. Therefore, according to Strong, God's immutability "is not that of the stone, that has no internal experience, but rather that of the column of mercury, that rises and falls with every change in the temperature of the surrounding atmosphere."[8]

Thus we see that it is a principle of God's immutable being (as revealed by him in Scripture) that he punishes the wicked and recalcitrant but blesses and forgives the righteous and repentant. If God were to reveal himself as such (as, in fact, he has done), only to punish the repentant and bless the recalcitrant, this would constitute real change and thus destroy immutability. God's declaration of intent to punish the Ninevites because of their sinful behavior and wickedness is *based on the assumption that they are and will remain wicked.* However, if and when they repent (as they did), to punish them notwithstanding would constitute a change, indeed reversal, in God's will and word, to the effect that he now, as over against the past, punishes rather than blesses the repentant.

Conclusion

What all this means, very simply, is that God is dependable! Our trust in him is therefore a confident trust, for we know that he will not, indeed cannot, change. His purposes are unfailing, and his promises unassailable. It is because the God who promised us eternal life is immutable that we may rest assured that nothing, not trouble or hardship or persecution or famine or nakedness or danger or sword, shall separate us from the love of Christ. It is because Jesus Christ is the same yesterday, today, and forever that neither angels nor demons, neither the present nor the future, no, not even powers, height, depth, nor anything else in all creation, will be able to separate us from the love of God that is in Christ Jesus our Lord (Rom. 8:35–39)!

---

[8] Augustus H. Strong, *Systematic Theology* (1907; repr., Old Tappan, NJ: Revell, 1970), 258.

Recommended Reading

Nash, Ronald H. *The Concept of God: An Exploration of Contemporary Difficulties with the Attributes of God*. Grand Rapids: Zondervan, 1983.

Roy, Steven C. *How Much Does God Foreknow? A Comprehensive Biblical Study*. Downers Grove, IL: IVP Academic, 2006.

Ware, Bruce A. *God's Lesser Glory: The Diminished God of Open Theism*. Wheaton, IL: Crossway, 2000.

4

Could Jesus
Have Sinned?

I "know" sin. I say this not because I can define sin, although I can. I say this not because I can identify sin when I see it, although I can also do that. I say it because I am a sinner. I "know" sin because I commit it, sadly, on a daily basis. My acquaintance with sin, therefore, does not come from associating with others who transgress or from reading a book on *hamartiology* (the technical, theological term for the study of sin). I "know" sin, as I said, because I, like David, was

> brought forth in iniquity,
>   and in sin did my mother conceive me. (Ps. 51:5)

I "know" sin because I sin.

Jesus, on the other hand, "knew no sin" (2 Cor. 5:21). Again, the apostle Paul doesn't mean by this that Jesus was unaware of the existence of sin or that he lived in isolation from those who committed sin. He was not intellectually ignorant of sin or unacquainted with its devastating consequences. He "knew no sin" in the sense that he never personally committed one. He was sinless.

How often do we pause and give thanks for the sinlessness of Christ? Were he not sinless, the entire scheme of reconciliation that Paul outlines in 2 Corinthians 5:18–21 would fall flat on its face. The glorious and gracious work of God in reconciling the world to himself hinges on God "not counting" our trespasses against us because he has counted our trespasses against Christ. But this would be to no avail if Christ himself had committed trespasses that ought to have been "counted" against him. The reckoning or imputing of our guilt to Jesus, for which he then suffered the wrath of God in our stead, is only redemptive if he was himself personally guilt free.

The New Testament is crystal clear on this point. Although 2 Corinthians 5:21 is the only explicit affirmation of Christ's sinlessness in Paul's writings, we should also take note of his reference to the "obedience" of the Son in both Romans 5:19 and Philippians 2:8.

Jesus gave the religious leaders of his day every opportunity to identify some sin in his life. "Which one of you convicts me of sin?" he asked them in public (John 8:46). The author of Hebrews reminds us that "we do not have a high priest who is unable to sympathize with our weaknesses, but one who in every respect has been tempted as we are, *yet without sin*" (Heb. 4:15). Jesus, he later tells us, was "holy, innocent, [and] unstained" (Heb. 7:26). He was "a lamb without blemish or spot" (1 Pet. 1:19) and "committed no sin" (1 Pet. 2:22).

The Main Question

That he *didn't* sin is a settled and undeniable fact. But *could* he have sinned? Was it in any way a *possibility* for him to have sinned, or was it in every way *impossible* that he should ever have transgressed? Or, to use theological terms, was Jesus *impeccable* (incapable of sinning), or *peccable* (capable of sinning, although remaining sinless)?

I intentionally avoid technical theological language, but bear with me for a moment as I appeal to four Latin phrases that shed light on this issue. The first is *non posse non peccare*, which means "not able not to sin." This describes unregenerate people and the fallen angels (i.e., demons). In other words, they necessarily sin.

Two other phrases are *posse peccare* ("able to sin") and *posse non peccare* ("able not to sin"). These describe Adam before the fall, regenerate people, and Jesus if one *denies* his impeccability. Finally, there is *non posse peccare*, or "not able to sin." This would be true of God, the saints in heaven, and Jesus if one *affirms* his impeccability.

My question is this: Was Jesus Christ sinless because he *could* not sin (*non posse peccare*) or because he *would* not sin? Was he constitutionally *incapable* of sinning or merely volitionally *unwilling* to sin? To say that Jesus could have sinned, even though he did not, is to say he was peccable. To say that Jesus could not have sinned, and therefore didn't, is to say he was impeccable.

The most helpful concrete illustration of this issue is the confrontation Jesus had with Satan in the wilderness (cf. Luke 4:1–13). When Satan came to him with those three temptations, *could* Jesus have succumbed? We know he didn't, and we are eternally grateful. But was it *possible* for him *not* to have resisted? Those who affirm impeccability respond with a definitive *no!* Those who deny impeccability counter with three observations, only two of which, in my opinion, are helpful.

First, those who deny impeccability argue that if he could not sin, he was not truly human. After all, "to err is human." This argument is weak, for it is not necessary to human nature that one be capable of sinning. When finally in heaven, having been glorified, the saints will be incapable of sinning, but they will not for that reason be less human than they are now on earth.

A second argument often heard is that if Jesus could not have sinned, he was not genuinely tempted. True temptation requires the possibility of sinning. That he refused to yield to Satan's temptations no one denies. But yielding must have been *possible* or the encounter was a sham.

Some respond by saying that perhaps *Jesus didn't know* he was impeccable. In other words, even though he couldn't yield to temptation, he was unaware of the impossibility. Therefore, at least so far as his own conscious experience is concerned, the temptation would have been quite genuine. But I find it hard to believe that Jesus lacked such self-awareness. Even if he did, we don't, so what benefit is there to us in his having resisted the Devil's overtures? In other words, we find encouragement in Jesus's example only if we know he could have sinned, but didn't (1 Pet. 2:21–23). So long as *we* know that his sinning was absolutely impossible, the force of his example is undermined, regardless of what *he* may have known.

A third and final argument by those who deny impeccability is that the doctrine is based on the belief that Jesus resisted the Devil from the strength of his divine nature. Satan was tempting God, and God, by definition, cannot sin. Regardless of the strength of his seductive appeals, Satan didn't stand a chance. After all, the finite cannot conquer the infinite. The presence of a holy and omnipotent divine nature within the incarnate second person of the Godhead made it impossible for him to have yielded to Satan's overtures.

For many years I strongly advocated the impeccability of Christ, insisting that because he was God incarnate, he was incapable of sinning. Now, make no mistake, he was and forever is God incarnate. But I'm not so sure about his impeccability, and here's why.

I believe Jesus lived and ministered as a *human, dependent on the power of the Holy Spirit*. Because he was human, the possibility existed that he *could* have sinned, but by virtue of his unceasing reliance on the power of the Holy Spirit he *did not* sin. Like the first Adam, Jesus could have sinned. But as the second Adam, he chose not to.

This means that in becoming a man, says Gerald Hawthorne, "the Son of God willed to renounce the exercise of his divine powers, attributes, prerogatives, so that he might live fully within those limitations which inhere in being truly human."[1] That which he had (all the divine attributes), by virtue of what he was (the second person of the Trinity), he willingly chose not to use. Thus we see a human being doing superhuman things and ask *how?* The answer is: *not from the power of his own divine nature, but through the power of the Holy Spirit.*

---

[1] Gerald F. Hawthorne, *The Presence and the Power: The Significance of the Holy Spirit in the Life and Ministry of Jesus* (Dallas: Word, 1991), 208.

Thus the Son chose to experience the world through the limitations imposed by human consciousness and an authentic human nature. The attributes of omnipotence, omnipresence, and omniscience were not lost or laid aside, but became *latent* and *potential* within the confines of his human nature. They were present in Jesus in all their fullness, but they were no longer in conscious exercise. The incarnation thus means that Jesus "actually thought and acted, viewed the world, and experienced time and space events strictly within the confines of a normally developing human person."[2]

Look again at the various accounts of Jesus's temptation by Satan. We are told that he not only was led *into* the wilderness by the Spirit (Matt. 4:1) but also was being led by the Spirit *in* the wilderness during the entire course of the forty days (Luke 4:1; it was, no doubt, the Spirit who led Jesus to fast).

> If he was being tempted by Satan for forty days (Mark 1:13), he was being led by the Spirit for those same forty days (Luke 4:1). It is impossible to escape the conclusion that these Gospel writers want their readers to understand that Jesus met and conquered the usurping enemy of God not by his own power alone but was aided in his victory by the power of the Holy Spirit.[3]

He was fortified and energized by the continual infusion of divine power from the Spirit of God (see also John 3:34).

Someone might ask, But why or how did the human Jesus *always* choose to rely on the power of the Spirit and thereby not sin? The answer would be that the Spirit was always antecedent to any choice that Jesus was to make, enabling and energizing him to continue in his conscious reliance on the power the Spirit was providing. Is that not also the case with us? To whatever degree and however frequently we choose not to sin, it is because the Spirit antecedently empowered us to choose to avail ourselves of his presence and supply.

It could conceivably be said, therefore, that Jesus was peccable when it came to the *metaphysical potential* for sin in his own

---

[2] Ibid., 210.
[3] Ibid., 139.

human nature (in other words, there was nothing inherent within the person of Christ that made it impossible for him to sin, any more than it was so in the case of Adam), but impeccable insofar as it was impossible for the Spirit to fail to energize Jesus's will to depend upon the power that the Spirit supplied.

Conclusion

The implications of this for you and me are profound, and I defer, in conclusion, to the words of Hawthorne to make the point:

> Not only is Jesus their [our] Savior because of who he was and because of his own complete obedience to the Father's will (cf. Heb. 10:5–7), but he is the supreme example for them of what is possible in a human life because of his own total dependence upon the Spirit of God. Jesus is living proof of how those who are his followers may exceed the limitations of their humanness in order that they, like him, might carry to completion against all odds their God-given mission in life—by the Holy Spirit. Jesus demonstrated clearly that God's intended way for human beings to live, the ideal way to live, the supremely successful way to live, is in conjunction with God, in harmony with God, in touch with the power of God, and not apart from God, not independent of God, not without God. The Spirit was the presence and power of God in Jesus, and fully so.[4]

Recommended Reading

Hawthorne, Gerald F. *The Presence and the Power: The Significance of the Holy Spirit in the Life and Ministry of Jesus.* Dallas: Word, 1991.

Piper, John. *Seeing and Savoring Jesus Christ.* Wheaton, IL: Crossway, 2001.

Ware, Bruce A. *The Man Christ Jesus: Theological Reflections on the Humanity of Christ.* Wheaton, IL: Crossway, 2012.

---

[4] Ibid., 234.

5

What Did Jesus Mean When He Said, "Judge Not, that You Be Not Judged"?

Whereas it comes as no surprise that most Christians have at least one favorite verse of Scripture, it is somewhat startling to learn that most non-Christians have one as well. Even more fascinating than the fact that non-Christians *have* favorite passages of Scripture, which they have committed to memory, is the curious fact that in most cases it is *the same verse*! Non-Christians may know little of the Bible, but as certainly as night follows day, they can quote for you Matthew 7:1: "Judge not, that you be not judged." And, ironically, this verse which they love most, they understand least.

A Text Abused

Never has a passage of Scripture been so utterly abused, misunderstood and misapplied as this one. Non-Christians (and not a few misguided believers as well) use this text to denounce any and all who venture to criticize or expose the sins, shortcomings, or doctrinal aberrations of others. One dare not speak ill of homosexuality, adultery, gossip, cheating on your income tax, fornication, abortion, non-Christian religions, humanism, and so on without incurring the wrath of multitudes who are convinced that Jesus, whom they despise and reject(!), said that we shouldn't judge one another!

This problem is due in large measure to the fact that *people hate absolutes*, especially moral ones. To suggest that there really is an absolute difference between good and evil, truth and falsity, is to risk being labeled as medieval and close-minded. In his widely praised book *The Closing of the American Mind*, Allan Bloom (professor of social thought at the University of Chicago) says this:

> There is one thing a professor can be absolutely certain of: almost every student entering the university believes, or says he believes, that truth is relative. If this belief is put to the test, one can count on the students' reaction: they will be uncomprehending. That anyone should regard the proposition as not self-evident astonishes them, as though he were calling into question $2 + 2 = 4$. . . . That it is a moral issue for students is revealed by the character of their response when challenged—a combination of disbelief and indignation: "Are you an absolutist?," the only alternative they know, uttered in the same tone as "Are you a monarchist?" or "Do you really believe in witches?"[1]

Bloom explains:

> The danger they have been taught to fear from absolutism is not error but intolerance. Relativism is necessary to openness; and this is the virtue, the only virtue, which all primary education for more than fifty years has dedicated itself to inculcating. Openness—and the relativism that makes it the only plausible stance in the face of various claims to truth and various ways of life and kinds of human beings—is the great insight of our times. The true believer is the real danger. . . . The point is not to correct the mistakes and really be right; rather it is not to think you are right at all.[2]

---

[1] Allan Bloom, *The Closing of the American Mind: How Higher Education Has Failed Democracy and Impoverished the Souls of Today's Students* (New York: Simon & Schuster, 1987), 25.
[2] Ibid., 25–26.

In brief, for many (if not most) students today, "there is no enemy other than the man who is not open to everything."[3]

Needless to say, we encounter in this a fundamental logical mistake called the fallacy of the faulty dilemma. The non-Christian believes that there are but two alternatives that are mutually exclusive. *Either* we never open our mouths to question or comment or express an opinion on the behavior and beliefs of others, *or* we do so and fall under the condemnation of Jesus in Matthew 7:1. To the prevailing way of thinking, this verse demands that we never exercise ethical discernment in our evaluation of others, indeed that we never evaluate others at all. We are told we must always manifest complete and uncritical tolerance toward every conceivable lifestyle or belief. What shall we say to this?

The irony, of course, is that in judging us for judging others they are themselves violating the very commandment to which they want to hold us accountable! To insist that it is wrong to pronounce others wrong for embracing a particular belief or moral practice is itself an ethical position, a moral stand. To insist on uncritical tolerance of all views is extremely intolerant of those who embrace a different perspective. But enough of that. Let's return to the words of Jesus.

What Jesus Does Not Mean

First of all, note what Jesus is *not* saying. John Stott reminds us that

> our Lord's injunction to "judge not" cannot be understood as a
> command to suspend our critical faculties in relation to other
> people, to turn a blind eye to their faults (pretending not to notice
> them), to eschew all criticism and to refuse to discern between
> truth and error, goodness and evil.[4]

Neither does this verse "command the sons of God, the disciples of Jesus, to be amorphous, undiscerning blobs who never under

---

[3] Ibid., 27.
[4] John R. W. Stott, *Christian Counter-Culture: The Message of the Sermon on the Mount* (Downers Grove, IL: InterVarsity, 1978), 175.

any circumstance whatsoever hold any opinions about right and wrong."[5] That Jesus was not forbidding us from expressing our opinion on right and wrong, good and evil, truth and falsity, can be demonstrated by noting two factors: the immediate context and the rest of the New Testament teaching on judging.

Let's start with the immediate context. Virtually all of the Sermon on the Mount, both preceding and following this text, is based on the assumption that we will (and should) use our critical powers in making ethical and logical judgments. Jesus has told us to be different from the world around us, to pursue a righteousness that exceeds that of the Pharisees (because theirs is a "bad" or inadequate righteousness), to do "more" than what unbelievers would do (because what they do isn't enough, another judgment), to avoid being like the hypocrites (now there's a word of judgment if ever I saw one!) when we give, pray, fast, and so on. "But how can we possibly obey all this teaching unless we first evaluate the performance of others and then ensure that ours is different from and higher than theirs?"[6]

Not only this, but immediately following this word of exhortation in Matthew 7:1 Jesus issues two more commands: don't give what is holy to dogs or pearls to pigs (again, powerfully critical words of judgment!), and beware of false prophets (there it is again!). "It would be impossible to obey either of these commands without using our critical judgment," says Stott. "For in order to determine our behavior toward 'dogs,' 'pigs' and 'false prophets' we must first be able to recognize them, and in order to do that we must exercise some critical discernment."[7] Furthermore, such critical judgments can only be made if there is an absolute standard against which such behavior can be measured.

As for the rest of the New Testament, I simply direct your attention to such texts as Matthew 18:15–17; Romans 16:17–18; 1 Corinthians 5:3; Galatians 1:8; Philippians 3:2 (where Paul refers to his enemies as "dogs . . . evil workers . . . false circumcision"!

---

[5] D. A. Carson, *The Sermon on the Mount: An Evangelical Exposition of Matthew 5–7* (Grand Rapids: Baker, 1978), 98.
[6] Stott, *Christian Counter-Culture*, 176.
[7] Ibid.

NASB); Titus 3:10–11; 1 John 4:1–4; 2 John 9–11; 3 John 9–10; and especially John 7:24, where Jesus himself says, "Do not judge by appearances, but *judge with right judgment*."

What Jesus Does Mean

What, then, does Jesus mean here in Matthew 7:1–6? Having already denied that Jesus is prohibiting all judging and critical discernment, we must still be extremely careful in this arena. The temptation to be sinfully judgmental is very real and powerful. Christ's call to holiness in Matthew 5–6, the call to be different, can lead to arrogance and a condescending attitude to others if we forget that all that we are is wholly of grace.

It would appear that Jesus is prohibiting the sort of judgmental criticism that is *self-righteous* (in that we think we are wholly free of the sin we so readily see in others), *hypercritical* (in that it often is excessive and beyond what is necessary to achieve the end in view), and *destructive* (in that it does not edify or restore but tears down the person whom we attack). He is prohibiting the kind of judgment we pass on others not out of concern for their spiritual health and welfare but solely to parade our alleged righteousness before men. Martyn Lloyd-Jones comments:

> The fact of the matter is that we are not really concerned about helping this other person; we are interested only in condemning him. We pretend to have this great interest; we pretend that we are very distressed at finding this blemish (in his life). But in reality, as our Lord has already shown us, we are really glad to discover it.[8]

Thus, Jesus is prohibiting not loving rebuke and constructive criticism, but rather self-serving censoriousness. To be censorious, Stott explains,

> does not mean to assess people critically, but to judge them harshly. The censorious critic is a fault-finder who is negative and

[8] D. Martyn Lloyd-Jones, *Studies in the Sermon on the Mount*, vol. 2 (Grand Rapids: Eerdmans, 1974), 180.

destructive towards other people and enjoys actively seeking out their failings. He puts the worst possible construction on their motives, pours cold water on their schemes and is ungenerous towards their mistakes.[9]

To sum up, "the command to *judge not* is not a requirement to be blind, but rather a plea to be generous. Jesus does not tell us to cease to be men (by suspending our critical powers which help to distinguish us from animals) but to renounce the presumptuous ambition to be God (by setting ourselves up as judges)."[10]

But we must not stop with verse 7:1, for Jesus has much more to say on this subject in the verses that follow. The reason he gives for not judging others in a self-righteous and censorious manner is that "with the judgment you pronounce you will be judged, and with the measure you use it will be measured to you" (v. 2). The problem here is determining whether this refers to the judgment we experience at the hands of men or of God. If we are censorious and sinfully critical of others, we should not expect to be treated any better by them. But I'm inclined to think this is God's judgment, which may come in one of two forms: either chastisement in this life for persistent sin (1 Cor. 11:32) or assessment of our lives for the purpose of reward in the age to come (2 Cor. 5:6–10). In either case, when we set up a standard to which *others* must conform, we are no less obliged to keep it than they are. That is why humility and love must govern our judgments. *All criticism must be preceded by confession*. Before we point out a fault in others, let us first confess its presence in our own lives.

An illustration of this principle is given in Matthew 7:3–5: "Why do you see the speck that is in your brother's eye," asks Jesus, "but do not notice the log that is in your own eye? Or how can you say to your brother, 'Let me take the speck out of your eye,' when there is the log in your own eye? You hypocrite, first take the log out of your own eye, and then you will see clearly to take the speck out of your brother's eye."

This principle applies to any number of situations, such as

---

[9] Stott, *Christian Counter-Culture*, 176.
[10] Ibid., 177.

denouncing the external, visible sins of the flesh, like adultery, theft, murder, in order to excuse or minimize the internal, less visible sins of the heart, such as jealousy, bitterness, greed, or lust. Related to this is the tendency to point out the faults of others precisely to throw them off the scent of our own sin. This form of judgment is nothing more than self-justification. We think that if we can just make known to others the gravity of their sins, we will by comparison come out smelling like a rose.

Again, far from forbidding all criticism and rebuke, Jesus actually commands it in verse 5. What he opposes is judgment that precedes rather than follows self-examination. So, says Stott, "again, it is evident that Jesus is not condemning criticism as such, but rather the criticism of others when we exercise no comparable self-criticism; nor correction as such, but rather the correction of others when we have not first corrected ourselves."[11] The danger in all this is stated in Romans 14:10ff. Judgment must always be restricted to those areas and issues on which Scripture speaks and gives a definitive yes or no. The problem is that Christians are inclined to treat as matters of law what Scripture leaves to freedom of choice.

There is also an opposite and equal danger. In verse 6 of Matthew 7, Jesus says, "Do not give dogs what is holy, and do not throw your pearls before pigs, lest they trample them underfoot and turn to attack you." Here Jesus points out the danger of being overindulgent and undiscerning. In loving our enemies, going the extra mile, and not judging unjustly, there is the peril of becoming wishy-washy and of failing to make essential distinctions between right and wrong and truth and falsehood. Whereas the saints are not to be judges, neither are they to be simpletons!

The terms "dogs" and "pigs" (perhaps wild boars) in this text are not what we normally think of when we hear the words. The "dogs" to which Jesus refers are not the cuddly household pets of the twenty-first century, but rather wild and savage street hounds that carried disease and filth. The apostle Peter likewise refers to false teachers and portrays them as dogs that return to their vomit

---

[11] Ibid., 179. See Ps. 51:10–13; Gal. 6:1.

(2 Pet. 2:22). He describes them as sows that are washed, only to return to wallowing in the mud. D. A. Carson explains:

> Jesus sketches a picture of a man holding a bag of precious pearls, confronting a pack of hulking hounds and some wild pigs. As the animals glare hungrily, he takes out his pearls and sprinkles them on the street. Thinking they are about to gulp some bits of food, the animals pounce on the pearls. Swift disillusionment sets in—the pearls are too hard to chew, quite tasteless, and utterly unappetizing. Enraged, the wild animals spit out the pearls, turn on the man and tear him to pieces.[12]

Jesus is not saying that we should withhold the gospel from certain people we regard as unworthy of it, but he is a realist and acknowledges that after multiple rejections and mockery of the gospel, the time may come to move on to others. There are those who are persistently vicious and calloused, who delight not in the truth of Scripture but only in mocking it. Therefore, the "dogs" and "pigs" are not simply unbelievers, but *defiant, persistently hateful, and vindictive unbelievers*. "It ought to be understood," wrote Calvin, "that dogs and swine are names given not to every kind of debauched men, or to those who are destitute of the fear of God and of true godliness, but to those who, by clear evidences, have manifested a hardened contempt of God, so that their disease appears to be incurable."[13]

Conclusion

In conclusion, then, several points should be made. First, it's important to note that Jesus speaks of "pearls" and not "gravel." We must always keep in mind the priceless treasure and incalculable value and glory of the gospel message. Second, there are going to be different sorts of people to whom we witness, and we must learn to discriminate among them (see Acts 17:32–34). Third, we need not present the gospel with the same emphasis at all times

---

[12] Carson, *The Sermon on the Mount*, 105.
[13] John Calvin, *Commentary on a Harmony of the Evangelists, Matthew, Mark, and Luke*, vol. 1 (Grand Rapids: Baker, 2005), 349. See also Prov. 9:7–8; Matt. 10:14; 15:14; Luke 23:8–9; Acts 13:44–51; 18:5–6; 28:17–28.

in an unthinking and mechanical way. Some are already weighed down with sin and guilt and conviction of the Holy Spirit and thus need to hear of God's love in Christ. Others need to hear of the holiness and wrath of God. Others need to come to grips with the depravity of their hearts, while still others need to be confronted with divine mercy and forgiveness. Remember that this instruction is set in the context of loving our enemies. Thus, whereas we are not to cast our pearls before swine, neither are we to be nasty and vicious and uncaring.

Finally, Matthew 7:6 probably does not need to be taught in certain churches or to certain Christians. Their problem is not that they are inclined to be undiscerning and often cast their pearls before swine. *Their problem is that they aren't casting their pearls at all!* This verse is addressed to those who are so zealous for evangelism that they fail to discern the scoffer from the hungry soul. Most likely, our problem is that we have no such zeal to evangelize in the first place.

Recommended Reading

Copan, Paul. *"True for You but Not for Me": Overcoming Objections to Christian Faith*. Minneapolis: Bethany House, 2009.

Wilson, Jared C. *Your Jesus Is Too Safe: Outgrowing a Drive-Thru, Feel-Good Savior*. Grand Rapids: Kregel, 2009.

6

What Is Blasphemy
of the Holy Spirit?

Blessed is the one whose transgression is forgiven,
 whose sin is covered.
Blessed is the man against whom the LORD counts no iniquity.
 (Ps. 32:1–2)

I seriously doubt if David, king of Israel, ever spoke more comforting and encouraging words than those. Listen again: "Blessed is the one whose transgression is forgiven"! There is perhaps no greater joy than knowing that one's sins have been forgiven.

There is in the reality of divine forgiveness a healing for the human soul that passes comprehension. There is a refreshing, a renewing power that can be found nowhere else. A prominent psychiatrist was once quoted as saying, "Half of my patients could go home in a week if they knew they were forgiven." That is why it is so comforting to know that our God is a forgiving God.

The LORD passed before him [Moses] and proclaimed, "The LORD, the LORD, a God merciful and gracious, slow to anger, and abounding in steadfast love and faithfulness, keeping steadfast

love for thousands, forgiving iniquity and transgression and sin."
(Ex. 34:6–7)

For you, O Lord, are good and forgiving,
    abounding in steadfast love to all who call upon you.
        (Ps. 86:5)

Bless the LORD, O my soul,
    and forget not all his benefits,
who forgives all your iniquity;
    who heals all your diseases. (Ps. 103:2–3)

Who is a God like you, pardoning iniquity
    and passing over transgression
    for the remnant of his inheritance? . . .
He will again have compassion on us;
    he will tread our iniquities underfoot.
You will cast all our sins
    into the depths of the sea. (Mic. 7:18–19)

It is into the brilliant and blessed light of this truth concerning forgiveness that Mark 3:22–30 casts such a dark and depressing shadow. Here is Jesus declaring that "whoever blasphemes against the Holy Spirit never has forgiveness, but is guilty of an eternal sin" (v. 29).

Are you confused by this? On the one hand, Jesus says in John 6 that whoever comes to him he will by no means ever cast out. Yet, on the other hand, here in Mark 3 he says that whoever blasphemes the Holy Spirit will never be forgiven, neither now nor in the age to come. Both statements must be true. What, then, do they mean?

This ominous declaration by Jesus doesn't occur in a vacuum. Something happened to provoke it. So let's look at the context. The religious leaders had just witnessed Jesus cast out a demon from someone, and they concluded from it that Jesus was himself possessed by Beelzebul or Satan and that it was in fact Satan himself who enabled Jesus to do this.

Mark doesn't give us any more information about this incident, but Matthew does. In Matthew 12 we are told that a man who was both blind and mute was brought to Jesus. Jesus proceeded to cast out the demon and heal the man. Instantly he could see and speak. The miracle was incontestable and beyond dispute. No one doubted that he was truly blind and mute. And the scribes didn't doubt that he was also demonized.

Matthew says that "all the people were amazed" (12:23): they were astounded, knocked back on their heels; they were left breathless. This was an unusually overwhelming miracle. It was so undeniably supernatural that the people began to wonder whether Jesus might in fact be the Son of David, the Messiah.

Their options were limited. There were *only two possible explanations* for what happened. This was no magical sleight of hand. This wasn't a case of some slick magician pulling a rabbit out of a hat or doing amazing things with a deck of cards. This man was blind and mute and everyone knew it. Either his healing was the work of God, or it was of the Devil. Since they refused to acknowledge that it was of God, they had no other options than to conclude that Jesus did it by the power of Satan himself.

Our Lord's response is profound. In essence he says, "Satan may be evil, but he's not stupid!" Any kingdom or house or city that develops internal strife will ultimately self-destruct. Satan's domain is no different. Aside from God himself, Satan is probably the most intelligent being in the universe. He is not so insane as to permit internal division or civil war among his demons. Satan is, above all else, committed to self-preservation. He will do nothing that might threaten or reduce his power. In other words, Satan would never be guilty of spiritual suicide. Jesus isn't saying that there is harmony or trust or loyalty in Satan's kingdom. Undoubtedly every demon in existence is selfish and perverted. But Satan would never allow any demon to undermine his efforts. Quite simply, Satan does not cast out Satan.

But Jesus doesn't stop there. Look again at Matthew 12:29 (Mark 3:27). Satan is the "strong man"; his "house" or palace is this present world; and his "goods" or property are the men and women whom he holds in darkness and spiritual bondage. But with the coming of Jesus, someone stronger has appeared and has assailed and conquered him. Jesus has come to plunder Satan's kingdom by rescuing the men and women who have been held captive to do his will. With the coming of Jesus, the Devil's power has been broken. His kingdom has been conquered. His captives have been set free. Jesus "binds" Satan, the "strong man," by virtue of his sinless life, his resistance to the temptation in the wilderness, his authoritative teaching in which truth prevails over falsehood, and ultimately by virtue of his death, resurrection, and exaltation to the right hand of the Father. This, then, is the setting or context in which Jesus utters these ominous words about a sin that is beyond forgiveness.

All sins can be forgiven, says Jesus in Mark 3:28. Whatever blasphemies you utter, they too can be forgiven. In Matthew's Gospel, Jesus says that even sins committed against him, the Son of Man, can be forgiven. But "whoever blasphemes against the Holy Spirit never has forgiveness, but is guilty of an eternal sin" (v. 29). I'll return to this in just a moment, but before I try to explain what the unforgivable or unpardonable sin is, I need to explain *what it is not*.

People have often said that the unforgivable sin is *murder*. If you kill an innocent human being, God will never forgive you. But consider Moses, David, and Paul, all of whom were guilty of murder and yet received the forgiveness of God.

Others have argued that *adultery* is the unforgivable sin. But again, David committed adultery, and yet it was he who wrote the words I quoted earlier from Psalm 32:1–2! And what about the woman taken in adultery in John 8, whom Jesus forgave and told to go and sin no more? And what about the Samaritan woman at the well in John 4?

Maybe the unpardonable sin is *denying Jesus under pressure or threat of persecution*. But consider Peter. One can hardly imagine a more grievous sin in which he three times denied that he knew Jesus. Yet we know that he was gloriously forgiven and restored to God and to ministry.

Some have argued that *suicide* is the unforgivable sin. But no text in either the Old or New Testament ever says any such thing.

Maybe you have lived in fear that you've committed the unforgivable sin when you have *taken the Lord's name in vain*. Perhaps in a moment of rage or bitterness or disappointment you cursed the Lord or strung together a bunch of expletives or used the *f* word repeatedly or some such thing. Or perhaps in your frustration and confusion you angrily declared that God doesn't exist or that he has miserably failed you. As serious as these sins are, they are not beyond forgiveness!

What Is the Unforgivable Sin?

Jesus is very specific in identifying the nature of the unforgivable sin: it is blasphemy against the Holy Spirit! The religious leaders were not being accused of blaspheming against Jesus himself. In fact, in Matthew's Gospel Jesus says that "whoever speaks a word against the Son of Man [i.e., against Jesus] will be forgiven, but whoever speaks against the Holy Spirit will not be forgiven" (12:32).

Why was their sin against the Holy Spirit and not against Jesus? Their sin was against the Holy Spirit because it was by the power of the Spirit that Jesus performed his healings and miracles. Jesus himself said in Matthew 12:28 that it was "by the Spirit of God" that he "cast out demons." Once again we see that the life Jesus lived, he lived in the power of the Spirit. The miracles he performed, he performed in the power of the Spirit.

What the religious leaders were saying comes down to this: "Jesus, we don't deny that a great healing miracle has occurred. We don't deny that you cast out a demon from that man. But the power by which you did it was the power of Satan." Thus their sin was attributing to the Devil what the Spirit did. They didn't deny the existence of the supernatural. They didn't deny the reality of the miracle. They simply said, in a remarkable display of hardness of heart and spiritual blindness, "The Devil enabled and empowered you to do it."

But we still don't know *why* Jesus regarded this as so heinous of a sin that it was beyond forgiveness. Why was this blasphemy of the Holy Spirit and his work so horrible, so reprehensible, so utterly outrageous that forgiveness becomes impossible?

The answer is found in the relationship between Jesus and the religious leaders and how they responded to him. Their repudiation of Jesus was not the result of ignorance or lack of evidence, or because they believed the negative report of someone else who didn't like Jesus. Blasphemy of the Holy Spirit is willful, wide-eyed slandering of the work of the Spirit, attributing to the Devil what was undeniably divine. These people had seen as clearly as anyone could see and understood as lucidly as anyone could understand that Jesus performed his miracles by the power of the Spirit. Yet they defiantly insisted, contrary to what they knew to be true, that it was Satan who empowered him.

The miracles Jesus performed were credentials of heaven. The religious leaders declared them to be the credentials of hell. According to Mark 3:30, they actually charged Jesus himself with being demonized! They didn't merely deny Jesus's deity. They, in effect, declared him to be a demon! His family may have thought he was mentally deranged, but the Pharisees declared him to be morally demonic.

This, then, was not a one-time, momentary slip or inadvertent mistake in judgment. This was a persistent, lifelong rebellion in the face of inescapable and undeniable truth. Blasphemy of the Holy Spirit is not a careless act committed only once in a moment of rage or rebellion, but a calloused attitude over time, a persistent defiance that hardens and calcifies the heart. The Pharisees were present when Jesus healed the sick. They saw him perform miracles up close and personal. They witnessed him raise the dead. They watched with their very eyes as skin infected with leprosy suddenly and decisively became clean and smooth and whole. They heard him teach with power and authority. They watched as demons fled his presence as he set free those in bondage. They watched with their own eyes as he gave sight to the blind. Notwithstanding all this, they openly and persistently and angrily and arrogantly declared that he did it all by the power of the Devil!

Blasphemy of the Holy Spirit, therefore, is *not just unbelief*, the sort of unbelief or rejection or doubt that is typical in our world. Blasphemy of the Holy Spirit is defiance of what one knows beyond any shadow of doubt to be true. It is not mere denial, but determined denial; not mere rejection, but wanton, willful, wicked, wide-eyed rejection. This sin, therefore, is unforgivable not because there is a defect in the atoning death of Jesus. It is unforgivable not because there is a limit to God's grace and mercy or because of some other shortcoming in the character of God.

Mark makes it plain that sins are forgiven only if a person repents. We read in Mark 1:4, "John appeared, baptizing in the wilderness and proclaiming a baptism of *repentance* for the forgiveness of sins." Again, in Mark 1:14–15, "Jesus came into Galilee, proclaiming the gospel of God, and saying, 'The time is fulfilled, and the kingdom of God is at hand; *repent* and believe in the gospel'" (see also 4:12; 6:12; Acts 2:38; 5:31). In order for people to receive forgiveness of sins, they have to repent. They must turn from sin to God and cast themselves on his grace and follow him. So when Jesus says in Mark 3:28, "All sins will be forgiven the children of man, and whatever blasphemies they utter," he means, all sins and blasphemies *from which you genuinely repent*.

Why, then, in verse 29 does Jesus seem to exclude one sin and one blasphemy from this promise: the blasphemy against the Holy Spirit? I think the reason is that blasphemy against the Holy Spirit puts you *beyond repentance*, and *therefore beyond forgiveness*. Verse 29 is *not* an exception to verse 28. Jesus is *not* saying that all *blasphemies you repent of* will be forgiven except blasphemy against the Spirit. He is saying that all blasphemies you repent of will be forgiven, but blasphemy against the Holy Spirit will not be forgiven because by its very nature it precludes repentance. It is the sort of sin that issues from a heart so incorrigibly calloused that a person simply isn't able to repent of it. If a sin makes it impossible for you to repent, then that is an unforgivable sin, because forgiveness is promised only for those sins from which we genuinely repent (cf. Mark 4:12).

This sin precludes pardon because by its very nature it precludes repentance. A sin of which one may repent is not the unpardonable sin. Therefore, those who are most worried that they may have committed the unpardonable sin have not. This is a sin for which there is no concern, no conviction, no anxiety, and thus no repentance. It is a sin that is so hard-hearted and willful and persistent and defiant that the one committing it couldn't care less that he or she is committing it.

So, yes, it is possible to put yourself beyond the possibility of forgiveness. But that is not God's fault. It is not for lack of mercy in him. It is not because he is limited in compassion or power or grace. It *is* because someone who has seen the truth and heard the truth and even tasted the truth has chosen to harden his heart to the point that he has rendered himself impervious to repentance and conviction.

Conclusion

Let me speak to those of you who are convinced you have committed the unforgivable sin, or at least are fearful that you may have. A particular sin in your life may have caused you profound internal anguish, an indescribable emotional pain. Perhaps you are living with an incessant and piercing guilt that makes life almost unbearable. Some even describe their shame as being so heavy and paralyzing that they feel as if every breath of spiritual life is being squeezed out of them.

Trust me, I know about this because dozens and dozens of you have come to talk to me over the years. I can't begin to count the number of people who are broken and shaking and weep endlessly and lose sleep—and when they do sleep, experience horrid nightmares—because they are convinced they have committed a sin that God cannot or will not forgive.

Trust me: if I've just described you, I tell you on the authority of the Word of God, I tell you with absolute confidence and joy, you have *not* committed the unforgivable sin!

- People who are ashamed of their sin have not committed the unforgivable sin.
- People who feel the conviction of the Holy Spirit in their hearts, who sense the piercing presence of guilt for having violated God's Word, have not committed the unforgivable sin.

- People who are in fear they have committed the unforgivable sin have not committed the unforgivable sin!
- People who are broken by their sin, who are grieved by their sin, have not committed the unforgivable sin.

The bottom line is that *I know with complete confidence when you have not* committed the unforgivable sin. But *I don't know when, if at all, a person has committed* a sin that puts him or her beyond the forgiveness of God.

In the final analysis, it doesn't matter if other people don't or won't forgive you. It doesn't matter if you can or can't forgive yourself (assuming that is even a legitimate possibility). The only thing that ultimately matters is whether God has or has not forgiven you. That's easy to find out: have you trusted Jesus Christ as your only hope for heaven? When you think about the cross, do you see what Jesus did there, dying for sinners, satisfying the wrath of God for sinners, and do you see there your only hope for forgiveness and reconciliation with God? If so, I assure you yet again, you have not committed blasphemy of the Holy Spirit. You have not transgressed in such a way that forgiveness is impossible.

Recommended Reading

Cole, Graham A. *Engaging with the Holy Spirit: Six Crucial Questions.* Nottingham: Apollos, 2007.

———. *He Who Gives Life: The Doctrine of the Holy Spirit.* Wheaton, IL: Crossway, 2007.

7

Does the Bible Teach the Doctrine of Original Sin?

Ugh! Original sin? It sounds so archaic, so pessimistic, so grimly medieval. For heaven's sake, this is the era of the Mars rover and the Human Genome Project. And haven't the most learned psychologists and sociologists assured us that people are by nature good, having been turned to their evil ways not by some inner instinct but through the influence of a deviant culture and substandard education?

Clearly, there are obstacles to our understanding and acceptance of this notion of original sin. Perhaps the first thing we should do, therefore, is to define our terms. The terminology of *original sin* has been used in any one of three ways. Often people think immediately of the *original* original sin—the first sin of Adam. Others use this language to refer to *inherited* sin, the idea that all humans are born morally corrupt and spiritually alienated from God.[1] Finally,

---

[1] This is what John Calvin had in mind when he wrote: "Original sin, therefore, seems to be a hereditary depravity and corruption of our nature, diffused into all parts of the soul, which first makes us liable to God's wrath, then also brings forth in us those works which Scripture calls 'works of the

by *original sin* some are referring to the causal relationship between Adam's sin and our sin. In this chapter we will be touching on all three elements.

The Contribution of Romans 5:12–21

The key text for our study of original sin is Romans 5:12–21. A central point to keep in mind in studying this passage is that Paul's thought is distinctly *corporate* in nature. Douglas Moo explains:

> All people, Paul teaches, stand in relationship to one of two men, whose actions determine the eternal destiny of all who belong to them. Either one "belongs to" Adam and is under sentence of death because of his sin, or disobedience, or one belongs to Christ and is assured of eternal life because of his "righteous" act, or obedience. The actions of Adam and Christ, then, are similar in having "epochal" significance. But they are not equal in power, for Christ's act is able completely to overcome the effects of Adam's. Anyone who "receives the gift" that God offers in Christ finds security and joy in knowing that the reign of death has been completely and finally overcome by the reign of grace, righteousness, and eternal life (cf. vv. 17, 21).[2]

Here is what Paul says:

> Therefore, just as sin came into the world through one man, and death through sin, and so death spread to all men because all sinned—for sin indeed was in the world before the law was given, but sin is not counted where there is no law. Yet death reigned from Adam to Moses, even over those whose sinning was not like the transgression of Adam, who was a type of the one who was to come.
>
> But the free gift is not like the trespass. For if many died through one man's trespass, much more have the grace of God and the free gift by the grace of that one man Jesus Christ abounded for many. And the free gift is not like the result of that one man's sin. For the judgment following one trespass brought condemnation, but the free gift following many trespasses brought justifica-

---

flesh' [Gal. 5:19]." *Institutes of the Christian Religion*, ed. John T. McNeill, trans. Ford Lewis Battles (Philadelphia: Westminster, 1975), 2.1.8.
[2] Douglas J. Moo, *The Epistle to the Romans* (Grand Rapids: Eerdmans, 1996), 315.

tion. For if, because of one man's trespass, death reigned through that one man, much more will those who receive the abundance of grace and the free gift of righteousness reign in life through the one man Jesus Christ.

Therefore, as one trespass led to condemnation for all men, so one act of righteousness leads to justification and life for all men. For as by the one man's disobedience the many were made sinners, so by the one man's obedience the many will be made righteous. Now the law came in to increase the trespass, but where sin increased, grace abounded all the more, so that, as sin reigned in death, grace also might reign through righteousness leading to eternal life through Jesus Christ our Lord. (Rom. 5:12–21)

There are five phrases in verse 12 that call for comment.

1. In verse 12 Paul says that "through one man" sin came into the world. Adam was a historical figure. He had a mind, a body, and a spirit, just as we do. He lived in space-time history, just as we do, in a geographical location no less than you or I (see Matt. 19:4; Mark 10:6; 1 Cor. 15; 1 Tim. 2:13–15).

2. Through this one man, says Paul, "sin entered into the world." Literally, sin *invaded* the world. This does not mean Adam was the first sinner; Eve was. It does not mean that sin began its existence at that time in the garden of Eden. Paul says sin *entered*, not that it began to be. Sin already existed as a result of Satan's rebellion. This text speaks of sin's inaugural entry into the world of humanity. Sin, therefore, is portrayed as an *intruder*. It was not a constituent element in the original creation.

3. The next important phrase reads, "and death through sin" (see Gen. 2:17; Ezek. 18:4; Rom. 6:23; James 1:15). Paul's point is that sin is the cause of death. Thus, death is a penal evil; it is punishment. Death was not inevitable for Adam and Eve. It was the punishment for rebellion. Death in Scripture may be portrayed in three ways. There is, first of all, *spiritual death* (the alienation of the soul from God and the subsequent spiritual corruption of the whole person; cf. Eph. 2:1–2). Second is *physical death*, which needs no explanation. Finally, there is the *second death*, which is the perpetuation of spiritual death into eternity. The second death

entails eternal separation and alienation from God (cf. Rev. 2:11; 20:6, 14; 21:8). The remedy for spiritual death is regeneration or the new birth. The remedy for physical death is the bodily resurrection. There is no remedy for the second death. It is irremediable, irrevocable, and eternal.

4. This death, says the apostle, "spread to all men." In other words, Adam's sin and its consequences did not stop with him. Physical death as a penal sanction is universal. But why do all die? The answer is found in our fifth important phrase.

5. The declaration "because all sinned" is surely the most difficult statement in this complex paragraph and has been interpreted in a number of different ways. We will focus on the major views.

First, is the doctrine of *Pelagianism*. According to this view the only reason people die is that they themselves personally sin. It is true, of course, that we die because we sin. But this view argues that the only link or connection between Adam's sin and us is that he *set a bad example*, which we have unwisely followed. We each individually reenact Adam's transgression in our own experience. As for Paul's statement in Romans 5:12, Pelagius insisted that we sinned in Adam only in the sense that we imitated his decision to rebel against God. Consequently, all men come into being in the exact condition as Adam's before the fall. Pelagius believed each soul is created immediately by God and thus cannot come into the world contaminated or corrupted by the sin of Adam.

The doctrine of *transmitted* sin, says Pelagius, is blasphemous. Sin cannot be passed along from one person to another. It cannot come upon another by propagation from an ancestor. Sin is not born with man but only committed afterward by man. Sin is not a defect in human nature, he insists, but consists solely in freely chosen acts of our will. Thus, according to Pelagius, an infant is not born in sin, nor does he or she possess any innate moral characteristics. Such are obtained only by the exercise of the will and the habits that develop from it. In other words, we are "socialized" to sin or "conditioned" to sin because of continual exposure to a family and society that are themselves sinful for the same reasons.

There are several problems with the view advocated by Pelagius. For one thing, it is historically and experientially false: not all die because they voluntarily sin (e.g., infants). Also, in Romans 5:15–19 Paul says six times that only *one* sin, the sin of Adam, is the cause of death. Furthermore, if all die because they are guilty of actual transgression, then they die because they sinned as Adam did. But verse 14 says some did *not* sin that way. This interpretation would also destroy the analogy or parallel that Paul draws between Adam and Jesus in verses 15–21. If this view were correct, Paul would be saying that since all men die personally because they sin personally, so also men become righteous personally because they personally obey (which, by the way, is precisely what Pelagius himself believed!). But the point of these verses is that just as we died because of the sin of one, so also we live because of the obedience of one (namely, Jesus). Finally, as Moo points out, "this interpretation fails to explain why it is that, as Paul makes clear, *everyone* does, in fact, sin. Surely there must be *something* inherent in 'being human' that causes everyone, without exception, to decide to worship idols rather than the true God (cf. 1:22–23)."[3]

A second view is known as *realism* and asserts that "human nature" existed in its unindividualized unity in Adam. This organic, physiological solidarity of the race in its natural head, according to which the human nature of the latter is numerically and specifically one with that of the former, is the ground on which the guilt of Adam is imputed to his posterity.[4] In other words, this view asserts that all of humanity were present in Adam naturally, biologically, physically, or seminally. It is from Adam and Eve that all have descended; thus it may be said that we were all in his loins (much in the same way that Levi, being in Abraham's loins, paid tithes to Melchizedek—Heb. 7:10). Thus, when Adam sinned, you were *really* present, being *in* Adam, and thus you participated in his transgression. When *he* partook of the fruit, *you* partook of the fruit. Augustine advocated this view based on his reading of

---

[3] Ibid., 324n51 (emphasis his).

[4] The best defense of realism as a theory of original sin is provided by William G. T. Shedd, *Dogmatic Theology*, vol. 2 (1889; repr., Minneapolis: Klock & Klock, 1979), 3–257. For a critical assessment of this view, see G. C. Berkouwer, *Sin*, trans. Philip C. Holtrop (Grand Rapids: Eerdmans, 1971), 436–48.

Romans 5:12 in the Latin translation of the New Testament. In that version, the final phrase of verse 12 is rendered "*in whom* [a reference to Adam, the "one man" of v. 12] all sinned," not "*because* all sinned."

Thus, according to Augustine, all men *really* and *actually* sinned when Adam sinned, not as individual persons but as participants in the generic human nature that existed in Adam. Infants, therefore, because they participated in the common human nature present in Adam, are born guilty of his (*their?*) sin and subject to that corruption of nature to which it gives rise.

Contrary to Pelagius, Augustine argued that Adam's nature and that of all his posterity became subject to corruption and evil principles. The penalty pronounced on Adam was pronounced on them; the corruption of his nature became the corruption of their nature. Thus, in Adam the whole human race became "a mass of perdition" (*massa damnata*). Therefore, sin is universally present in all, not by way of imitation (Pelagius) but by way of generation.

Although this is certainly an improvement on the view of Pelagius, there are a number of problems with it. For example, how can we *act* before we *exist*? In other words, how can we personally and individually sin before we are individual persons? If this view were correct, would we not also be guilty of all Adam's subsequent sins? Again, according to Paul, it is the sin of *one* man, not of all men in Adam, that accounts for death. Realism says that all die because all really sinned in Adam, but this again destroys the parallel in verses 15–21. Surely it cannot be said that all live because all personally obeyed (contra Pelagius). We were not physically or seminally in Christ when he obeyed. The point of verses 15–21 is that just as men are justified for a righteousness not their own, so also are they condemned for a sin not personally their own. Paul's point is that death came by one man so that life might come by one man. As for the appeal to Hebrews 7:9–10, observe that if this were taken literally, "all actions of all progenitors would have to be ascribed to each of their descendants, which is nearly absurd."[5]

We come now to the third view, known as *federalism* or *cov-*

---

[5] Henri Blocher, *Original Sin: Illuminating the Riddle* (Grand Rapids: Eerdmans, 1997), 115.

enant representation. This view does not deny the reality of a seminal or realistic union of the species in Adam. Nor does it deny that the sinful disposition is transmitted from Adam to his posterity by means of natural propagation. However, advocates of what is called the "representative" or "federal headship" doctrine do deny that this natural solidarity is sufficient to explain the imputation of Adam's sin to his posterity. The representative view insists that by divine appointment, in addition to being the *natural* head of the species, Adam was constituted the *covenant* head of his posterity. Therefore, the ground on which the guilt of the first sin is imputed to the species is that divinely ordained representative principle on the basis of which the species is reckoned to have stood its probation in Adam.

Thus the issue between these two schools of thought is not the existence of a seminal, or natural, union. Both acknowledge the validity of that notion. The point of dispute, rather, is this:

> Was Adam a person in whom human nature existed as an entity, a specific and numerically one entity (that is, all the individuals who come from Adam are specifically one [belong to the same species], and at one time in Adam they were numerically one, but now by propagation have become individualized into a multitude of persons), or was Adam by divine ordination a representative person who stood the probation for his posterity?[6]

The view of covenant headship points to verse 12 of Romans 5, where Paul says all die because all sinned. But in verses 15–19 Paul says all die because *Adam* sinned. In both statements Paul is saying the same thing. But how can it be that the sin of *one* man, Adam, is also the sin of *all* men? The answer is that there is some kind of union or solidarity between Adam and us. It can't simply be a physical or natural union, as the realists contend. It must be a *legal* or *representative* union, that is, a *covenant union*. God entered into covenant with Adam as representative head of the human race. God dealt with Adam as with all his posterity.

---

[6] S. Lewis Johnson, "Romans 5:12—An Exercise in Exegesis and Theology," in *New Dimensions in New Testament Study*, ed. Richard N. Longenecker and Merrill C. Tenney (Grand Rapids: Zondervan, 1974), 309.

Thus, we became guilty of Adam's sin and suffer its penalty not because we personally committed a sin like Adam's sin, as the Pelagians argue, or because we sinned in Adam as our physical or biological root, as the realists insist, but because Adam served in the capacity as covenant head of the human race. Similarly, we become righteous because of Christ's obedience, and experience the life it brings, not because we personally obeyed, but because our covenant head, Jesus, obeyed (see 1 Cor. 15:21ff.).

Two Men, Two Deeds, Two Destinies

What the doctrine of original sin means is that whereas Adam ruined us, Christ renewed us. As we are condemned for the sin of the first Adam, we are justified for the obedience of the last Adam. This is why Adam is called the *type* of Christ in Romans 5:14. According to this view, God has not dealt with men as with a field of corn, each standing for himself, or as pebbles of sand on the shore, each person isolated and independent of all others. Rather he has dealt with men as with a tree, all the branches sharing a common root. While the root remains healthy, the branches remain healthy. When the axe cuts and severs the root, all die.

The primary objection to this view is what appears to be the injustice of it. To hold all of the human race eternally accountable for the sin of one of its members *seems* morally inconceivable. But let's give the apostle Paul a chance to vindicate himself!

When we turn to verses 13–14 we see that Paul's point is to demonstrate that personal death is not always the result of personal sin. He has in mind that period in Old Testament history stretching from Adam to the Mosaic law. During this period people certainly sinned. But in the absence of law, their sin was not imputed to them (v. 13). Nevertheless, *they died*. But why did they die if God did not impute their sins against them? The answer would seem to be that they died because of the sin of another, someone who *had* indeed violated a divinely revealed law. That other person, of course, would be Adam.

Moreover, says Paul, death reigned even over those who did not sin like Adam did. In other words, there is a class of people who never sinned voluntarily and personally as Adam did, as the majority of the people during this period did, *but they still died!* Whom does he have in mind? Infants, most likely. But if infants don't sin voluntarily and personally, why do they die? If death comes only as a penalty for sin, why do infants, who commit no sin, still die? It must be because of the sin of another. It must be that those who die in infancy, before they commit conscious, personal sin, die because of the sin of their representative head, Adam.

The parallels and ethical contrasts in verses 15–21 between Adam and Jesus are crucial to Paul's argument.

- The offense of one brought death; the obedience of one brought the free gift of grace (v. 15).
- One sinned, bringing condemnation; one obeyed, bringing justification (v. 16).
- Through one offense death reigns; through one act of obedience life reigns (v. 17).
- The offense of one brings judgment; the righteousness of one brings justification (v. 18).
- By virtue of one man's disobedience men are made sinners; by virtue of one man's obedience men are made righteous (v. 19).
- Through Adam sin reigned unto death; through Christ righteousness reigns unto life (v. 21).

So, before you object to the doctrine of covenant or representative headship, remember this: *only if Adam represents you in the garden can Jesus represent you on Golgotha.* It was on the cross that Jesus served as your representative head: his obedience to the law, his righteousness, and his suffering the penalty of the law were all the acts of a covenant head acting in the stead and on behalf of his people. If Adam stood for you in the garden, Christ may also hang for you on the cross. If you insist on standing your own probation before God, instead of submitting to the covenant representation of Adam, you must also stand on your own in regard to righteousness. And how do you think you will fare? In other words, if you fall individually and by your own doing, it would appear you must be saved individually and by your own doing.

We need to take note of one more issue in verse 18. Adam's act has brought condemnation to all men. Must we not also conclude, as this verse seems to assert, that Christ's act has brought justification and life for all men? In other words, does this verse teach the doctrine of *universalism*? Moo's answer is helpful:

> Paul's point is not so much that the groups affected by Christ and Adam, respectively, are coextensive, but that Christ affects those who are his just as certainly as Adam does those who are his. When we ask who belongs to, or is "in," Adam and Christ, respectively, Paul makes his answer clear: every person, without exception, is "in Adam" (cf. vv. 12d–14); but only those who "receive the gift" (v. 17; "those who believe," according to Rom. 1:16–5:11) are "in Christ." That "all" does not always mean "every single human being" is clear from many passages; it is often clearly limited in context (e.g., Rom. 8:32; 12:17, 18; 14:2; 16:19), so this suggestion has no linguistic barrier. In the present verse, the scope of "all people" in the two parts of the verse is distinguished in the context, Paul making it clear, both by his silence and by the logic of [Rom. 5] vv. 12–14, that there is no limitation whatsoever on the number of those who are involved in Adam's sin, while the deliberately worded v. 17, along with the persistent stress on faith as the means of achieving righteousness in 1:16–4:25, makes it equally clear that only certain people derive the benefits from Christ's act of righteousness.[7]

Conclusion

This brief discussion of the notion of original sin serves to confirm what we already know from experience: we are by nature, from birth, universally wicked. The so-called enlightened man of the twenty-first century may prefer not to think of himself in this way, choosing instead to dismiss what we've seen in this chapter as an overly pessimistic and outmoded view of human nature. But it is only when we fully realize and acknowledge in personal confession that "in Adam's fall, we sinned all," and that we are indeed morally corrupt and spiritually alienated from God that the salvation provided in Christ Jesus will be appealing to our souls.

There is, however, one more gut-wrenching issue that must be

---

[7] Moo, *The Epistle to the Romans*, 343–44.

addressed. If our portrayal of the human condition at birth is that we are, in the words of Paul, "by nature children of wrath" (Eph. 2:3), what becomes of those who die in infancy? To that question we turn in the next chapter.

Addendum: An Alternative Interpretation of Romans 5:12–14

One of the principal issues in the interpretation of Romans 5 is Paul's statement that death spread to all men "because all sinned." On this reading, Paul's point would be that all men die because, when Adam sinned, they were reckoned by God to have sinned in him, their representative head.

An alternative reading has recently been proposed by Tom Schreiner, first in his commentary on Romans[8] and more recently in his treatise on the theology of Paul.[9] Schreiner contends that we should translate this enigmatic phrase not "because" but "upon the basis of which." His point is that the sinning of all people is a *consequence* or *result* of that death which entered the world through Adam. He writes:

> As a result of Adam's sin death entered the world and engulfed all people; all people enter the world alienated from God and spiritually dead by virtue of Adam's sin. By virtue of entering the world in the state of death (i.e., separated from God), all human beings sin. . . . Our alienation and separation from God are due to Adam's sin, and thus we sin as a result of being born into the world separated from God's life.[10]

Paul's point is not that we sinned when Adam sinned, whether "seminally" or by virtue of his representative role, as a result of which we died spiritually. Rather, Adam's sin brought spiritual death into the world, as a result of which death we sinned personally. The objection to this view is that Paul often argues that death is the result of sin, whereas Schreiner is arguing here that sin is

---

[8] Thomas R. Schreiner, *Romans* (Grand Rapids: Baker, 1998).
[9] Thomas R. Schreiner, *Paul: Apostle of God's Glory in Christ* (Downers Grove, IL: InterVarsity, 2001).
[10] Schreiner, *Romans*, 275–76.

the result of death. The resolution of this problem, notes Schreiner, is not difficult.

> We should not opt for an either-or answer here. Paul does indeed claim that people die because of sin, but he also insists that they sin because they are dead (i.e., separated from God [and he points particularly to Eph. 2:1–3 as proof of this]). All human beings enter the world alienated from God, and as a result of this alienation they sin. It is also true that they will experience eschatological death if they sin.[11]

If Schreiner is correct, what is the meaning of Romans 5:13–14? Contrary to the view explained earlier, Paul is not suggesting that people between Adam and Moses died solely because of Adam's sin and not because of their own personal rebellion. Romans 2:12 makes this clear, for there Paul asserts that "those who sin without the law perish without the law." Schreiner explains:

> It would be inconsistent for Paul to assert in Romans 2:12 that Gentiles without the law perish because they transgress the unwritten law and then to say in Romans 5:13–14 that sin is not charged to the account of those without the Mosaic law. Moreover, Paul was well aware of the early chapters of Genesis in which the world was destroyed by a flood and those building the tower of Babel were judged. Such punishments would be indefensible if judgment was only valid after the law of Moses was disseminated. The judgment of the flood generation and Babel fits with the Pauline principle that those who sin without the law will perish without the law (Rom. 2:12).[12]

What, then, does Paul mean in 5:13 when he says that "sin is not counted when there is no law"? He does not mean that people aren't punished for their personal sin simply because the law of Moses had not yet been given. His point is simply that sin committed before the Mosaic law is not *technically* reckoned as sin. In other words, "there was not a technical register of sin; sin was present, just like heat and cold are present whether we have a

---

[11] Ibid., 276–77.
[12] Schreiner, *Paul*, 147.

thermometer or not. But one could not, in a sense, *measure* sin before the giving of the law."[13] It's true that people between Adam and Moses didn't sin as Adam did in that they did not violate a revealed commandment. But this doesn't mean they weren't held accountable by God for their actions. It simply means their sin couldn't be measured as sin without the violation of written commandments.

Paul's point, then, is that death reigns or exercises its power over people even if no explicit and divinely encoded law exists, for even in the absence of the law sin is still sin and will be punished. Once that written law is revealed, the seriousness of sin increases "in the sense that the sin is now more defiant and rebellious in character."[14]

Two brief observations are in order, neither of which is a critique of Schreiner. First, if Schreiner is correct, the sinful plight of the human race is *still* traceable to Adam and his sin. Whether we die spiritually because we are reckoned to have sinned in Adam or we sin personally because of the spiritual death that came from Adam's sin, the fact remains that it is "by the transgression of the one," Adam, that "the many died" (5:15, NASB). Second, if Schreiner is correct, he has provided a helpful way of understanding Romans 5:12–14, but not one that is any more successful than the earlier view in addressing the ethical dilemma of how the human race can find itself sinful, not ultimately because of personal, conscious sin, but because of the sin of another, Adam.

Recommended Reading

Blocher, Henri. *Original Sin: Illuminating the Riddle.* Grand Rapids: Eerdmans, 1997.

Jacobs, Alan. *Original Sin: A Cultural History.* New York: HarperOne, 2008.

Plantinga, Cornelius, Jr. *Not the Way It's Supposed to Be: A Breviary of Sin.* Grand Rapids: Eerdmans, 1995.

---

[13] Ibid., 148.
[14] Schreiner, *Romans*, 279; cf. Paul's statement to this effect in Rom. 7:7–11.

8

Are Those Who Die in Infancy Saved?

There are days that we never forget. Some are indelibly imprinted in our minds because of the joy they evoke, while others we can't shake because of the emotional pain and distress surrounding them. One of the latter occurred for me in 1978 as I was summoned to the hospital with news that a lady in our church had given premature birth to two baby girls. Upon arriving at the hospital I was informed that one of the girls had died. I never anticipated the question that came my way as I walked into the room of the grieving mother. Before anyone could say so much as hello, the words came: "Sam, is my baby in heaven?" Years of seminary training had failed to prepare me for such a moment. I felt so helpless and somewhat ashamed that I stumbled to respond in a way that would touch the hearts of these grieving parents.

A few years later the young child of a good friend was killed in a car accident. The parents asked me to perform the funeral, once again putting me in the position of having to think through and articulate in a biblical and compassionate way what I believed about the eternal destiny of their child. So, what conclusion did I reach?

If human nature is corrupt and guilty from conception, the consequence of Adam's transgression (Ps. 51:5; Eph. 2:1ff.), are those who die in infancy lost? The same question would apply to those who live beyond infancy but because of mental disability or some other handicap are incapable of moral discernment, deliberation, or volition. This is more than a theoretical issue designed for our speculation and curiosity. It touches one of the most emotionally and spiritually unsettling experiences in all of life: the loss of a young child. Let's take a look at the variety of options that have been suggested.

Problematic Views

One view insists that those dying in infancy are saved for the simple reason that there is nothing in them or done by them that merits condemnation. In other words, they are born in a state of moral neutrality or moral equilibrium. They do not possess a sin nature, nor are they corrupt. They are, in a word, characterless. They lack moral standing. There is nothing in their souls that is properly the object of divine judgment. Hence all who die in that state are saved for no other reason than that they are not condemnable. Several texts would seem to contradict this view, among them Genesis 8:21; Job 15:14–16; Psalms 51:5; 58:3; Proverbs 22:15; and Ephesians 2:3.

Another viewpoint simply asserts that all will be saved, inclusive of those dying in infancy. None will suffer eternal condemnation. God's saving grace extends effectually to the entire human race. Again, countless texts could be cited to disprove this idea, among them Matthew 7:13–14, 21–23; 8:11–12; 10:28; 13:37–42; Luke 16:23–28; 2 Thessalonians 1:9; Jude 6; Revelation 14:10–11; 20:11–15.

Based on a certain (misguided) interpretation of 1 Peter 3:18–19 and 4:6, it is asserted that those who die without having the opportunity to hear the gospel of Christ and make a cognitively and morally informed decision will be granted a "second chance" (though it would be, in fact, a *first* chance if they never had a legitimate opportunity in this life). As for infants in particular, it is said that God will bring them to a state in which they are sufficiently mature to understand and choose responsibly.

There are several problems with this view. First, how can they be brought into a state of maturity by God without the influence of parents, education, peers, experience, and so on, which contribute to our own intellectual and spiritual framework and on the basis of which we ourselves make an informed choice? Would they be brought into a state of moral equilibrium, having had no history of personal sin that so decisively shapes who people are? If God is the one who somehow directly educates and nurtures them, has he not then prejudiced their minds and wills in a way that is altogether different from the way we are educated and nurtured? The problems associated with this are innumerable.

Furthermore, the two texts on which this view is based say nothing about postmortem evangelism for either those dying in infancy or pagans who never hear the name of Jesus. Finally, from a pastoral point of view, this theory does nothing to ease the anxieties of parents who want to know whether their baby is in heaven, for there is no guarantee, on this view, that even if given an opportunity after death they will respond in faith.

Others have appealed to 1 Corinthians 7:14–16 to argue that the infants or children of a believing parent or parents are, for that reason, granted special salvific privilege in the kingdom of God. Again, this view is only as cogent as is that particular interpretation of 1 Corinthians 7. A related perspective advocated by a number of Reformed theologians is that *some* who die in infancy are elect, and therefore saved, while others are nonelect, and therefore condemned.

Certain traditions within Christianity have affirmed baptismal regeneration, according to which the waters of baptism are used by God to effect the regeneration, spiritual cleansing, and forgiveness of the infant. Needless to say, this view is only as cogent as the case for baptismal regeneration, which is worse than weak. In addition, it fails to address the question of what happens to the vast majority of infants in the history of the world who have died without the benefit of Christian baptism.

The Roman Catholic Church has acknowledged the possibility of a state of natural blessedness or happiness in which unbaptized infants experience a form of eternal peace (limbo) but not the consummate joy of heaven itself.[1] The concept of limbo in Roman Catholic theology is tied to its doctrines of original sin and the necessity of baptism for salvation. The Catechism of the Catholic Church defines baptism as follows:

> Holy Baptism is the basis of the whole Christian life, the gateway to life in the Spirit, and the door which gives access to the other sacraments. Through Baptism we are freed from sin and reborn as sons of God; we become members of Christ, are incorporated into the Church and made sharers in her mission: "Baptism is the sacrament of regeneration through water and in the word."[2]

According to Roman Catholicism, two things are accomplished in water baptism: first, the individual is purified from the guilt of both original sin and all personal sins (the latter, of course, would be relevant only in the case of adults); and second, the person experiences regeneration or the new birth. In the catechism, we read that "baptism not only purifies from all sins, but also makes the neophyte 'a new creature,' an adopted son of God, who has become a 'partaker of the divine nature,' member of Christ and co-heir with him, and a temple of the Holy Spirit."[3]

Children are likewise to be baptized. According to the catechism:

> Born with a fallen human nature and tainted by original sin, children also have need of the new birth in Baptism to be freed from the power of darkness and brought into the realm of the freedom of the children of God, to which all men are called. . . . The Church and the parents would deny a child the priceless grace of becoming a child of God were they not to confer Baptism shortly after birth.[4]

Does this mean, then, that those infants who die without the

---

[1] The word "limbo" comes from the Latin *limbus*, meaning a hem, edge, or boundary.
[2] The Catechism of the Catholic Church, 1213.
[3] Ibid., 1265.
[4] Ibid., 1250.

sacrament of baptism remain in their sin, unregenerate, and condemned to hell? Augustine (d. 430) said yes, although they do not suffer the full extent of hell's misery because they have committed no personal sin. Medieval Catholic theologians were uncomfortable with this and wanted to mitigate what they perceived as the harshness of Augustine's doctrine, so they formulated the concept of limbo, a place or experience in the afterlife in which unbaptized infants enjoy a natural happiness, blessedness, or peace, but are excluded from the beatific vision, or sight of God (and the supernatural joys that living in his presence brings).

The catechism does not use the word *limbo* but contains the following explanation:

> As regards *children who have died without Baptism*, the Church can only entrust them to the mercy of God, as she does in her funeral rites for them. Indeed, the great mercy of God who desires that all men should be saved, and Jesus' tenderness toward children which caused him to say: "Let the children come to me, do not hinder them," allow us to hope that there is a way of salvation for children who have died without Baptism.[5]

The Catholic Church has never formally recognized or denied the existence of limbo in its official teaching. Thus one cannot characterize it as either a dogma or a heresy.

In December of 2005, thirty leading theologians met at the Vatican to discuss what should be done with the concept. They had been summoned a year earlier by the late John Paul II to develop a "more coherent and illuminating" doctrine. In 1984, then Cardinal Ratzinger, now Pope Benedict XVI, told Catholic author Vittorio Messori that limbo had "never been a definitive truth of the faith" and that it was "only a theological hypothesis" and should be dropped. Although nothing has been done as yet, one expects Benedict to make it "official" that unbaptized infants enter into the fullness of heavenly bliss.

There are two interesting corollaries to this development. In a recent *Time* magazine editorial, David Van Biema writes that "in

---

[5] Ibid., 1261.

the absence of limbo . . . the rite of baptism may not seem as imperative to many Catholics as it once appeared. Despite its continued centrality as the sacramental entry to the body of Christ, some of its ASAP urgency will presumably fade."[6] Whereas that may well be true for many Catholic parents, I doubt that the Church's more conservative theologians will countenance such a thought.

Many see this impending decision as consistent with the church's stance on abortion as murder. Recently Pope Benedict asserted that the embryo, despite its lack of physical development, is a "full and complete" human being. In the same *Time* article the author observes that "if you are going to call a fetus' termination murder, then it seems somehow inconsistent to deny heaven to the blameless, full and complete victim."[7] I won't comment on the cogency of such reasoning or its theological implications, but it does provide the Catholic Church a way of granting grieving parents a measure of consolation following the loss of a child.

Salvation for All Who Die in Infancy

The view that I embrace is that *all* those dying in infancy, as well as those so mentally incapacitated that they are incapable of making an informed choice, are among the elect of God chosen by him for salvation before the world began. The evidence for this view is scant, but significant.

First, in Romans 1:20 Paul describes people who are recipients of general revelation as being "without excuse." That is to say, they cannot blame their unbelief on a lack of evidence. There is sufficient revelation of God's existence in the natural order to establish the moral accountability of all who witness it. Does this imply that those who are *not* recipients of general revelation (i.e., infants) are therefore *not* accountable to God or subject to wrath? In other words, would not those who die in infancy have an "excuse" in that they neither receive general revelation nor have the capacity to respond to it?

Second, there are texts that appear to assert or imply that in-

---

[6] *Time*, January 9, 2006, 68.
[7] Ibid.

fants do not know good or evil and hence lack the capacity to make morally informed and thus responsible choices. According to Deuteronomy 1:39 they are said to "have no knowledge of good or evil." This in itself, however, would not prove infant salvation, for they may still be held liable for the sin of Adam.

Third, we must take account of the story of David's son in 2 Samuel 12:15–23 (esp. v. 23). The firstborn child of David and Bathsheba was struck by the Lord and died. In the seven days before his death, David fasted and prayed, hoping that "the LORD will be gracious to me, that the child may live" (v. 22). Following his death, David washed himself, ate food, and worshiped (v. 20). When asked why he responded in this way, he said that the child "is dead. Why should I fast? Can I bring him back again? I shall go to him, but he will not return to me" (v. 23).

What does it mean when David says "I shall go to him"? If this is merely a reference to the grave or death, in the sense that David, too, shall one day die and be buried, one wonders why he would say something so patently obvious! Also, it *appears* that David draws some measure of comfort from knowing that he will "go to him." It is the reason why David resumes the normal routine of life. It *appears* to be the reason David ceases from the outward display of grief. It *appears* to be a truth from which David derives comfort and encouragement. How could any of this be true if David is simply saying that he will die like his son? It would, therefore, *appear* that David believes he will be reunited with his deceased infant. Does this imply that at least *this one particular infant* is saved? Perhaps. But if so, are we justified in constructing a doctrine in which we affirm the salvation of *all* who die in infancy?

Fourth, there is the consistent testimony of Scripture that people are judged on the basis of sins voluntarily and consciously committed in the body (see 1 Cor. 6:9–10; 2 Cor. 5:10; Rev. 20:11–12). In other words, eternal judgment is always based on conscious rejection of divine revelation (whether in creation, conscience, or Christ) and willful disobedience. Are infants capable of either? There is no explicit account in Scripture of any other judgment based on any other grounds. Thus, those dying in infancy are saved because they do not (indeed cannot) satisfy the conditions for divine judgment.

Fifth, and related to the above point, is what R. A. Webb states. If a deceased infant

> were sent to hell on no other account than that of original sin, there would be a good reason to the divine mind for the judgment, but the child's mind would be a perfect blank as to the reason of its suffering. Under such circumstances, it would know suffering, but it would have no understanding of the reason for its suffering. It could not tell its neighbor—it could not tell itself—why it was so awfully smitten; and consequently the whole meaning and significance of its sufferings, being to it a conscious enigma, the very essence of penalty would be absent, and justice would be disappointed of its vindication. Such an infant could feel that it was in hell, but it could not explain, to its own conscience, why it was there.[8]

Sixth, we have what appears to be clear biblical evidence that at least *some* infants are regenerate in the womb, such that if they had died in their infancy, they would be saved. This at least provides a theoretical basis for considering whether the same may be true of all who die in infancy. That is to say, "if this sort of thing happens even once, it can certainly happen in other cases."[9] These texts include Jeremiah 1:5 and Luke 1:15.

Seventh, some have appealed to Matthew 19:13–15 (Mark 10:13–16; Luke 18:15–17), where Jesus declares, "Let the little children come to me and do not hinder them, for to such belongs the kingdom of heaven." Is Jesus simply saying that if one wishes to be saved, he or she must be as trusting as children, that is, devoid of skepticism and arrogance? In other words, is Jesus merely describing the *kind* of people who enter the kingdom? Or is he saying that *these very* children were recipients of saving grace? If the latter were true, it would seem to imply that Jesus knew either that the children whom he was then receiving would all die in their infancy or that they would continue to live and all be saved. Is that credible?

---

[8] R. A. Webb, *The Theology of Infant Salvation* (Harrisonburg, VA: Sprinkle, 1981), 288–89.
[9] Ronald Nash, *When a Baby Dies* (Grand Rapids: Zondervan, 1999), 65.

Eighth, Millard Erickson argues for the salvation of deceased infants in an unusual way. He reasons that notwithstanding Adam's sin, there must be a conscious and voluntary decision on our part to embrace or ratify it. Until such is the case, the imputation of Adam's sin to his physical posterity, as is also true of the imputation of Christ's righteousness to his spiritual posterity, is *conditional*. Thus, prior to reaching the "age of accountability" all infants are innocent. When and in what way does this ratification of Adam's sin come about? Erickson explains:

> We become responsible and guilty when we accept or approve of our corrupt nature. There is a time in the life of each one of us when we become aware of our own tendency toward sin. At that point we may abhor the sinful nature that has been there all the time. We would in that case repent of it and might even, if there is an awareness of the gospel, ask God for forgiveness and cleansing. . . . But if we acquiesce in that sinful nature, we are in effect saying that it is good. In placing our tacit approval upon the corruption, we are also approving or concurring in the action in the Garden of Eden so long ago. We become guilty of that sin without having to commit a sin of our own.[10]

But there are at least two problems with this. First, if we are born with a corrupt and sinful nature, as Erickson concedes we are, our willing ratification of Adam's transgression, and the guilt and corruption of nature that are its effects, is *itself* an inevitable effect of the corrupt nature to which we are now ostensibly giving our approval. In other words, how else *could* a person who is born corrupt and wicked respond but in a corrupt and wicked way, namely, by ratifying Adam's sin? If Erickson should suggest that such a response is *not* inevitable, one can only wonder why *every single human being* who ever lived (except Jesus) ratifies and embraces the sin of Adam and its resultant corruption of nature. Surely someone, somewhere would have said no. Erickson would have to argue that at the point when each soul becomes morally accountable, it enters a state of complete moral and spiritual equi-

---

[10] Millard J. Erickson, *Christian Theology*, vol. 2 (Grand Rapids: Baker, 1984), 639.

librium, in no way biased by the corruption of nature and wicked disposition with which it was born.

But that leads to the second problem, for it would mean that each of us experiences our own garden of Eden, as it were. Each human soul stands its own probation at the moment the age of moral accountability is reached. But if that were so, what would be the point of trying to retain any connection at all between what Adam did and who or what we are? If ultimately I become corrupt *by* my own first choice, what need is there of Adam? And if I am corrupt *prior to* that first choice, we are back to square one: my guilt and corruption inherited from Adam, the penal consequence of *his* choice as the head and representative of the race.

Conclusion

As we bring this most difficult chapter to a close, we must ask the question, Given our understanding of the character of God as presented in Scripture, does he appear as the kind of God who would eternally condemn infants on no other ground than that of Adam's transgression? Admittedly, this is a subjective (and perhaps sentimental) question. But it deserves an answer, nonetheless. And mine is no.

So, I can only speak for myself, but I find the first, third, fourth, and fifth points sufficiently convincing. Therefore, I do believe in the salvation of those dying in infancy. I affirm their salvation, however, neither because they are innocent nor because they have merited God's forgiveness but solely because God has sovereignly chosen them for eternal life, regenerated their souls, and applied the saving benefits of the blood of Christ to them apart from conscious faith.

Recommended Reading

Nash, Ronald. *When a Baby Dies*. Grand Rapids: Zondervan, 1999.

Webb, R. A. *The Theology of Infant Salvation*. Harrisonburg, VA: Sprinkle, 1981.

9

Will People Be Condemned for Not Believing in Jesus though They've Never Heard His Name?

In an interview with Sally Quinn of *The Washington Post*, Rob Bell, author of the best-selling book *Love Wins*, again muddied the waters over the question of the fate of those who've never heard about Jesus. In doing so he also greatly misrepresented the evangelical answer to this question. Here are his words:

> If, billions and billions and billions of people, God is going to torture them in hell forever—people who never heard about Jesus are going to suffer in eternal agony because they didn't believe in the Jesus they never heard of—then at that point we will have far bigger problems than a book from a pastor from Grand Rapids.

Bell is responding to evangelicals who purportedly believe that people "are going to suffer in eternal agony because they didn't believe in the Jesus they never heard of." Let me say this as clearly as I can: *No one will ever suffer for any length of time in hell or anywhere else for not believing in the Jesus they never heard of.* Should I say that again or is it enough to ask that you go back and read it again?

Romans 1: God Is Revealed to All

Bell and others who make this sort of outrageous claim have evidently failed to look closely at Romans 1:18ff. There we read that the wrath of God revealed from heaven is grounded in the persistent repudiation by mankind of the revelation God has made of himself in the created order. In other words, there is a reason for God's wrath. It is not capricious. God's wrath has been deliberately and persistently provoked by man's willful rejection of God as he has revealed himself.

The revelation is both *from* God and *about* God. Therefore, in this case if the pupil does not learn, it is not because the teacher did not teach. The phrase "evident to them" (v. 19, NASB) is better rendered either ". . . in them" or ". . . among them," probably the latter. In other words, God has made himself known among people (and thus, in a manner of speaking, to them, in their minds and hearts) in his works of creation and providence.

Observe Paul's paradoxical language in verse 20: he refers to God's invisible attributes (cf. 1 Tim. 1:17) as clearly seen (an oxymoron). Paul's point is that the invisible is made visible via creation or nature. Divine wisdom, power, eternity, and goodness, for example, are not in themselves visible, but their reality is undeniably affirmed and apprehended by the effects they produce in nature. That there is a God who is supreme, eternal, infinite in power, personal, wise, independent, and worthy of glory and gratitude is clearly evident in the creation.

How are these truths about God made known, and where may we see them? Paul's answer is, "in the things that have been made" (Rom. 1:20). God has left the indelible mark of his fingerprints all across the vast face of the universe. Those who do not have a Bible in which to read of his existence and nature can still look at the moon in its beauty, the sun in its brightness, the stars in their order, the thunder and lightning in their power, the human body in its exquisite detail, the mountains in their grandeur, the oceans in their expanse, and the vast array of species in the animal kingdom and see without mistake that there is a God of power and majesty and holiness and love. Herman Bavinck put it succinctly in declaring that "there is not an atom of the universe in which God's power and divinity are not revealed."[1]

Paul's point here in Romans 1 is that this revelation is sufficiently clear and inescapable to render all *without excuse* (see v. 20). Consequently, there is no such thing as "an innocent native in Africa," any more than there is "an innocent pagan in America."

What does Paul mean when he says that all humanity is without excuse? R. C. Sproul explains:

> The excuse that is banished, the excuse every pagan hopes in vain to use, the excuse that is exploded by God's self-revelation in nature is the pretended, vacuous, dishonest appeal to ignorance. No one will be able to approach the judgment seat of God justly pleading, "If only I had known you existed, I would surely have served you." That excuse is annihilated. No one can lightly claim "insufficient" evidence for not believing in God.[2]

The problem is not a lack of evidence. The problem is the innate, natural, moral antipathy of mankind to God. The problem is not that the evidence is not open to all humanity. The problem is that humanity is not open to the evidence. Note well Paul's words: "For even though they knew God" (v. 21). Again, "that which is known about God is evident within them" (v. 19, NASB)—not hidden, obscure, uncertain, but disclosed, clear, and inescapable. There is no such thing as an honest atheist! All people know God. There is a distinction, of course, between a cognitive apprehension of God— knowing that there is a God and that he is worthy of obedience, worship, and gratitude—and a saving or redemptive knowledge of God. All people experience the former, whereas only the redeemed

---

[1] Herman Bavinck, *The Doctrine of God*, trans. and ed. William Hendriksen (Edinburgh: Banner of Truth, 1977), 63.
[2] R. C. Sproul, Arthur Lindsley, and John Gerstner, *Classical Apologetics: A Rational Defense of the Christian Faith and a Critique of Presuppositional Apologetics* (Grand Rapids: Zondervan, 1984), 46.

experience the latter. Thus the problem, again, "is not a failure to honor what was not known, but a refusal to honor what was clearly known."[3]

Paul saw the unbeliever's knowledge of God as *real* though not *saving*. Unbelievers have more than an awareness of God. They know both that he exists and is of a certain moral character and that they themselves are accountable to him. In other words, their knowledge of God brings *subjective* understanding, but not *saving* understanding. The God they truly and really know, they hate and refuse to honor. Their response, however, is borne not of ignorance but of willful rebellion and self-centered sinfulness.

But Paul is equally clear that all persistently suppress this knowledge (see vv. 21–32). He does not say that they began in darkness and futility and are slowly but surely groping their way toward the light. Rather, they began with the clear, inescapable light of the knowledge of God and regressed into darkness.

The reference to them as "futile" and "fools" (vv. 21–22) does not mean all pagans are stupid. It is not human intelligence that is in view but one's disposition. The problem with the unsaved isn't that he can't think with his head. The problem is that he refuses to believe with his heart. The unsaved man is a fool not because he is of questionable intelligence. He is a fool because of his immoral refusal to acknowledge and bow to what he knows is true.

What is the response of the human heart to this revelatory activity of God? Paul describes it in verses 21–23. What he has in mind involves a distortion or deliberate mutation when one substitutes something artificial or counterfeit for that which is genuine. Clearly, then, the person who rejects God does not cease to be religious. Indeed, he becomes religious in order to reject God. He substitutes for God a deity of his own making, often himself.

This leads to three important conclusions. First, the revelation of God in creation and conscience is sufficient to render all people without excuse, sufficient to lead to their condemnation if they repudiate it, but not sufficient to save. No one will be saved solely because of his or her acknowledgment of God in nature, but

---

[3] Ibid., 51.

many will be lost because of their refusal of him as revealed there. In other words, general revelation lacks redemptive content. It is adequate to provide all humankind with a general knowledge that God exists and of what he is like, but in itself it does not save anyone. It makes known that there is a God who punishes sin but not that he pardons it.

Second, and please note this well, *the so-called heathen are not condemned for rejecting Jesus, about whom they have heard nothing, but for rejecting the Father, about whom they have heard and seen much*. Whatever about God is included in Paul's words, "his invisible attributes, namely, his eternal power and divine nature" (Rom. 1:20), the knowledge of such is universal and inescapable and renders all people without an excuse for their unbelief, without an excuse for their failure to honor God, without an excuse for their refusal to thank God, and without an excuse for turning from the one true God to the worship of idols.

Third, general revelation is the essential prerequisite to special revelation. And special revelation is that which redemptively supplements and interprets general revelation. Therefore, if by God's gracious and sovereign enablement and enlightenment any unbeliever responds positively to the revelation of God in nature (and conscience), God will take the necessary steps to reach that person with the good news of Christ whereby he or she may be saved.

Conclusion

What we have seen from this brief look at Romans 1 is that God has made his existence and attributes known to all humanity in every age, people of every religion in every nation on earth. These people may never hear the name of Jesus. They may never hear the gospel proclaimed. They may never hear of the cross or the resurrection. They may never hold in their hands a Bible in their own language. But they are totally and justly and righteously "without excuse" before God for their failure to honor him as God and their subsequent idolatrous turn to created things as a substitute for the Creator.

They will not be judged for their rejection of Jesus, of whom they have heard nothing. For Rob Bell or anyone else to suggest that we believe they will is a distortion of what we affirm and, worse still, is a distortion of what Paul clearly taught. People will be held accountable and judged on the basis of the revelation God has made of himself to them. This revelation is unmistakable, unavoidable, and sufficiently pervasive and clear that their failure to respond, as well as their turning to idolatry, renders them "without excuse." They will be righteously judged for rejecting the Father, not for rejecting the Son.

Recommended Reading

Nash, Ronald H. *Is Jesus the Only Savior?* Grand Rapids: Zondervan, 1994.

Piper, John. *Jesus: The Only Way to God: Must You Hear the Gospel to Be Saved?* Grand Rapids: Baker, 2010.

Sanders, John, ed. *What about Those Who Have Never Heard? Three Views on the Destiny of the Unevangelized.* Downers Grove, IL: InterVarsity, 1995.

10

What Can We Know about Angels?

For many years I readily acknowledged the *existence* of both holy angels and fallen demonic spirits, but relegated their activity to the pages of the Bible. As one who affirms biblical authority, I couldn't deny the reality of such beings, but they played little if any role in the daily affairs of my life (or so I thought). Angels and demons were fine (in a manner of speaking), but only if they remained tucked safely away inside the two covers of my Bible. That I should ever encounter an angelic being, or a demonic one, was not something I expected, but was something I would have quickly explained away lest I be regarded as theologically naïve or given to charismatic sensationalism. What I hope this chapter will do is awaken all of us to the inescapable reality of angelic and demonic activity and the necessity of our preparation for the battle in which we are engaged.

We'll look at eight key questions.

Eight Questions about Angels

1. Our first question is simply, *Do angels really exist, and if they do, does it matter?* The evidence for the existence of angels is

spread throughout Scripture. The words translated "angel" occur in 34 of the 66 books of the Bible: 108 times in the Old Testament and over 165 times in the New, which is nearly 275 times in the Bible.

Jesus believed in the presence of angels and was even the recipient of their ministry of encouragement and strengthening. Just consider how pervasive and influential angels were in his earthly life: his conception was announced by an angel (Gabriel); his birth was announced by angels; he was tempted by a fallen angel; he was ministered to by angels subsequent to the temptation; his teaching is filled with references to angelic beings; he experienced the ministry of angels in Gethsemane; he could have appealed to twelve legions of angels to deliver him from death (Matt. 26:53); angels were present at his tomb following the resurrection and they were present at his ascension. The point is that angels were an integral part of Christ's birth, life, ministry, teaching, death, resurrection, and ascension, and will even accompany him at his second advent. Thus to deny the reality of the angelic world is to undermine the integrity of Jesus himself.

2. *Where did angels come from?* Angels, no less than humans, were *created* at a point in time (Ps. 148:2–5; John 1:1–3; Col. 1:16). They are *not* eternal beings. Each angel is a direct creation. That is to say, they did not descend from an original pair as we did; they do not procreate as we do (Matt. 22:28–30). We don't know *when* angels were created, but it is likely this happened before the events of Genesis 1:1 (see Job 38:4–7). They must have been created righteous and upright for the simple fact that God does not directly create evil. Several texts assert or imply an original act of rebellion (Colossians 1; Revelation 12; more on this in the chapters on Satan and demons).

3. *What are they like?* That's sort of an open-ended question, so I'll limit myself to just a few important points. First, let's think in terms of *personality*, the basic elements of which are intellect, emotion, will, self-consciousness, self-determination, and a sense

of moral obligation (i.e., conscience) and the power to pursue it. Angels certainly are intelligent but not omniscient (Mark 13:32; 1 Pet. 1:12), experience emotion (Job 38:7; Luke 15:10; Revelation 4–5), and exercise their wills (Revelation 12).

People often ask whether angels were created in the image of God, as were humans. The Bible nowhere explicitly affirms or denies this. Of course, it all depends on how one defines the "image" of God. If it entails such things as personality, reason or intellect, a capacity for relationship, self-consciousness, the exercise of authority and dominion, and moral accountability to God, I suppose it would be possible to say yes, they are in the image of God. But we can't be certain.

We know that angels are *spirit* beings in that they are immaterial or incorporeal. They have no flesh or blood or bones. They are, as Hebrews 1:14 declares, "ministering *spirits*." However, although they are spirits, they have spatial limitations. In other words, angels are not omnipresent (see Dan. 9:21–23; 10:10–14, where we find both spatial movement and temporal limitations). They are always in only one place at any one time.

There is a sense in which as spirit beings they also have *form* or *shape*. That is to say, they are spatially confined (their being is not distributed throughout space). They are localized. Do angels have literal "wings"? The seraphim (see below) are portrayed as having wings in Isaiah 6:2 and 6 (see also Ezek. 1:5–8). Gabriel is portrayed as flying to Daniel's side (Dan. 9:21; cf. Rev. 14:6–7). Whether or not all angels are winged is simply impossible to say. I'm inclined to think that angels do not have gender (see Matt. 22:28–30); hence they do not procreate. I should point out, however, that they are always described in the masculine gender (but see Zech. 5:9). Finally, angels cannot die (Luke 20:36). Their immortality, though, is not inherent but is surely a gift of God.

As for their *powers*, they are able to assume the form and appearance of humans. We have record of them appearing as such to the naked eye (Matt. 28:1–7; Luke 1:11–13, 26–29), as well as in visions and dreams (Isaiah 6; Matt. 1:20). In Genesis 18:1–8 angels appear in the form of men. In this case they are sufficiently "real" in their appearance that the homosexuals in Sodom and Gomorrah lust after them (see also Mark 16:5).[1]

Regardless of the shape or form they might assume, in virtually all instances the reaction to angelic appearances is some expression of mental and emotional agitation, fear, even loss of composure and consciousness! This certainly speaks volumes in response to those who talk carelessly and even comically (and often somewhat arrogantly) of their rather chummy, buddy-buddy relationship with angelic beings. The typical response in the Bible for one who sees an angel is to be scared witless!

All angelic power is subject to God's power and purpose (Ps. 103:20; 2 Pet. 2:11). In Genesis 19:12–16 angels are used of God to destroy Sodom and Gomorrah. In 2 Kings 19:35 one angel is empowered to kill 185,000 Assyrians. According to Matthew 28:2 an angel moved the stone from Christ's tomb. In Acts 12 an angel enters a locked prison and releases Peter. In Acts 12:23 we read that an angel killed Herod in a most gruesome way. Angels appear in the book of Revelation (see esp. Rev. 7:2–3) to influence the phenomena of nature.

As for their *position*, angels are of two moral orders or categories: elect-holy (Mark 8:38; 1 Tim. 5:21) and evil (Luke 8:2). Evidently, after the rebellion and fall of Satan and his hosts, all angels were *confirmed* in their moral state. That is to say, God preserves the elect-holy angels in their righteous condition and will not redeem the evil ones. Why do we deny the possibility of redemption for fallen angelic beings (i.e., demons)? For one reason: there is no record of such anywhere in Scripture. Nor is there any record in Scripture of demonic repentance. Whenever we read about the impact of the cross on demons, it is always portrayed as judgment, never salvation. Nowhere do we read of justification, forgiveness, redemption, adoption, or regeneration being true of any angelic being. And, of course, Hebrews 2:14–17 declares that whereas Jesus "partook" of human flesh and blood, "it is not angels that he helps," but rather "the offspring of Abraham" (see also Rev. 5:8–14).

---

[1] For other appearances and the forms angels might assume, see Dan. 10:5–6; Matt. 28:3; Rev. 4:6–8.

4. *What are they called?* The word *angel* itself typically means messenger. They are also called "ministers" who serve both God (Ps. 104:4) and the elect (Heb. 1:14). They are referred to as "hosts" (Ps. 46:7, 11) and "watchers" (Dan. 4:13, 17; that is, supervisors employed by God in governing the world).[2] Other designations include "sons of the mighty" (Ps. 89:6, NASB), "sons of God" (Job 1:6; 2:1; 38:7), and "holy ones" (Ps. 89:6–7).

There appear to be a few special classifications or categories or kinds of angelic beings. The *cherubim* are the highest order or rank and are characterized by splendor, power, and beauty. They guard Eden and prevent man's return (Gen. 3:24) and are said to hover above the mercy seat (Ex. 25:17–22; cf. Heb. 9:5, "cherubim of glory"; see also Ezek. 1:1, 28; 10:4, 18–22). Cherubim are never explicitly called "angels" because they are not messengers. Rather they proclaim and protect the glory and holiness of God.

Seraphim (lit., "burning ones"; Isaiah 6) are known for their consuming devotion to God; they are "afire" or "ablaze" with adoration of God, and their principal task is worship. The "living creatures" of Revelation 4:6–9 could be either cherubim or seraphim, or another class altogether.

Only two angels are named. Michael (lit., "who is like God?" Dan. 10:13, 21) is assigned to protect Israel. He is the "archangel" (Jude 9) and the leader of the angelic host in their war against Satan (Rev. 12:7). In each of his appearances in Scripture, Gabriel (lit., "mighty one of God"; Dan. 9:21; Luke 1:26) communicates or interprets divine revelation concerning God's kingdom purposes.[3]

The angel of the Lord, also called "the angel of God" or "the angel of the presence" (Gen. 22:9–18; Ps. 34:7; etc.), appears to be a unique case. The question we face is whether this is the preincarnate Logos, the second person of the Trinity, or merely a created angelic being. On occasion this angel is distinguished from the Lord and sometimes, even in the same passage, he is identified with the Lord. When confronting Hagar (Genesis 16) the angel

---

[2] However, in some intertestamental writings, such as the book of Jubilees and the Dead Sea Scrolls, the word "watchers" is used for evil spirits, not angels.

[3] In the apocryphal book of Tobit, another angel is named: Raphael. If one includes 2 Esdras under the apocryphal books, another name occurs: Uriel.

of the Lord speaks to her in the first person: "I will surely multiply your offspring so that they cannot be numbered for multitude" (v. 10). Hagar even describes him as "a God of seeing" (v. 13). The angel says to Jacob, "I am the God of Bethel" (Gen. 31:13). However, Abraham clearly distinguishes the angel from God: "he [God] will send his angel before you" (Gen. 24:7). It was "the angel of the LORD" who appeared to Moses in the burning bush (Ex. 3:2; cf. Acts 7:35, 38), yet it was clearly God himself whom Moses encountered (Ex. 3:13–14).

Arguments for identifying the angel of the Lord with God himself are significant: the angel explicitly identifies himself with the Lord on several occasions; those to whom he makes his presence known often identify and speak of him as divine; and the biblical authors often explicitly refer to him as "the Lord." However, there are also good arguments for identifying the angel of the Lord with a created spirit being: God often so completely invests and authorizes his ambassadors or representatives with his character and word that they become indistinguishable from him when they speak his message (see Ex. 23:21); the Old Testament prophets display this kind of identity with God when they identify his message with their message; the "angel of the Lord" appears in the New Testament *subsequent* to the incarnation and thus would have to be regarded as someone or something other than the second person of the Trinity; "yet his actions (for example, Acts 12:7,15) are also described as an act of the Lord himself, and he sometimes speaks in the first person for the Lord himself (Rev. 22:6, 7, 12)."[4]

5. *How many angels are there?* A "multitude" announced Jesus's birth (Luke 2:13–15). God is Yahweh "of hosts" (Ps. 46:7, 11; etc.), which is to say he is head over a vast army of angels. Jesus refers to "twelve legions" of angels (Matt. 26:53; a legion is six thousand, hence seventy-two thousand angels). Often angels are associated with the stars, leading some to suggest they are equal in number (Job 38:7; Ps. 148:1–3; Rev. 9:1–2; 12:3–4, 7–9). Some suggest

---

[4]Andrew J. Bandstra, *In the Company of Angels: What the Bible Teaches. What You Need to Know* (Ventura: Gospel Light, 1995), 49–50.

that since each angel is a guardian of a Christian (Heb. 1:14), the number of the elect equals the number of angels. It has even been argued that Jesus won't return until enough people are saved to correspond to each angel![5] But no text says that every angel serves in this capacity. Many, it would seem, never leave the throne of God (see Revelation 4–5). Regardless of how many there are, their number seems to be fixed, for they neither procreate nor die (Matt. 22:28–30; Luke 20:36). Revelation 5:11 refers to "myriads" (a "myriad" is ten thousand), but nothing here suggests that these are all the angels there are. Finally, Daniel 7:10 refers to "a thousand thousands" and "ten thousand times ten thousand" angels who stood before the Lord, and Deuteronomy 33:2 mentions "ten thousands of holy ones" (cf. Jude 14). So how many angels are there? A lot!

6. *How are they organized?* Michael is the "archangel" (a word found only in 1 Thess. 4:16 and Jude 9), which means chief or first. In Revelation 12 he is head of the angelic host (see Dan. 10:13). Job 1:6 and 2:1 indicate that there was a regular, periodic assembly of the angels (cf. Ps. 89:5–6 and "the assembly of the holy ones"), perhaps to report on service and to receive instructions from God (see Ps. 103:20–21).

The fact that there are different classes or categories or types of angels would imply some form of organization. In Ephesians 1:21; 3:10; 6:12; and Colossians 1:16; 2:10, 15, Paul uses six terms to describe them and thus perhaps hints that there are at least six classes or categories of angelic (demonic) beings. These include:

- Principalities or rulers (*archē*; a ruler must have someone or something over which to exercise dominion; see Rom. 8:38; Eph. 1:21; 3:10; 6:12; Col. 1:16; 2:10).
- Authorities (*exousia*; again, authority, by definition, demands a subordinate; see Eph. 1:21; 3:10; Col. 1:16).
- Powers (*dynamis*; Rom. 8:38; Eph. 1:21). In Mark 9:29 Jesus refers to a type of demon that "cannot be driven out by anything but prayer." The point seems to be that some demons are stronger and more powerful than others. Hence, there is implied a hierarchy or differentiation based on spiritual strength.

---

[5]Augustine suggested that the number of the elect corresponds to the number of fallen angels, as if Christians must for some reason fill up what was "lost" in heaven by the rebellion led by Satan.

- Dominions (*kyriotētos*; again, "lordship" or "dominion" over what, whom, and where?—see Eph. 1:21; Col. 1:16).
- Thrones (*thronoi*, used of angels only in Col. 1:16).
- World rulers (*kosmokratoras*, used of angels only in Eph. 6:12).

If all angels and demons are of the same type or rank or carry the same authority, why are they described by such a variety of terms? It would also seem that with difference in rank comes difference in power, task, and so forth.

7. *What is their ministry or what do they do?* We've already seen that their primary role is to worship (Isaiah 6; Rev. 4:6–11; 5:11) and serve God (Ps. 103:19–21; this latter text seems to suggest open-ended service in that they do whatever God should desire or decree). People will often question the claim that an angelic being is responsible for some event by saying, "Where is that in the Bible?" as if to say angels can only do what they are explicitly recorded as already having done during biblical times. But there is no basis for restricting angelic activity to what is explicitly recorded in Scripture. If, as Psalm 103 indicates, they exist to fulfill God's will and perform his commands, the scope and variety of their activity could be virtually limitless.

They also provide guidance and direction for God's people (see Gen. 24:7, 40, where the servant of Abraham pursues a bride for Isaac; and Ex. 14:19, where an angel guides Israel in the wilderness; cf. also Ex. 23:20; Num. 20:16; Acts 5:17–20; 8:26; 10:3–7, 22; 16:9). In a related way they also guard and protect (see 1 Kings 19:5–7; Pss. 34:7; 78:23–25; 91:11; Dan. 6:20–23; 12:1; Acts 12:15).

Several passages call for extended comment. Considerable debate has surrounded the reference to the "angels" of the seven churches in Revelation 2–3.[6] When I was still an active member of a Southern Baptist church, I heard my pastor (who will remain unnamed) argue that the "angel" in each case was the senior pastor of the congregation! This isn't to say that all Southern Baptist pastors see themselves in this text, but it is a view that

---

[6]The following discussion has been adapted from my book *To the One Who Conquers: 50 Daily Meditations on the Seven Letters of Revelation 2–3* (Wheaton, IL: Crossway, 2008), 21–24.

warrants comment. There are several reasons why I find this theory unlikely.

First of all, it is contrary to the New Testament portrait of church structure. Nowhere in the New Testament is a single individual described as exercising pastoral authority over a congregation. Rule by a *plurality of elders* is the standard biblical perspective. To argue otherwise is to assume, falsely in my opinion, that there was an evolutionary development in biblical ecclesiology in which a plurality of leadership in the early years of the church's existence gradually gave way to a singular pastoral authority. In terms of *historical* development, subsequent to the closing of the biblical canon, this is precisely what happened. The first indication of a single pastor or bishop is found in the writings of Ignatius, c. 110, and Clement of Rome. But that is far removed from saying it occurred within the canon itself.

Second, the word *angel* is used some sixty times in Revelation and always means a supernatural or spiritual being. This is not a decisive objection, but it does place the burden of proof on the one who contends that the word here deviates from its standard use in the Apocalypse.

Third, the word *angel* is nowhere else in the New Testament used to designate an ecclesiastical office. Again, that doesn't mean it can't be applied that way in the seven letters, but it would be unique in the biblical revelation if it were.

Fourth, and finally, we know from Acts 20:17–38 that the Ephesian church was ruled by a plurality of elders. So, although I do believe in the legitimacy of a "senior" or "lead" pastor of a congregation (although he remains one elder among a plurality who govern the body), I seriously doubt this is what Jesus had in mind when he used the word *angel* in these seven letters.

Another possibility is that the *angel* refers to a prophet or delegated representative of the church. This person may have functioned in an ambassadorial role, or perhaps as something of a secretary responsible for maintaining communication with those outside the congregation, as well as other tasks that may have been assigned. This view stresses the literal meaning of the Greek term *angelos* as messenger (cf. Luke 9:52; James 2:25).

Yet a third, more likely option points to the fact that in Revelation 1:11 (cf. 1:4) the letters are directed to "the churches" (plural). So also at the end of each letter we read, "Let him hear what the Spirit says to the *churches*." Thus the Lord speaks to the *whole church* and not just to an "angel." This leads some to conclude that the angel *is* the church, that is, a personification of the church. The Greek text would certainly allow (but by no means require) this interpretation, in which case we would translate, "to the angel *which is* the church in Ephesus." Needless to say, this view suffers from the same weakness as the first two options in that it requires that we deviate from the regular use of the term *angel* in the book of Revelation (where it refers to a supernatural, nonhuman, being). There is also the fact that in Revelation 1:20 the angels of the seven churches are described as distinct from the seven churches themselves, making their identification less likely.

Another theory is that the "angel" of each church is its guardian angel. Although some scoff at the notion of angels providing this kind of service or ministry to the body of Christ, we should not dismiss it too quickly. Angels are described as "ministers" (*leitourgos*), a word that suggests a priestly service (Heb. 1:7, 14; cf. Ps. 103:19–21). They provide guidance and direction for God's people (Gen. 24:7, 40; Ex. 14:19; see also 23:20; Num. 20:16; Acts 5:17–20; 8:26; 10:3–7, 22; 16:9), as well as comfort and encouragement (Matt. 4:11; Luke 22:43; Acts 27:22–24). Angels also guard and protect the children of God, as is clear from 1 Kings 19:5–7; Psalms 34:7; 78:23–25; 91:11; Daniel 6:20–23; and 12:1.

Acts 12:15 is an unusual passage, in that we read of believers who mistook Peter himself for "his angel." It's possible that Luke is only describing their belief without himself endorsing it (but I find this unlikely). Others argue that he intends to teach not only that each of us has a guardian angel but also that our guardian angel may assume our physical characteristics. Yes, it seems odd, but why else would the believers have concluded that the person at the door was Peter's angel and not someone or something else?

Matthew 18:10 is especially interesting. There Jesus warns against the neglect of little children and reminds his disciples that "their angels always see the face of my Father who is in heaven." An ancient custom prevailed in eastern court settings according to which those who stood "before the king" or were allowed to "see his face" were officers who enjoyed the king's special favor and were privileged to enjoy the closest possible fellowship. The implication may be that *the highest ranking angels* are assigned and commissioned by God to watch over his "little ones" with loving care. Thus Jesus is saying, in effect, "Don't despise my 'little ones,' for they are so highly regarded that God has appointed his most illustrious angels to keep watch over them."

Their continual presence before God, beholding his face, may mean one of two things: (1) our condition and needs are ever before God; he is always and ever alert to our situation in life; or (2) these angels of high rank are constantly present before him for the purpose of quickly responding to whatever tasks God may assign them in their ministry to us. (One might be tempted to ask, If these angels "continually" stand before the face of God in heaven, how can they serve as daily or continual "guardians" of people on earth?)

The most basic and obvious problem with this view is that it doesn't make sense why Jesus would address the letter to the guardian angel of a church rather than directly to the congregation itself. What need would there be to do so, and what purpose would it serve? Perhaps a good answer for this is forthcoming. But at this point, I don't know what it would be.

As you can see, there is no definitive explanation for who these angels were or what function they discharged. If pressed to make a choice, I would opt for either the third (church as angel) or fourth (guardian angel) interpretation. In any case, our responsibility to heed the counsel of Christ in each letter does not hang on our ability to decipher the identity of the "angel" to whom each letter was sent.

According to 2 Kings 6:8–23 angelic armies fight God's battles and thus influence earthly affairs. It's important to note that our knowledge of angelic armies and their role counters fear and instills confidence. Similarly, angels are said to comfort and encourage people (Matt. 4:11; Luke 22:43; Acts 27:22–24). Angels also reveal and interpret divine revelation. Note the role they play in the giving of the Mosaic law (Acts 7:38, 52–53; Gal. 3:19; Heb. 2:2). They also communicate and then interpret God's will (Daniel 9; the entire book of Revelation).

Angels provide assistance in response to prayer (Dan. 9:20–24; 10) and are used by God in the execution of judgment, as described in Genesis 18–19; Exodus 12:23, 29 (Is "the destroyer" an angelic being?); 2 Samuel 24:15–17; 2 Kings 19:35; Psalm 78:49; Acts 12:23; and of course, Revelation.[7]

8. *What should be our response to angels?* As noted before, our immediate reaction should be one of respect and awe (Dan. 8:16–17; 10:1–18; Luke 1). We are also to learn from their example in worship (Revelation 4–5). We must be careful never to worship them, as they themselves worship only God. One passage that appears to address this issue head on is Colossians 2:18. But what does it mean?

On the one hand, it could refer to the worship that the angels themselves offer to God (cf. Revelation 4–5). If so, the false teachers in Colossae were claiming to be extraordinarily spiritual because their worship of God was not in association with that of other merely human participants, but was an elevated and exceptionally unique experience in which they joined with the angelic hosts in heaven to praise God.

I'm not inclined to accept this view for two reasons. First, although it is grammatically possible, it is not probable. But second, and more importantly, why would it be regarded as illicit for Christians to join with the angels in the worship and honor of God? On what grounds would a select few claim that they alone had this privilege? We are told in Hebrews 12:22 that we "have come to Mount Zion and to the city of the living God, the heavenly Jerusalem, and to innumerable angels in festal gathering." This may well refer to angels engaged in worship. And there is no indication in Revelation 4–5 that John was in danger of sinning were he to have

---

[7] We should observe that in Gen. 19:12–13 the angels say that they will execute judgment on Sodom and Gomorrah, yet in 19:23–25 it is God who does so.

praised God in the midst of the myriads of angelic hosts who were doing so. So, I find it a stretch to say that Paul was denouncing the idea of worshiping with angels. This would be grounds for rebuke only if it were a claim made by an exclusive and elitist inner circle who insisted they had an access to the heavenly celebration that other, lesser saints did not.

Then, of course, Paul could mean that these heretics were worshiping angels, giving to them the praise and honor that only God is due (cf. Rev. 19:10; 22:8–9). However, if this were the case, why didn't Paul more severely and explicitly denounce such a practice as the blasphemous idolatry that it is?

There is another option. As David Garland points out:

> Some have claimed that the Colossian errorists understood these angels to be involved in creation and the government of the world, and they worshipped them as their link to God. These angels could be regarded as malevolent and needing appeasement or as benevolent and bestowing blessing. Their so-called "worship" may only have involved propitiating them to ward off their evil effects or beseeching them for protection.[8]

In other words, the word translated "worship" could well mean something more along the lines of "invoke" or "conjure." These folk, then, were guilty of engaging in the somewhat magical solicitation of angels to ward off evil or to provide physical protection or to bestow blessing and success on their daily endeavors.

In any case, there was in Colossae (and oftentimes is in our own day) an excessive and inappropriate preoccupation with angels and their involvement in human life that Paul regarded as detracting from the centrality and supremacy of Jesus Christ. We would do well to heed his warning!

Among numerous other important texts (such as Luke 16:22; 1 Cor. 6:2–3; 11:1–10; Heb. 12:22; 13:1), I want to take special note of 1 Timothy 5:21, where Paul refers to the "elect angels." Is this a way of referring to all angels that did not fall with Satan in his re-

---

[8] David E. Garland, *Colossians and Philemon: The NIV Application Commentary* (Grand Rapids: Zondervan, 1998), 177.

bellion? If so, were they elect before his fall? Or were they in some sense "chosen" only after the fall of those whom we now refer to as demons? Or are these angels a smaller "select" or special group, such as the cherubim and seraphim, who are assigned the unique responsibility of keeping watch over the conduct of church leaders or church affairs in particular (note the context in which they appear)? In the final analysis, Paul does not supply us with enough information to draw any firm conclusions.

Conclusion

Our brief study of what the Bible says about angels clearly reveals that they are a vital part of God's redemptive purposes and play an active role not only in the salvation of God's elect but also in the overall pursuit of his goal to glorify himself. We must not become obsessed with them. We must not worship them. But we cannot afford to ignore their existence or the manifold ways in which they implement the will of God in the earth.

Addendum: A Brief Overview of the Nature and Role of Angels in the Book of Daniel

Without going into any explanatory detail, I want to close this chapter by listing the numerous references to angels in the book of Daniel. If nothing else, we see here confirmation of what has preceded in terms of the significance and pervasive presence of angels in God's economy of revelation and redemption.

Daniel 3:28

- Angels obey God, being sent to fulfill his purposes.
- This "angel" (the preincarnate Son of God?) is unaffected by fire and has the power to protect humans from fire.

Daniel 4:13

- These are called "watchers" and "holy ones."
- They communicate revelation via dreams.
- They are empowered and authorized to mediate God's purposes ("decree," "decision").

- God delegates some measure of authority to them over the human realm (cf. v. 17b).

Daniel 6:22

- This "angel" (the preincarnate Son of God?) is sent by God, fulfilling his will.
- The angel has power to restrain violent impulses of the lions (power over the animal realm).

Daniel 7:10

- Innumerable angels are portrayed as (possibly) "attending" God.
- Innumerable angels are portrayed as (possibly) "standing before" God.

Daniel 8:13

- They are mediators of revelation.
- Conversation between two angels is "overheard" by Daniel.

Daniel 8:16

- Gabriel provides an interpretation of divine revelation.
- Gabriel is subject to God.

Daniel 8:17–18

- An angelic appearance is frightening to Daniel.
- The angel makes physical contact with Daniel's body.

Daniel 9:21–22

- An angel takes on the form or appearance of a man.
- An angel communicates with and teaches Daniel.

Daniel 10:5–9

- An angel(?) takes on the appearance of a human.
- The angel displays physical characteristics that symbolize spiritual truths (purity, royalty, holiness, power, etc.).
- The angel induces fear and physical phenomena in Daniel.

- The angel is capable of selective appearance; that is, only Daniel actually "sees" and "hears" the angel, whereas his companions are aware of the presence of something that terrifies them (cf. Acts 9:1–7).

Daniel 10:10–12

- The angel makes physical contact with Daniel's body.
- The angel is acting in obedience to a divine commission.
- Angels can be the means by which God answers human prayers.

Daniel 10:13–14

- Angels, both good and bad (demons), are engaged in conflict with each other. (What is the nature of this conflict? How do they harm each other? How do they resist each other? What constitutes a victory or loss in such conflict?)
- Neither good nor bad angels are omnipotent.
- Fallen angels (demons) evidently can impose hindrances and cause delays in the answers to prayers; apparently God has granted a measure of power to demons that enables them to resist and *temporarily* thwart his purposes.

Daniel 10:15–17

- The angel again makes physical contact with Daniel's body ("lips").
- The angelic presence is a humbling experience for Daniel (v. 17); he addresses the angel as "my lord" (= "sir") and asks how he, as a mortal man, could be allowed to converse with such a majestic being.

Daniel 10:18–21

- By physically touching a human being an angel can impart both physical and emotional strength.
- Both good and bad angels (demons) may be assigned (by God and Satan, respectively) a special authority or role with respect to entire nations.

Daniel 11:1

- Even good angels grow "weary" and need strengthening.
- Even good angels grow "discouraged" and need encouragement.

- Not even the highest angel (Michael, the archangel) is self-sufficient or omnipotent.

Daniel 12:1, 5–7

- The archangel Michael exercises "charge" over God's people, Israel.
- Angels are instruments of revelation concerning God's future purposes.

Recommended Reading

Bandstra, Andrew J. *In the Company of Angels*: *What the Bible Teaches. What You Need to Know*. Ventura: Gospel Light, 1995.

Noll, Stephen F. *Angels of Light, Powers of Darkness: Thinking Biblically about Angels, Satan and Principalities*. Downers Grove, IL: InterVarsity, 1998.

Oropeza, B. J. *99 Answers to Questions about Angels, Demons and Spiritual Warfare*. Downers Grove, IL: InterVarsity, 1997.

11

What Can We Know about Satan?

It bothers me that I should feel obligated to talk about my enemy. I would much prefer to ignore Satan altogether and give neither him nor his demonic hosts (in the next chapter) so much as a syllable of publicity. But if our ultimate struggle is not against flesh and blood (i.e., human beings) but rather against Satan and the principalities and powers who serve him, I don't have a choice. So let's begin and get these two chapters over with as quickly as we can.

The Existence and Activity of Satan

The first thing to remember about Satan is that he, like all other angels, was created at a point in time (John 1:1–3; Col. 1:16). Satan is not eternal. He is a finite creature. He is, therefore, *God's* Devil. Satan is *not* the equal and opposite power of God (contra *dualism*). His power is not infinite. He does not possess divine attributes. In sum, he is no match for God! At most, Satan is the equal and opposite power of the archangel Michael.

If originally created as an angel, how did Satan come to fall? Two Old Testament passages have been interpreted as descriptions of Satan's original demise: Isaiah 14:12–15 and Ezekiel 28:12–19. As Sydney Page points out:

> Each is part of a funeral dirge lamenting the death of a pagan king. In both, the king is portrayed as having come to ruin because he exalted himself beyond what was appropriate. Although the form of the two texts is that of a funeral dirge, the sorrow at the passing of the monarch is not genuine. Both passages virtually drip with sarcasm. In reality, the tyrant's death is welcomed.[1]

The question is, Do these laments allude to Satan and his primordial rebellion?

Isaiah 14:12–15 appears in a passage that is specifically identified as a taunt of judgment against the king of Babylon (vv. 3–4). The taunt may be directed at one particular king (most likely Sennacherib) or perhaps "at the whole Babylonian monarchy personified as a single individual."[2] Clearly, though, the mocking lament portrays (indeed, celebrates) the demise of an *earthly* power that both opposes and oppresses the people of God. The language used in verses 12–14 is certainly compatible with what we know of Satan's character, but may well be a use of poetic language to describe an earthly king. Many of the terms used here ("Day Star," "Dawn," and "the mount of assembly") have been found in texts dealing with ancient pagan mythology. Page notes that "the mythology was probably rooted in the observation of the brilliant rise of the planet Venus (the 'morning star') in the early morning sky and its rapid fading with the rise of the sun."[3] If this is true, Isaiah would be utilizing (without endorsing) motifs common in pagan mythology to describe the downfall of an earthly ruler.

Others have argued that whereas all this may be true, we can still see in this description of an earthly opponent of God (the Babylonian king) his model and heavenly inspiration (Satan). But is that what Isaiah had in mind when he wrote it? The word sometimes rendered "Lucifer," literally "shining one" or "star of the morning"

---

[1] Sydney H. T. Page, *Powers of Evil: A Biblical Study of Satan and Demons* (Grand Rapids: Baker, 1995), 37.
[2] Ibid., 38.
[3] Ibid., 39.

(v. 12, NASB), is called a "man" in verse 16 and is compared with other earthly kings in verse 18. "Lucifer" was first used in the Latin vulgate to translate the Hebrew word (*helel*) and eventually made its way into the King James Version. According to Gregory Boyd:

> Isaiah is simply comparing the king of Babylon to the planet Venus, the morning star. It rises bright at dawn and climbs to the highest point in the sky, only to be quickly extinguished by the brightness of the rising sun. Thus, Isaiah says, shall be the career of the presently shining king of Babylon. He appears on the stage of world history as the brightest star, ascending higher and higher. But in the end he shall quickly disappear in the light of the sun.[4]

So what about Ezekiel 28:12–19? Again, verses 1–10 refer to the "prince" or "ruler" of Tyre (a Phoenician port city about 125 miles northwest of Jerusalem). Verses 2 and 9–10 clearly indicate that he is human, not angelic. The historical setting is the siege of Tyre by Nebuchadnezzar from 587 to 574 BC. The king of Tyre during this period was Ithobaal II.

Verses 12–19 refer to the "king" of Tyre, suggesting to some a supernatural power behind the human ruler of verses 1–11. However, this word ("king") is used elsewhere in Ezekiel of *earthly* rulers (17:12; 19:9; 21:19; 24:2; 26:7; 29:2–3, 18; 30:10, 21; 31:2; 32:2, 11), leading most to believe that the "prince" of 28:1–11 and the "king" of verses 12–19 are one and the same ("prince" and "king" being synonymous). On the other hand, the "king" of verses 12–19 seems to be portrayed in terms that go beyond what is true of any earthly king (e.g., "perfection," "in Eden," "created," "cherub," "holy mountain of God," "blameless").

The identification of this king as an "anointed guardian cherub" in verse 14 is considered the strongest evidence that the reference is to Satan. Others have pointed out, however, that the Hebrew text may just as easily be translated, "*with* a cherub." Also, it is difficult to understand how dishonest or unrighteous trade and the

---

[4] Gregory A. Boyd, *God at War: The Bible and Spiritual Conflict* (Downers Grove, IL: InterVarsity, 1997), 158.

desecration of sanctuaries (v. 18) could have been involved in the fall of Satan. How, then, are we to understand the reference to the garden of "Eden" in verse 13? Most believe that the king of Tyre is being compared with Adam. Page suggests:

> Perhaps the king believed himself to be the re-embodiment of the first man, and Ezekiel is using arrogant claims made by the king himself to set his defeat in sharper relief. . . . In effect, Ezekiel would be holding the king's pretensions up to ridicule by charging that, whatever claims he might make about his relationship with the primeval period, there is at least one similarity—like Adam, he stands under divine judgment for rebelling against his Creator.[5]

Others, such as Lamar Cooper, contend that the description of the king of Tyre in Ezekiel simply cannot be exhausted by reference to this one earthly figure. He writes:

> Overlaid in these prophetic messages [in 28:1–19] are many elements that extend beyond the characteristics of the city or the king. . . . Ezekiel presented the king of Tyre as an evil tyrant who was animated and motivated by a more sinister, unseen tyrant, Satan. . . . The sinister character of the mastermind behind God's enemies is not always recognized. The real motivating force behind the king of Tyre was the adversary, the satan, who opposed God and his people from the beginning (28:6–19).[6]

I suppose we will have to settle for a measure of uncertainty as to whether either of these texts actually describes Satan's fall. So, *when* did Satan fall? The Bible gives no clear answer to this question. Some have argued that it could not have been prior to the sixth day of Genesis 1, since everything in God's creation until that time is said to have been "very good" (Gen. 1:31). However, this declaration may pertain only to the *material* creation in view. Perhaps Satan's rebellion antedates Genesis 1:1. Others insist that it occurred just before he approached Eve in the garden. We simply don't know.

---

[5] Page, *Powers of Evil*, 42.
[6] Lamar Eugene Cooper Sr., *Ezekiel*, The New American Commentary (Nashville: Broadman & Holman, 1994), 268–69.

Satan's Names

We learn much about the character of our enemy from the names by which he is designated in Scripture. The title *Satan* is used fifty-two times in the Bible. It literally means "the adversary," the one who opposes (see Zech. 3:1–2). This is its meaning in Numbers 22:22, 32; 1 Samuel 29:4; 2 Samuel 19:22; and 1 Kings 5:4; 11:14, 23, 25. In Psalm 109:6 it has the sense of "accuser" or "prosecuting attorney."

The use of *Satan* in the book of Job is especially instructive. The "sons of God" (1:6) refer to the angelic host (cf. Job 38:7). They constitute the heavenly council, God's courtiers surrounding the throne ready to obey his every command (see also 1 Kings 22:19 and Dan. 7:9–14). With them is, literally, "the Satan." Everywhere this word appears in Job it has the definite article ("the").[7] Hence, it is a title, descriptive of his function and character.

Satan is at a loss concerning Job's loyal obedience to God. Job is a complete puzzle to him. He doesn't doubt that Job is obedient and upright. There is no mistaking his godliness. But the Devil just can't bring himself to believe that anyone would want to be holy for nothing. The only thing left is to launch an assault against Job's motives. Whereas he can hardly question Job's righteousness, he does wonder about the reason for it. His diabolical conclusion is that Job serves God for what he can get out of him. Job's piety, reasoned the Devil, must be a calculated effort to milk God of his gifts. "Take away the pay and he'll quit the job," he thinks. Satan is persuaded that worship must be fundamentally selfish, that it is nothing more than a man-made device to flatter God into generosity. If God's generosity were cut off, thought Satan, Job's praise would turn to cursing.

In sum, Satan accuses God of having bought Job's loyalty with health and wealth: "Job doesn't serve you for free. Don't flatter yourself, God! No one else does either." In effect, he says, "He doesn't love you for *who* you are but only for *what* you've given him." In other words, it isn't Job that Satan accuses, but God!

---

[7] See Job 1:6, 7 (twice), 8, 9, 12 (twice); 2:1, 2 (twice), 3, 4, 6, 7.

The question that Job will face, the question we all face, is this: Is God worthy to be loved and deserving of our obedience for who he is, irrespective of all other considerations? Is Job sufficiently dedicated to remain loyal if no benefits are attached? Satan says no. He accuses God of being a deceptive fraud and Job of being a selfish hypocrite.

Note also how abrupt and rude Satan is. Traditional court etiquette in the ancient Near East avoided the use of personal pronouns when addressing a superior. Courtiers would say "my lord" instead of "you" and "your slave" instead of "I" or "me." But not Satan. He also uses imperative verbs, as if to *command* God what to do. We should also note in Job 1:12 that Satan has no power or authority beyond that which God grants or permits. It is God who sets the boundaries for what Satan can do. Thus *when given permission by God*, Satan is able to exercise tremendous destructive influence on nature, nations, and individuals. This would also indicate that there is an ongoing restraint by God put on Satan and what he can do.

Our enemy is also called the "Devil," a word that is used thirty-five times and literally means "slanderer" or "accuser" (*diabolos*; Luke 4:2, 13; Rev. 12:9, 12; see also 1 Sam. 29:4; 1 Kings 11:14). In other words, it is the Devil's aim to defame. He is a constant source of false and malicious reports. He lies to God, about you (Rev. 12:10; but cf. Rom. 8:33–39; 1 John 2:1), to you, about God (Genesis 3; Matthew 4), and to you, about yourself (Eph. 6:16; he seeks to undermine and subvert your knowledge of who you are in Christ).

Other names or descriptive titles for Satan include Lucifer (see above), the "ancient Serpent" (Rev. 12:9, 15, an obvious allusion to Genesis 3; cf. Rom. 16:20; 2 Cor. 11:3), and the "great dragon" (Rev. 12:3, 7, 9, 17). He is a terrifying, destructive beast. He is also the "ruler [or prince] of this world" (John 12:31; 14:30; 16:11). Scripture does not make clear how Satan came to exercise such authority over the world, although it is likely that he did so as people, through their sin, granted him power.

One particularly instructive title for Satan is the "ruler" or "prince of the power [lit., "authority"] of the air" in Ephesians 2:2.

The word translated "power" (or "authority") denotes the realm or sphere or empire of the Devil's influence (i.e., demonic hosts; see Col. 1:13). The word "air" could refer to the literal atmosphere around us (hence the abode of demonic spirits), or it could be synonymous with "darkness" (cf. Luke 22:53; Eph. 6:12; Col. 1:13) or could be a reference to the nature of the demonic hosts—they are unearthly, spiritual, and not human. Some insist that it could involve to some degree all these ideas and be "another way of indicating the 'heavenly realm,' which, according to Ephesians 6:12, is the abode of those principalities and powers, the 'world-rulers of this darkness' and 'spiritual forces of wickedness,' against which the people of Christ wage war."[8] The word does not have the modern sense of "moral atmosphere" or "world of opinion and ideas."

The next phrase has been rendered in several different ways. It could be understood as "the prince of the power of the air, [which is] the spirit that is now at work." The "air" would thus be the spiritual atmosphere controlling unbelievers. Or it could be taken as "the prince of the power of the air, [the prince being] the spirit that is now at work." Others suggest that we read it as "the prince of the power of the air, [the prince of] the spirit that is now at work." That is to say, Satan is the ruling lord or prince over that evil principle (i.e., spirit, mood, temper, disposition) which operates in the lost (cf. 1 Cor. 2:12 and "spirit of the world").

What is most important, however, is that Paul says Satan is "at work" (*energeō*) in the "sons of disobedience" (cf. Mark 3:17; Luke 10:6; 16:8; 20:34; Acts 4:36; Eph. 5:8; 1 Pet. 1:14), a phrase used earlier of God's activity in the world (Eph. 1:11) in general and in the resurrection of Jesus in particular (1:20). Here it refers to Satan's supernatural activity by which he exerts a negative influence over the lives of unbelievers. This does *not* mean that all unbelievers are demon-possessed. It does mean that "the whole world lies *in the power of* the evil one" (1 John 5:19).

Paul clearly says that Satan is working *"now"* in unbelievers. In other words, although the readers of this epistle and other Christians were in bondage to Satan in the *past*, this does not mean

---

[8] Peter T. O'Brien, *The Letter to the Ephesians* (Grand Rapids: Eerdmans, 1999), 160.

Satan's power ceased to exist. It is yet at work in the present in and among all who remain in unbelief.

The Greek preposition in Ephesians 2:2 translated "according to" in the NASB (*kata*) must mean something more than simply that the lost live "in conformity with" or "after the manner of" the Devil, as if Paul were saying unbelievers live like the Devil. The idea is that in some way they have come under the controlling influence of Satan. Paul speaks in Romans 8:4 about believers walking "according to" (*kata*) the Spirit (cf. 2 Cor. 10:2) rather than "according to the flesh," again with the idea of controlling influence.

Satan is also called "the god of this world" (2 Cor. 4:4; but see Ps. 24:1; 89:11) and "the evil one" (Matt. 6:13; 13:38; John 17:15; 1 John 2:14; 5:18). There are several reasons to conclude that the final petition in the Lord's Prayer is a reference to Satan. The use of the adjective "evil" (*ponēros*) with the definite article "the" in Matthew 13:19, 38; John 17:15; Ephesians 6:16; 2 Thessalonians 3:3; 1 John 2:13–14; 3:12; and 5:18 clearly refers to Satan. This petition is probably an allusion to Jesus's own encounter with Satan in the wilderness. Jesus's point is that we can expect to encounter the tempter in much the same way he did. Finally, the word translated "from" in the last petition is *apo*, used predominantly with persons, not things.

Satan is the prince or ruler of demons (Matt. 10:25; 12:26–27; Luke 11:15; 2 Cor. 6:15). The name or title "Beelzebul" has been taken to mean "lord of dung" (i.e., god of filth), "enemy," "lord of the dwelling" (i.e., the dwelling of demons), and "lord of the flies," a title given to one of the pagan gods of the Philistines and brought over into Judaism as a name for Satan.

He is the destroyer in Revelation 9:11, where the quoted Hebrew word "Abaddon" could mean ruin or destruction, and the Greek term "Apollyon," exterminator or destroyer. Finally, Satan is "the tempter" (Matt. 4:3; 1 Thess. 3:5), the one "who accuses" (Rev. 12:10), and "the deceiver" (Rev. 12:9; 20:3). He is a liar and a murderer (John 8:44; an allusion either to the murder of Abel by Cain or to the fall in Genesis 3; cf. 1 John 3:11–12), and a master of misrepresentation (2 Cor. 11:14–15; 2 Thess. 2:9). He is powerful but not omnipotent (see Matt. 4:5, 8), intelligent but not omniscient, and active but not omnipresent.

Satan's Activities

Satan has a plan. Although sinful, he is not stupid. He does not act haphazardly or without a goal in view. Paul states clearly in 2 Corinthians 2:10–11 that Satan has "designs," a strategy, an agenda to undermine unity in the church in Corinth (and no doubt in every city, yours included!). This is similar to what the apostle says in Ephesians 6:11 concerning the "schemes" (*methodeia*, lit., "method") of the Devil. In other words, he is cunning and wily and employs carefully orchestrated stratagems (cf. Eph. 4:14) in his assault against Christian men and women and the local church. Satan energizes and gives shape to worldly value systems, institutions, organizations, philosophical movements, and political, social, and economic systems. Satan sets his goals and then utilizes and exploits the most effective means, while avoiding all obstacles, to reach his diabolical ends. I've identified numerous examples of what Satan seeks to do, so let's look briefly at each.

(1) *He works in active opposition to the gospel.* Paul says that he blinds the minds of the unbelieving lest they should see the glory of the gospel and be saved. There are two factors in spiritual blindness: fleshly, sinful, self-resistance to the truth on the one hand, and satanic, demonic hardening or blinding, on the other. Before we ever arrive on the scene with the gospel, Satan is exerting a stupefying influence on the mind of the unbeliever. In other words, we face more than merely intellectual obstacles. We face supernatural opposition. How does Satan do it?

Sometimes he distracts people when an opportunity to hear the gospel is at hand through untimely interruptions, useless daydreaming, an intrusive telephone call, an emergency of some sort, the sudden remembrance of a job or other responsibility that needs immediate attention, or perhaps the appearance of a friend (cf. Acts 13:7b–8). He often stirs up hostility and suspicion in the person's mind concerning the competency and integrity of the individual presenting the gospel. The unbeliever suddenly imputes sinister motives to the Christian: "He's in it for the money," or "She only wants to gain control over me," or "He's just looking for another notch on his Bible so he can boast to others of one more convert." Sometimes the unbeliever will excuse his unbelief by questioning the educational and academic credentials of the believer: "She is so uneducated; what does she know anyway."

Satan stirs up the non-Christian to distort what is being said into something the speaker never intended (cf. Jesus and the Pharisees in John 2:19–21; 6:48–52; 7:33–36; 8:51–53). He stirs up their minds to draw false conclusions or implications from the gospel that make it seem absurd (e.g., the doctrine of Trinity implies three gods; the doctrine of grace means you can believe and yet live any way you please). He inclines their minds to link the Christian with people who've disgraced Christianity in the past, giving them an excuse to reject what is being said (i.e., guilt by association): "All you Christians are just like those hucksters on TV! You're in it for the gold and the glory!" He puts in their minds all sorts of questions and convinces them that if they can't get completely satisfying answers, Christianity can't be true. Right in the middle of hearing the gospel, she suddenly blurts out questions like: "What about evil?" "What about all the hypocrites in the church?" "What about the heathen in Africa?" "Why is there only one way? It seems egotistical." "Why are there so many denominations?"

Just as the gospel is beginning to make sense, Satan stirs up pride or produces feelings of independence and self-sufficiency: "I don't need a religious crutch. I'm my own man!" Before serious consideration is given to the message, Satan snatches the seed of the gospel (Matt. 13:4, 18–19) from the hearer's mind. How does he do it? Perhaps on the way home from church the car breaks down, or the conversation turns to politics or sports, or a sexy billboard diverts attention, or something on the radio captivates his mind. Satan might suddenly prompt him to place a higher value on things he might lose if one were to become a Christian: friends, fame, money, fleshly pleasures, approval of others (cf. John 9). Satan stirs up feelings of hopelessness: "Not even this will work. There's no hope. My life is a lost cause. Not even Jesus can help."

Consider what Paul says in 1 Thessalonians 2:18: "We wanted to come to you—I, Paul, again and again—but Satan hindered us." Paul doesn't say by what means Satan opposes and undermines missionary endeavors, but we may assume he disrupts travel plans, works on the minds of state officials to delay or deny the issuing of visas, inflicts illness, provokes military conflict—the list could go on. Neither does Paul tell us how he was able to discern whether it was God or Satan who was responsible for a change in plans (cf. Acts 16:6–7). Perhaps we shouldn't read too much into circumstances, but acknowledge that God can even use Satan's schemes to accomplish his purposes.

(2) *He is often, but not always, the source of sickness* (Matt. 8:16; Mark 9:17–18; Luke 13:10–17; Acts 10:38). (3) *He can inflict death as well as provoke the paralyzing fear of it* (Heb. 2:14; see also John 10:10; Job 1:13–19). (4) *He plants sinful plans and purposes in the minds of men* (Matt. 16:21–23; John 13:2; Acts 5:3). It is instructive to observe that in Acts 5, "it is not through some act of terrible depravity, but through an act of religious devotion, that Satan brings about the downfall of Ananias and Sapphira. . . . It is sobering to think that the very good that God's people attempt to do can be their undoing."[9]

(5) *On occasion, Satan will himself indwell a person.* Satan "entered into" Judas, according to John 13:27, language that is reminiscent of demonization (Luke 8:30, 32–33). It is important to note, however, that Judas's motive was also greed, and nowhere is he exonerated of his action simply because he was indwelt by the Devil.

(6) *He sets a snare or trap for people (perhaps with a view to exploiting and intensifying their sinful inclinations).* In 1 Timothy 3:6–7 Paul speaks of the danger of falling "into the condemnation of the devil," and in 2 Timothy 2:25–26 he speaks of people experiencing "the snare of the devil," having been "captured by him to do his will." Thus Satan is able to exploit any blemish on the reputation of a Christian leader. In the latter text Paul speaks of individuals who have been led astray through false teaching. Satan thus strives to hold people captive to do his will by deceiving them to believe what

---

[9] Page, *Powers of Evil*, 132.

is false and misleading. If nothing else, this text emphasizes how crucial sound doctrine is.

(7) *He tests or tries Christians.* Consider Satan's "sifting" of Peter in Luke 22. Clearly, Satan is unable to act outside the parameters established by the will of God. He must first ask permission of God. Satan's intent in "sifting" Peter was obviously malicious.[10] He wanted to destroy Peter by inciting him to deny Jesus. But God's intent in permitting Satan to do it was altogether different. God's purposes with Peter were to instruct him, humble him, perhaps discipline him, and certainly to use him as an example to others of both human arrogance and the possibility of forgiveness and restoration. The point is simply that often we cannot easily say "Satan did it" or "God did it." In cases such as this, both are true (with the understanding that God's will is sovereign, supreme, and overriding), but their respective goals are clearly opposite. Page's comments concerning this incident are important:

> Luke 22:31–32 reveals that Satan can subject the loyalty of the followers of Jesus to severe tests that are designed to produce failure. So intense are the pressures to which Satan is able to subject believers that the faith of even the most courageous may be found wanting. Satan is, however, limited in what he can do by what God permits and by the intercession of Jesus on behalf of his own [cf. Rom. 8:34; Heb. 7:25; 1 John 2:1]. Furthermore, those who temporarily falter can be restored and, like Peter, can even resume positions of leadership. It is implied that Satan cannot gain ultimate victory over those for whom Jesus intercedes.[11]

(8) *He incites persecution, imprisonment, and the political oppression of believers* (1 Pet. 5:8–9; Rev. 2:10), (9) *is the accuser of the Christian* (Rev. 12:10; see also Zech. 3:1–2), (10) *performs signs and wonders to deceive the nations* (2 Thess. 2:9–11), and (11) *seeks to silence the witness of the church* (Rev. 12:10–12). If one of the primary ways Satan is defeated is by our witness, he will go to any lengths necessary to mute our testimony.

---

[10] It should be noted that Satan evidently obtained permission to test all of the disciples. Observe Jesus's use of the plural "you" (meaning, all the disciples) in 22:31.

[11] Page, *Powers of Evil*, 124.

(12) *He seeks to incite disunity and division.* In 2 Corinthians 2:10–11 we find another instance in which Satan seeks to exploit the otherwise good intentions of the church. Certain people in Corinth, ostensibly to maintain the purity of the church, were reluctant to forgive and restore the wayward but now repentant brother. This harshness would give Satan an opportunity to crush the spirit of the repentant sinner and drive him to despair, most likely resulting in his being forever cut off from the church.

(13) *He promotes false doctrine* (1 Tim. 4:1–3; 2 Cor. 11:1ff.; Rev. 2:24), (14) *manipulates the weather* (when given permission to do so by God; Job 1:18–19; and perhaps Mark 4:37–39), and (15) *influences the thoughts and actions of unbelievers* (Eph. 2:1–2).

(16) *He attacks married couples in regard to their sexual relationship* (1 Cor. 7:5). Paul approves of the decision by married couples to refrain from sexual relations to devote themselves to prayer, but only for a season. To abstain entirely for a prolonged period of time exposes oneself to unnecessary temptation (i.e., lust and the satisfaction of one's sexual desires outside the bonds of marriage). Again, we see here an example of how the Enemy takes an otherwise godly intention and exploits it for his own nefarious purposes.

(17) *He exploits our sinful decisions, most likely by intensifying the course of action we have already chosen.* For instance, in Ephesians 4:26–27, Satan is not credited with or blamed for creating the anger in the first place. We are responsible for it. Satan's response is to use this and other such sins to gain access to our lives and to expand and intensify our chosen course of behavior. And finally, as we have come to expect, (18) *he confronts us with various temptations* (2 Sam. 24:1; 1 Chron. 21:1; 1 Thess. 3:5).

Conclusion

I refuse to conclude this chapter by leaving in your mind the ways in which Satan appears to succeed in his opposition to the gospel and the Christian. So, let's simply remember that "the reason the Son of God appeared was to destroy the works of the devil" (1 John 3:8). There is nothing Satan does that Jesus cannot reverse and overcome. He is God's Devil, and he is a defeated enemy. So simply remember this: "Submit yourselves . . . to God. Resist the devil, and he will flee from you" (James 4:7).

Recommended Reading

Arnold, Clinton E. *Powers of Darkness: Principalities and Powers in Paul's Letters*. Downers Grove, IL: InterVarsity, 1992.

Green, Michael. *I Believe in Satan's Downfall*. Grand Rapids: Eerdmans, 1981.

Page, Sydney H. T. *Powers of Evil: A Biblical Study of Satan and Demons*. Grand Rapids: Baker, 1995.

12

What Can We Know about Demons?

Given the fact that Satan is himself a *demon*, we should expect there to be considerable overlap between what the Bible says of demons and what we have just seen it to say about him. So let's begin by looking at the Old Testament and then move to the New.

Demons in the Old Testament

Several texts indicate that the idols worshiped by Israel during her time of rebellion were in fact demons. Visible images are but fronts for invisible demonic spirits (Deut. 32:17; Ps. 106:36–37; cf. Ps. 96:4–5).

The reference in such texts as Leviticus 17:7 and 2 Chronicles 11:15 is to he-goats, literally, "hairy ones" (cf. the "satyr," the half-goat and half-man of Greek mythology). This word refers to a male goat in Leviticus 16:7–10, 15, 18, 20–22, 26–27. Some believed that demons assumed the shape or form of a goat (Josh. 24:14; Ezek. 20:7). Others suggest that the references here are simply to goat idols (common in Egypt), behind which were demonic spirits. It is worth noting that the goat head is a common symbol or representation of Satan in modern occultic activity.

When we look at 1 Samuel 16:14–16, 23; 18:10; and 19:9, we discover that each of these texts describes a "harmful spirit" that comes "from God/the LORD" or is sent by God. Is this a reference to a good angel who is sent to afflict someone with evil, or is it a demon whose very character is evil but who is used by the sovereign God to accomplish his purposes? The latter seems most likely. We must remember that demons are subject to the will of God no less than good angels. The spirit is described as having "tormented" Saul. The precise nature of this suffering is not specified, but surely it was both physical and emotional. On two occasions the presence of this spirit led or induced or somehow prompted Saul to become violent and make an attempt on David's life (1 Sam. 18:10–11; 19:9–10). What, if anything, does this tell us about the relationship between demonic affliction and human sin? Note well that Saul himself acknowledges the sinfulness of his attempts to kill David, even though it was in some way prompted or stirred by the evil spirit (see 1 Sam. 24:16–21 and 26:21). Also, the sending of the evil spirit from God is portrayed as an act of divine judgment. It was in response to Saul's disobedience. Finally, the evil spirit left Saul whenever David played his harp (1 Sam. 16:16–23). Was it merely the fact that *music* was played, or was it the fact that it was *David* who played it (see esp. v. 18)?

Isaiah 13:21 and 34:14 (cf. Lev. 17:7) are especially instructive. The word used in these texts elsewhere simply means "male goat" (the sort presented as a sin offering). It is likely, however, that in the two texts from Isaiah it refers to demons. As Sydney Page notes:

> In both cases, the word appears in a prophecy of the destruction Yahweh will bring to an enemy of Israel. Chapter 13 describes the devastation of Babylon, and chapter 34 paints a similar picture for Edom. Both passages envisage a time when Israel's enemies will be utterly destroyed, when their centers of power will no longer be inhabited by humans but become a dwelling place for the

denizens of the desert. The *se'irim* are included among the future inhabitants of these waste places.[1]

Many believe that Revelation 18:2 is an allusion to Isaiah 13:21. In the former text we read,

Fallen, fallen is Babylon the great!
    She has become a dwelling place for demons,
a haunt for every unclean spirit,
    a haunt for every unclean bird,
    a haunt for every unclean and detestable beast.

Here again we see the association of demons with desolate places abandoned by humans. In Isaiah 34:14, another word occurs that probably refers to demons. It is the Hebrew word translated *Lilith*, rendered "night monster" by the NASB and "night bird" by the ESV.

In Babylonian demonology, Lilith could refer to several things: (1) a child-stealing witch; (2) Adam's first wife, before Eve, believed to be the mother of all demons; or (3) a night demon that prowled about in dark and desolate places. In postbiblical times, Lilith became the topic of much speculation in Judaism. "She came to be regarded primarily as a demon who seduced men in their dreams, who murdered young children, and who was a special threat at childbirth. More recently, she has emerged as a positive symbol for Jewish feminists."[2] Some have argued that the reference to "the terror of the night" in Psalm 91:5 is an allusion to Lilith.

Although *incubus* and *succubus* are not biblical terms, the purported existence of these demonic spirits needs to be addressed. Incubi (from the Latin, *incubare*, "to lie upon") are said to be demons who take on the shape or form of men to seduce sleeping women; succubi assume the shape or form of women to seduce men. Since demons are incapable of producing either semen or eggs, there is no reproductive fruit from such encounters. Their motivation is primarily to humiliate and corrupt their victims. Most often the alleged victim feels physically immobilized and thus raped. How-

---

[1] Sydney H. T. Page, *Powers of Evil: A Biblical Study of Satan and Demons* (Grand Rapids: Baker, 1995), 69.
[2] Ibid., 73.

ever, it is not uncommon for the demon to *deceive* the victim into thinking that he or she was a *willing* partner, thereby intensifying the feelings of deep, personal shame and self-loathing. Many often find it difficult to develop a healthy sexual relationship with their spouse. In the final analysis, there is no way to know with any degree of certainty whether such demons exist and whether they engage in this sort of nefarious activity.

In Psalm 82 God is portrayed as presiding or ruling over the divine assembly. He accuses the "gods" of failing in their duty to protect the poor and powerless and condemns them to death (v. 7). Who are these "gods"? Some argue that they are human beings or judges who are called "gods" because they represent God when they issue their verdicts. More likely this is a reference to supernatural beings. Several things indicate this. The setting of the psalm (see v. 1) is the heavenly council or divine assembly. The terms "gods" (v. 1) and "sons of the Most High" (v. 6) more naturally refer to celestial beings. In verse 7 it is said that they will die "like men," which assumes they are not human (otherwise, there is no purpose for the comparison with humans). And the idea that celestial beings have been given responsibility for the administration of justice in particular nations is found elsewhere in the Old Testament, such as Deuteronomy 32:8.

It may not be wise to draw too sharp a distinction between celestial beings and earthly human rulers, for "the psalmist may well have believed that the celestial 'gods' exercised their influence on earth through terrestrial rulers."[3] Thus, I conclude that the "gods" of Psalm 82 are fallen angels, originally assigned as patrons of various nations, who shirked their responsibility and abused their powers. Page explains:

> The text is silent about the circumstances of their fall from innocence, but obviously these are fallen beings whose sin had a devastating impact on human society. The angels stand accused of aiding and abetting the wicked in their exploitation of the poor and powerless. Indeed, the plight of the marginalized in society was exacerbated by the actions of these gods. So great was their influence that verse 5 says, "All the foundations of the

---

[3] Ibid., 58.

earth are shaken." When justice is perverted, the very structure of the cosmic order comes under attack, threatening chaos. Obviously, the psalmist saw the promotion of inequity and the absence of compassion as grievous sins that are not due to human moral deficiencies alone. So great is the evil of social injustice that it can only be accounted for by the activity of cosmic forces opposed to God.[4]

In Isaiah 24:21–22 we read of a time when God will punish "the host of heaven, in heaven" or "the powers in the heavens above" (NIV). In support of the interpretation that this is a reference to fallen angels, note the contrast in verse 21 with earthly rulers or kings. These demons are thus in some way allied with the kings of various nations; they are "patron" angels of earthly nations and are involved in the sins mentioned in v. 5. The word translated "powers" in the NIV (*saba*) is used elsewhere in the Old Testament to refer to angels (1 Kings 22:19). This passage also suggests that these demons will be imprisoned in an intermediate place of detention awaiting the final judgment (Isa. 24:22; cf. 2 Pet. 2:4 and Jude 6).

First Kings 22:19–23 (2 Chron. 18:18–22) is a fascinating passage. Ahab was seeking to form an alliance with Jehoshaphat, king of Judah, whereby they might together attack Ramoth Gilead, which was under Aramean control. Jehoshaphat insisted that they first consult a prophet to get God's perspective. Ahab, on the other hand, gathered four hundred of his prophets, who told him to attack Ramoth Gilead and he would be victorious. Jehoshaphat consulted with the prophet Micaiah, who told him of a vision he had had of a meeting of the heavenly council. In the vision, God asked who would go to entice Ahab into attacking Ramoth Gilead, in which battle Ahab would die. A "spirit" (angel?) volunteered to be a "lying spirit in the mouth of all his [Ahab's] prophets" (1 Kings 22:22). God agreed. The spirit went forth, Ahab heeded the voice of the prophets, and went forth in the battle where he eventually died.

The scene in Micaiah's vision is similar to that in Job 1: a heav-

---

[4] Ibid., 59.

enly council at which the angels are all present. Some have argued that the "spirit" was in fact Satan, but there is no indication of this in the text. The spirit is portrayed as simply one among many others. There is no evidence he held some superior or special position. Was this a fallen spirit, a demon? Probably. It performed an evil function: it prompted Ahab's prophets to speak lies. Although the spirit was not Satan himself, there are undeniable parallels between this text and Job 1. Also, the passage seems to draw a distinction between the spirit that inspired Ahab's prophets and the one that inspired Micaiah (see 1 Kings 22:24). "The implication is that Micaiah and Ahab's prophets could not both have received their messages from the same source. There are, of course, two distinct sources, but it is Micaiah who has the right one. After all, it is his prophecy that comes to pass."[5]

Perhaps most important of all is the fact that even this demonic spirit was absolutely subject to the will of God. It did God's bidding. Micaiah is clear that it was God who "put a lying spirit in the mouth of all these your prophets; the Lord has declared disaster for you" (v. 23). Thus God can and often does use demonic spirits to fulfill his purposes. Again we see that the question, Who did it, God or the devil? may be answered, *yes*. But God is always ultimate. A close parallel with this passage is the account in Judges 9:23, where God sends an evil spirit to provoke discord between Abimelech and the people of Shechem.

Demons in the New Testament

Much of the Jewish literature dating from the New Testament era focused on identifying demonic spirits by name (e.g., Raux, Barsafael, Artosael, Belbel). Aside from a single reference to Satan as Belial (2 Cor. 6:15), the apostle Paul does not identify any demonic being, but there are three terms he typically uses to describe them. The first is *daimōn* or *daimonion* ("demon"), used sixty-three times (fifty-four of which are in the Gospels). Then there is *pneumata*, most often translated "spirits" (cf. Luke 10:17 with 10:20). Also,

---

[5] Ibid., 79.

"unclean spirits" is used twenty-one times, about half of which are in Mark (see Luke 11:19–26) and "evil spirits" (only eight times in the Gospels and Acts; cf. Luke 8:2). Finally, demons are also called *angelos*, translated "angel" (see Matt. 25:41; 1 Pet. 3:22; Rev. 12:7). I should also point out that the term *devils* is technically incorrect. *Diabolos* is never used in the New Testament of demons, but only of the Devil, Satan.

Characteristics and Activities of Demons

Virtually everything I've said concerning the properties and powers of angels is true of demons as well. The only difference is that the demons are evil, serving Satan, and the angels are good, serving God. Several things in particular should be noted.

Although demons are rarely named in the New Testament (see Luke 8:30), it is reasonable to conclude that each has a name (holy angels have names: Michael, Gabriel). Demons can speak to and communicate with humans (Luke 4:33–35, 41; 8:28–30; Acts 19:13–17). They are intelligent (Luke 4:34; 8:28; Acts 19:13–17) and formulate and propagate their own doctrinal systems (1 Tim. 4:1–3).

We see from this that distortions and misrepresentations of the truth are not always the product of merely human misunderstanding or miscalculation. Paul believes that often they are demonically inspired. This does *not* mean, however, that everyone who disagrees with you on any particular point of doctrine is an unwitting tool of a demon! On the other hand, it is entirely possible that certain false doctrines that well-meaning Christians hold may be demonically energized. Demons are extremely active in promoting falsehood in the church. According to 1 John 4, behind false prophets (such as those who deny the incarnation) are supernatural agents of the Enemy.

Demons have emotions and experience a variety of feelings (Luke 8:28; James 2:19). There are also differences or degrees in their strength (Mark 9:29) and sinfulness (Matt. 12:45). Like the holy angels, demons can appear to us in various forms, both spiritual and physical (Matthew 4; Rev. 9:7–10, 17; 16:13–16). If holy angels can visit us without our knowing it (Heb. 13:1–2), there is every reason to believe that demons can do so as well.

Demons can infuse their victims with superhuman strength (Mark 5:3; Acts 19:16) and, like the holy angels, can move swiftly through space (Dan. 9:21–23; 10:10–14). Normal physical barriers do not restrict their activity (a "legion" of demons—six thousand—inhabited one man, and later two thousand pigs). Demons can also physically assault someone and cause physical affliction. Luke 9:39 (Matt. 17:15) speaks of a demon *seizing* a young boy. He is thrown to the ground or into fire or water, together with other violent symptoms. In Matthew 9:32–34 a man's inability to speak is attributed to a demon (cf. 12:22–24; Luke 11:14–15). Note, however, that Jesus healed several cases of blindness or the inability to speak that the Gospels do *not* attribute to demonic influence (Matt. 9:27–31; 20:29–34; Mark 7:31–37; 8:22–26; 10:46–52; Luke 18:35–43; John 9:1–7).

Demons inspire and energize the false wisdom of the world that all too often infiltrates the church and poisons interpersonal relationships in the body of Christ. James 3:13–18 describes two kinds of wisdom: that which comes from heaven and that which is characterized as "earthly, unspiritual, demonic" (*daimoniōdēs*). "James clearly considered the arrogant, sectarian spirit of his opponents to be demonic."[6]

Demons animate and energize all non-Christian religions and all forms of idolatry (1 Cor. 10:14–22). In Galatians 4:3, 8–9, Paul refers to the *stoicheia*, the "elementary principles" of this world, to which both Jews and Gentiles were held in bondage prior to their conversion to Christ. Many believe this term is a reference to demonic powers. Thus, according to Clinton Arnold:

> at one time they thought they were worshiping real gods and goddesses in their pagan worship, but they were soon to find out that these were mere idols—tools of the devil and his powers of darkness. The Galatians had appeared to have turned their backs on their pagan gods, but they were now tempted to add Jewish legal requirements to the pure gospel of Christ, which Paul had taught them. In Paul's mind this would be trading one form of slavery to

---

6 Ibid., 230.

the powers for another. . . . Both pagan religion and the Jewish law surface here as two systems that Satan and his powers exploit to hold the unbeliever in captivity and re-enslave the believer.[7]

Although we can't be certain on this next point, demons may have been responsible, in part, for the crucifixion of Jesus. In 1 Corinthians 2:6–8, Paul refers to the "rulers of this age" (vv. 6, 8) who "crucified the Lord of glory." Some insist that this is a reference to the *human* rulers of the day, such as Annas, Caiaphas, and Pilate. Others argue that the evidence points to *demonic* powers. Support for this latter view is twofold.

First, the term "ruler" is used elsewhere by Paul of Satan (Eph. 2:2). It is also used this way by Jesus (John 12:31; 14:30; 16:11). However, it is also used of human rulers in Romans 13:3. Second, these "rulers" are "doomed to pass away" or "are coming to nothing" (NIV), translations of the verb *katargeō*, a term used later in 1 Corinthians 15:24 of Christ's ultimate defeat and destruction of the principalities and powers. Paul never uses this verb for the ultimate doom of unbelieving humanity. It is also used in Hebrews 2:14 for Christ's defeat of the Devil.

If the "rulers" refer to demonic forces, then we must conclude, with Arnold, that

> Paul held the demonic rulers responsible for Christ's death. He assumes that these powers of Satan were working behind the scenes to control the course of events during the passion week. It was not a part of Paul's purpose to explain exactly how these demonic rulers operated. At the very least we can imagine they were intimately involved by exerting their devious influence in and through Judas, Pilate, Annas and Caiaphas, and by inciting the mob. Demonic victory over God's plan by putting Christ to death failed. The powers did not apprehend the full extent of God's wisdom—how the Father would use the death of Christ to atone for sin, raise him victoriously from the dead and create the church. Least of all did they envisage their own defeat![8]

---

[7] Clinton E. Arnold, *Powers of Darkness: Principalities and Powers in Paul's Letters* (Downers Grove, IL: InterVarsity, 1992), 131–32.

[8] Ibid., 104. Note, however, that an equally strong case can be made that the "rulers" here are human, earthly rulers.

Demons appear at present to be in one of three places. They are active in the earth or confined in the abyss (Luke 8:31, although this confinement may not be permanent—see Rev. 9:1–3, 11) or permanently imprisoned in hell/tartarus (2 Pet. 2:4; Jude 6; and possibly 1 Pet. 3:18–20). The verb *tartareō* ("to send to hell") occurs only in 2 Peter 2:4 in the New Testament, but is found frequently in Greek mythology, where it refers to the depths of the underworld. There is a textual problem in verse 4. Some manuscripts say that the demons were committed to "pits" of darkness, while others say "chains" of darkness. It has been suggested that since Peter's language is necessarily figurative, he may be interpreted as saying not that these demons are permanently confined but that they are only significantly restricted in what they can do in the earth. I find this suggestion highly unlikely.

Demons engage in cosmic level warfare with the holy angels (Rev. 12:1–12). New Testament scholars have generally acknowledged that there are four levels of spiritual conflict or warfare: (1) the conflict between God and Satan (Heb. 2:14; 1 John 3:8); (2) the conflict between the elect angels and the evil angels (Daniel 10; Revelation 12); (3) the conflict between Satan and the saints (either *direct* [a sensible, often tangible encounter between intelligent evil beings and the believer; Ephesians 6] or *indirect* [the inescapable conflict from simply living in a world that lies in the power of the Evil One (1 John 5:18–19), a world shaped by the values, ideologies, and institutions energized by Satan]); and (4) the conflict between Satan and the unsaved (Matt. 13:1–23; Acts 26:18; 2 Cor. 4:4; Eph. 2:2; Col. 1:12–14), although *conflict* is probably not a good word insofar as the unbelieving world willingly sides with Satan, even though they may not know they do. Our immediate concern is with level (2), and for this we turn to Revelation 12:1–12.

John introduces Revelation 12:7–12 to explain why the "woman" had to flee into the wilderness (vv. 1–6), why Satan's fury is now unleashed against the church of Jesus Christ *on earth*. The reason is that he has lost his place and position *in heaven*; his power has been curtailed. There are generally three theories about when this expulsion of Satan and his demons from heaven occurred.

Some believe it will occur in the future, during the so-called tribulation period. Others insist that this event is timeless. No specific moment in history is in view. It is simply a highly symbolic description of Satan's downfall. Most likely, however, it is because of the incarnation, life, death, and resurrection of Jesus that this defeat of the Devil occurs, indeed, *has already occurred*. Michael and his angels are given the task of expelling Satan consequent to the victory of Jesus *at the time of his first coming* (Luke 10:18). Christians carry on this victory over Satan (Rev. 12:11) as they stand on the achievements of the cross and boldly proclaim the authority of Jesus's name. I believe this third view is correct. In that light, four observations are in order.

First, we do know that when Satan rebelled, he enticed a large number of angels to follow him. Many believe this is what verse 4 is describing and thus we should conclude that a third of the original angelic host are fallen demonic spirits. But there may be a better explanation of this text.

The picture of the dragon sweeping away one-third of the stars of heaven is probably taken from Daniel 8:10. There we read of a "little horn" (v. 9) that "grew great, even to the host of heaven. And some of the host and some of the stars it threw down to the ground and trampled on them" (v. 10). The "little horn" is clearly a reference to Antiochus Epiphanes IV, eighth ruler in the Seleucid line, 175–164 BC (he died in 163).[9] In view of the statement in Daniel 8:24 (that he will "destroy mighty men and the people who are the saints"), most likely the references to the "host" and the "stars" in 8:10 form a symbolic allusion to the people of God as shining lights or glorious ones.

The point of this is that the "stars of heaven" in Revelation 12:4 that Satan throws to the earth are probably *not* those in the angelic host who fall with him in a primordial rebellion and subsequently constitute the demonic hosts of which we read in both the Old Testament and the New. Thus the "stars" of verse 4 are not to be

---

[9] The best description of the rule of Antiochus and his oppression and persecution of the Jews is provided in the apocryphal work of 1–2 Maccabees (esp. the former; see the preface, 1:10–15, 20–24, 29–35, 41–50, 54–64 (cf. 2 Macc. 6:1–6; 7); 4:36–59; 6:5–16.

identified with the dragon's "angels" in Revelation 12:7–8. Verse 4 is probably describing Satan's persecution of God's people, perhaps even their martyrdom.

In addition to the background in Daniel 8:10, two other facts support the view that Revelation 12:4 is not talking about the rebellion of formerly holy angels. First, the time of Revelation 12:4 is immediately before the birth of Jesus, whereas most believe that the angelic rebellion occurred prior to creation, or at least no later than the events of Genesis 6. Second, Gregory Beale makes this important point:

> The observation that the "tails" of Satan's demons afflict people on earth in Rev. 9:10 and 9:19 also points to the idea that the tail of the dragon here is afflicting people and not merely or primarily angels. This is confirmed further by the close relation of 12:4 to 12:1. The portrayal of the stars in v. 4 must have a close relationship with the "twelve stars" only three verses earlier. The falling stars must symbolize an attack on Israel, since the twelve stars in v. 1 represent the heavenly identification of the true Israel . . . . Though ultimately protected . . . genuine Israel, nevertheless, will still suffer Satanic attack.[10]

That a "third" of the stars are thrown down reminds us of other references in Revelation to a "third" of earth, trees, the sea and its creatures, the rivers, and the heavenly luminaries being affected by divine judgment. In each case it refers to a relative fraction of the total or a significant minority, always short of complete destruction.

Whether or not Satan led precisely a third of the angelic host in rebellion, or even whether this is what is in view here in Revelation 12, is not important. What is important is that the demonic hosts are now regarded as "his angels" (Rev. 12:7, 9).

Second, Satan's accusations no longer have any legal or moral force following his defeat at the cross. This, I believe, is the meaning of his being "thrown down" and there no longer being a "place found for them in heaven." In other words, this is not a description

---

[10] G. K. Beale, *The Book of Revelation: A Commentary on the Greek Text* (Grand Rapids: Eerdmans, 1999), 637.

of a literal or spatial or geographical change in the Devil's dwelling place. "Rather we should recognize that Satan's power was broken through what happened on the cross so that he can no longer successfully bring accusations against God's people."[11] After all, verse 10 affirms that the one who "has been" (the Greek tense is aorist, or past) thrown down is the one who "accuses" (present tense) believers "day and night before our God." This ongoing work of accusation is countered by the intercessory ministry of Jesus (Rom. 8:33–34; Heb. 7:25; 1 John 2:1–2).

Third, we learn from this that events in the heavenly or angelic realm have consequences for us on earth. Fourth, Michael and his elect angels are more powerful than Satan and his demonic hosts (Rev. 12:8). Why? Because of the cross and resurrection of Jesus! Two other texts substantiate this point.

The first is 2 Peter 2:10–11, where "angelic majesties" (NASB), or "celestial beings" (NIV)—lit., "glories," meaning evil angelic beings or demons—come in for ridicule. The false teachers mock and insult them, something not even the elect angels do. Elect angels (a reference to all holy angels or only archangels such as Michael?) are "greater in might and power" than evil angels. This superior strength isn't by virtue of creation; it isn't inherent within them. Rather, it is by virtue of the victory of the cross and resurrection and exaltation of Jesus.

Why would false teachers speak disdainfully of demons? Richard Bauckham explains:

> The most plausible view is that in their confident immorality the false teachers were contemptuous of the demonic powers. When they were rebuked for their immoral behavior and warned of the danger of falling into the power of the devil and sharing his condemnation, they laughed at the idea, denying that the devil could have any power over them and speaking of the powers of evil in skeptical, mocking terms. They may have doubted the very existence of supernatural powers of evil.[12]

The second text is Jude 8–9. Here we see that Michael, though

---

[11] Page, *Powers of Evil*, 215.
[12] Richard J. Bauckham, *Jude, 2 Peter*, Word Biblical Commentary (Waco, TX: Word, 1983), 262.

greater and more powerful than Satan (2 Pet. 2:11; Rev. 12:8) because of Christ's victory, did not pronounce a judgment against his rival. There is no reference in the Old Testament to this dispute. It comes from Jude's reconstruction of the lost ending of the *Testament of Moses* (first century BC; see Deut. 34:1–6). According to *T.Mos*, Michael was sent by God to Mount Nebo to remove Moses's body to its burial place. Before he could do so, Satan, making one last effort to gain power and authority over Moses, tried to obtain the body (hoping, perhaps, to make it an object of worship among the Israelites [idolatry] or at least to deprive Moses of the honor of burial by the archangel). It was a legal dispute, as Satan sought to prove Moses unworthy of honorable treatment, accusing him of murder (Ex. 2:12). Michael, not tolerating such slander, appealed to divine authority and said, "May the Lord rebuke you, devil!"

This is *not* designed to teach us to show reverence for the Devil. Rather, the point is that Michael, unlike the false teachers, did not presume to be a law unto himself but referred the matter to the proper moral authority: God. Again, Bauckham explains:

> The point of contrast between the false teachers and Michael is not that Michael treated the devil with respect, and the moral is not that we should be polite even to the devil. The point of the contrast is that Michael could not reject the devil's accusation on his own authority. Even though the devil was motivated by malice and Michael recognized that his accusation was slanderous, he could not himself dismiss the devil's case, because he was not the judge. All he could do was ask the Lord, who alone is judge, to condemn Satan for his slander. The moral is therefore that no one is a law to himself, an autonomous moral authority.[13]

This does *not* mean that we, as Christians, are forbidden to rebuke or verbally resist or pronounce judgment against demonic beings. Neither unbelievers (the false teachers) nor even the holy angels have the authority we have received by virtue of our being in Christ. In Christ, with his authority, we both can and must resist and rebuke the Enemy (see Luke 10:1–20; Acts 5:16; 8:7;

---

[13] Ibid., 61.

16:16–18; 19:12). Jude makes no attempt to extend to Christians the restriction placed on Michael.

Conclusion

It seems only right to bring this chapter to a close with the same note of victory over demons that we saw in the previous chapter in relation to their leader, Satan. The defeat of the hosts of hell does not come by our efforts or energetic shouting or wild gesturing, or by turning up the volume when we worship, as if demonic spirits cannot tolerate loud music! Paul was clear and to the point in writing to the Colossians, "He [God the Father, or perhaps the Son] disarmed the rulers and authorities and put them to open shame, by triumphing over them in him [that is, in Christ, or perhaps in "it," the cross]" (Col. 2:15). The good news is that we have been granted authority "over all the power of the enemy" (Luke 10:19). Satan and his henchmen are powerful, but they are no match for those who go forth in the name of Jesus (Luke 10:17)!

Recommended Reading

Cuneo, Michael W. *American Exorcism: Expelling Demons in the Land of Plenty*. New York: Doubleday, 2001.

Warner, Timothy M. *Spiritual Warfare: Victory over the Powers of This Dark World*. Wheaton, IL: Crossway, 1991.

White, Thomas B. *The Believer's Guide to Spiritual Warfare*. Ann Arbor, MI: Servant, 1990.

13

Can a Christian Be Demonized?

I find it strangely intriguing that of all the thorny topics addressed in this book, the one presently under consideration often provokes more heat and contention than all the others. Let's jump directly into the fray! Can a Christian be demonized? Can a Christian be indwelt by a demonic spirit? Three answers have been given: yes, no, and yes/no! But before I turn to evaluate these arguments, we need to define our terms.

What Does It Mean to Be Demonized?

Some of you are probably wondering why I have chosen the term *demonization* rather than the more popular *demon possession*. This may actually come as a surprise to you, but the Bible never once talks about demon "possession." That phrase was popularized by its appearance in the King James Version, although it had appeared in other English versions prior to the 1611 edition.[1] Lack of support for that rendering should be reason enough to avoid

---

[1] Clinton E. Arnold, *Three Crucial Questions about Spiritual Warfare* (Grand Rapids: Baker, 1997), 205n11.

using such language, but in addition we need to consider the emotional impact of the phrase, which I believe detracts from an objective discussion of the subject. It is difficult for many to dissociate the concept of demon possession from scenes in the movie *The Exorcist.* I would also point out that the term *possession* implies ownership, and it is questionable to say that Satan or a demon owns anything.

When we turn our attention to the New Testament, we discover four ways in which it describes demonic influence. First, there is the Greek term *daimonizomai*, which is used thirteen times in the New Testament (all in the Gospels). It's unfortunate that the KJV always translates this word as "demon possession" (see Matt. 4:24; 8:16, 28, 33; 9:32; 12:22; 15:22; Mark 1:32; 5:15, 16, 18; Luke 8:36; John 10:21, the last being a disparaging remark concerning Jesus).

What's important for us to note is that every case of demonization involves someone under the influence or control, in varying degrees, of an *indwelling* evil spirit. The word *demonization* is never used in the New Testament to describe someone who is merely oppressed or harassed or attacked or tempted by a demon. In every case, reference is made to a demon either entering, dwelling in, or being cast out of the person. Matthew 4:24 and 15:22 at first appear to be exceptions to this rule, but the parallel passages in Mark 1:32ff. and 7:24–30 indicate otherwise. Hence, to be "demonized," in the strict sense of that term, is to be *inhabited* by a demon with varying degrees of influence or control.

On sixteen occasions in the New Testament, reference is made to a person who "has" a demon. This language is twice used of John the Baptist by his accusers (Matt. 11:18; Luke 7:33). Six times the enemies of Jesus use it of him (Mark 3:30; John 7:20; 8:48, 49, 52; 10:20). Eight times it describes someone under the influence of a demonic spirit (Mark 5:15; 7:25; 9:17; Luke 4:33; 8:27; Acts 8:7; 16:16; 19:13). Hence to "have" a demon is to be "demonized" or inhabited by a demon (see esp. John 10:20–21).

On two occasions (Mark 1:23; 5:2) we find reference to someone who is "with" (Gk. *en*) a demon or spirit. To say a person is "with" a demon is to say he "has" a demon, which is to say he is "demonized" or is indwelt by a demon.

Finally, the terminology of being vexed or "afflicted" by or with an unclean spirit is used only once, in Acts 5:16.

In summary, if a demon indwells or inhabits a person, it is a case of demonization. Merely to be tempted, harassed, afflicted, or oppressed by a demon is not demonization. *Demonization always entails indwelling.* We are now ready to take note of the three answers to our question, Can a born-again Christian be inhabited or indwelt by a demonic spirit?

Arguments for a Modified Demonization of Christians

Several authors suggest that a believer can be demonized, but in a somewhat modified or restricted sense. Based on the doctrine of *trichotomy*, according to which a person is made of three faculties—body, soul, and spirit—they affirm that a demon can inhabit a Christian's soul and body, but not his spirit. The body is one's physical constitution. The soul comprises one's mind, emotions, and will. The spirit is that element or faculty which relates to God and at regeneration is born anew, sealed, and permanently indwelt by the Holy Spirit.

Although this view has become increasingly popular, I find it lacking in several ways. In the first place, there is no explicit evidence for this in Scripture. Nowhere in the Bible do we read of a demon indwelling a person's "soul" or "body" but being excluded from the "spirit." Furthermore, this view assumes the validity of trichotomy (1 Thess. 5:23), a doubtful doctrine (see Mark 12:30). Man is dichotomous: both material and immaterial, both physical and spiritual, the latter often called the soul and at other times the spirit. On numerous occasions in Scripture *spirit* and *soul* are used interchangeably, as simply different names for the same immaterial dimension of our constitution, thus prohibiting us from drawing rigid distinctions between the two.

I would also argue that the whole person is renewed by the Holy Spirit, not just one faculty or element within that person (2 Cor. 5:17). To restrict a demon to a person's soul and body, excluded from his spirit, is to suggest that there is a rigid, spatial compartmentalization of our beings. But *where* is the soul in the body? *Where* is the spirit? These are biblically illegitimate questions. They are attempts to apply physical categories to spiritual realities. Clinton Arnold offers a slightly different interpretation. Without drawing a distinction between soul and spirit, he refers to "the core of the person, the center of his or her being, his or her ultimate nature and identity."[2] It is this within each person that undergoes a radical, indeed supernatural, transformation in the new birth. He explains:

> At the center of this person's being now lies a desire for God and a passion to please him in every respect. *This is the place of the Holy Spirit's dwelling. No evil spirit can enter here or cause the Holy Spirit to flee. To extend the image of the temple, we might say that this is the inviolable "holy of holies."*[3]

Here again we see an attempt to restrict the access of a demonic spirit to certain "places" or "spiritual regions" within the individual. Does Arnold's model successfully avoid the weaknesses and criticisms of the "trichotomist" theory noted above? I don't think so.

Arguments against the Demonization of Christians

Those who insist that a Christian cannot be inhabited or indwelt by a demonic spirit appeal to several lines of evidence. Let's look at each one in turn.

They begin by pointing to those biblical *texts that describe the defeat of Satan*, specifically John 12:31; 16:11; Colossians 2:14–15; Hebrews 2:14–15; and 1 John 3:8. The argument is that if Satan has been judged and stripped, and his work "destroyed" (1 John 3:8), how can he or his demons indwell a believer?

But these passages do not by themselves settle the issue. It is true that Jesus has "bound" (Matt. 12:25–29) the strong man (i.e., Satan), but it is equally the case that Satan can exert a significant influence in the lives of believers (Matt. 16:23; Acts 5:3; 1 Pet. 5:8).

[2] Ibid., 85.
[3] Ibid., 84 (emphasis mine).

Jesus has defeated the Devil (John 12:31; 16:11), but he must also continue to pray that God will guard us against the attacks of the Evil One (John 17:15). On the one hand, all demonic powers have been subjected to the lordship of Jesus and placed beneath his feet (Eph. 1:19–22). But on the other hand, Paul warns us that our struggle is still against principalities and powers and the forces of this present darkness (Eph. 6:10–13). We have been delivered from Satan's domain, and Jesus has triumphed over the demonic (Col. 1:13; 2:14–15), but Satan can still hinder Paul's missionary efforts (1 Thess. 2:18). My point is simply that the reality of Satan's defeat does not eliminate his activity and influence in the present age.

Appeal is also made to *texts that describe the promise of divine protection.* Yes, Jesus instructed us to pray for deliverance from the Evil One (Matt. 6:13), but this is clearly dependent (and not automatic) on our prayer for it. What happens if we do *not* pray? No one can snatch us from the hand of our heavenly Father (John 10:28–29), so if a demon could indwell a believer, wouldn't that mean our security is in doubt? No, because this text simply asserts the same truth we find in Romans 8:35–39—that nothing, not even a demon, can separate us from the love and life we have in God. It says nothing about the possibility of demonization.

I'm grateful, as I'm sure you are, that Jesus prayed in John 17:15 that the Father would guard us against the Enemy. But this text cannot mean that Jesus was asking the Father to make us utterly invulnerable to demonic attack. Indeed, it was after this prayer that Jesus told Peter of Satan's request to "sift" him like wheat. This prayer is more likely for our eternal preservation, or it may be that the fulfillment or answer to it is dependent on our availing ourselves of the Father's protection (Ephesians 6).

Paul prays in 2 Thessalonians 3:3 that the Lord would "guard" us from Satan. But again, we must ask, guard from *what* regarding the enemy, and on what, if any, conditions that we are responsible to meet? This promise of protection does not rule out attack or temptation from the Enemy (see 2 Cor. 12:7; 1 Thess. 2:18; 1 Pet. 5:8; etc.). Therefore, either this is a promise pertaining to the eternal preservation of the believer (i.e., no matter how vicious the attack, no matter how bad life gets, Satan can't separate you from God), or it is a promise conditioned upon the obedient response of the believer. In other words, it is a promise based on the truth of verse 4. Fred Dickason explains:

> This promise, then, is for those who walk in obedience to the Lord. Satan will not be able to take them unaware and render them weak, unfaithful, and unproductive in Christian life and service. It is a great promise for the obedient and watchful Christian, but is not a blanket protection promised to all. It does not promise that no Christian will ever be attacked or seriously affected by demonic forces. It does not address the matter of demonization.[4]

One of the most encouraging texts in the New Testament is 1 John 4:4, where the apostle assures us that greater is he who is in us (Jesus Christ) than he who is in the world (Satan). But this text does not mean that all Christians are always automatically guaranteed of never being deceived by error. It does mean that we *need not* ever be deceived, for the Holy Spirit is more powerful than Satan.

I often hear reference made to 1 John 5:18 and the assurance that the Enemy cannot touch the believer. The argument is made that it makes little sense to say, on the one hand, that the Evil One cannot "touch" a Christian and, on the other hand, that he could conceivably indwell him. But let's think about this more closely. For one thing, we can't press the term "touch" to exclude the attack and influence of Satan, for according to 1 Peter 5:8 it is possible to be "devoured" by the Devil! We should also consider Revelation 2:10, where Jesus himself says that Satan can imprison and even kill the Christian. Thus, whatever "touch" means, it does not suggest that all Christians are automatically insulated against demonic attack. Also, to "touch" a believer may mean to rob him or her of salvation. If so, then Satan cannot "grasp so as to destroy" the spiritual life of the believer. Finally, it may well be that the promise is conditional, perhaps suspended on the fulfillment of 1 John 5:21, "Little children, keep yourselves from idols."

---

[4] C. Fred Dickason, *Demon Possession and the Christian* (Chicago: Moody, 1987), 91.

Clearly, no Christian can be swallowed up by Satan or robbed of the salvation, life, and love of the Father. He or she cannot be owned by Satan, or separated from the love of God in Christ. But none of these texts explicitly rules out the possibility of demonization. The promises of protection are of two sorts: either (1) a promise pertaining to the security of the believer's salvation, or (2) a promise dependent on the believer's taking advantage of the resources supplied by the Spirit.

Another line of argumentation is based on *texts that describe the indwelling presence of the Holy Spirit.* The argument is this: A demon cannot enter and dwell within a believer because the Holy Spirit lives there. Since the Spirit is greater and more powerful than any demon, there is no possibility that he would grant access into a Christian's heart.

But I must again ask, is this protection against demonic invasion automatic? What if the believer grieves the Holy Spirit through repeated and unrepentant sin? What if the believer fails to faithfully and prayerfully adorn himself or herself with the armor of God (Ephesian 6)? Several texts are relevant to this issue.

In Psalm 5:4 we read,

> For you are not a God who delights in wickedness;
> evil may not dwell with you.

Does this text really mean to suggest that God cannot dwell alongside an evil spirit inside a person? Observe that the two lines of verse 4 are in synonymous parallelism: "evil may not dwell with you" is simply another way of saying that God does not delight in wickedness. The point is not that God cannot be in close spatial proximity with evil. We must not forget that the *omnipresent* God is in close spatial proximity with *everything*! The point of the passage is simply that God detests evil and has no fellowship with it.

Matthew 12:43–45 is a famous passage that needs to be cited in full. Jesus says:

> When the unclean spirit has gone out of a person, it passes through waterless places seeking rest, but finds none. Then it says, "I will

return to my house from which I came." And when it comes, it finds the house empty, swept, and put in order. Then it goes and brings with it seven other spirits more evil than itself, and they enter and dwell there, and the last state of that person is worse than the first. So also will it be with this evil generation.

The argument is that if the house *is* occupied (presumably by Jesus or the Holy Spirit), demons can't enter. But does this mean that the person himself cannot "open the door" to intrusion by a demon through willful, unrepentant sin or idolatry? Also, the text does not say what the demon would have done had he found his previous home occupied. It does not say that *that* in itself would have prevented his reentry. It may well have made reentry more difficult, but not necessarily impossible.

In 1 Corinthians 10:21 Paul warns Christians: "You cannot drink the cup of the Lord and the cup of demons. You cannot partake of the table of the Lord and the table of demons." But the "cannot" in Paul's language refers to a moral, not a metaphysical, impossibility. If I say to a Christian who is contemplating committing adultery, "But you *cannot* do that!" I don't mean that it is physically impossible for him to commit adultery, but that it is *morally or spiritually incompatible* with his being a Christian. In other words, you can't expect to enjoy close intimacy with Christ and simultaneously give yourself to the influence of demons. It is a moral and spiritual contradiction to affirm your love for God while you simultaneously expose yourself to the influence of demons by participating in activities they energize. In fact, far from ruling out the possibility of a Christian participating in or fellowshiping with demons, Paul warns us to be careful of that very thing.

Two texts in the Corinthian letters describe Christians as the "temple" of the Holy Spirit in whom he dwells, and the danger in being "unequally yoked" with unbelievers and of seeking "fellowship" with darkness (1 Cor. 3:16–17; 2 Cor. 6:14–16). The argument from these texts at first glance seems persuasive: surely a Christian cannot simultaneously be both the temple of God and the temple of a demon!

But Paul is not referring (in 2 Corinthians 6) to the physical impossibility of a Christian being "yoked" in "fellowship" with evil or with an unbeliever. The fact is, we know it happens all the time (unfortunately). Rather, he is denouncing the *moral or spiritual incongruity* of such fellowship. The temple of God has no moral or spiritual harmony with idols. Therefore, avoid all such entangling alliances.

The argument from 1 Corinthians 3 is based on the idea that a demon indwelling a Christian is a *spatial* and *spiritual* impossibility. As for the former, it is argued that there is "not enough room" for both the Holy Spirit and a demonic being to coexist in the same human body. It would be too crowded! But this is to think of spiritual beings in physical terms. I could as easily ask: How can the Holy Spirit and the human spirit both indwell the same body? Wouldn't that be just as "crowded"? Mary Magdalene at one time had "seven demons" inhabiting her (Luke 8:2). The Gadarene demoniac (Mark 5) was inhabited by a "legion" of demons (six thousand), enough, at any rate, to enter and destroy two thousand pigs. And if the presence of the Holy Spirit "crowds out" demons, then demons couldn't exist *anywhere* because the Holy Spirit exists *everywhere*.

The second argument is that this would be a spiritual impossibility. That is to say, how can the *Holy* Spirit inhabit the same body with an *unholy* demon? But again we must remember that the Holy Spirit in a certain sense "inhabits" everything and everyone in the universe, even unbelievers (though, of course, not in a saving or sanctifying way). The Holy Spirit is, after all, omnipresent. He dwells everywhere! You may also recall from the book of Job that Satan had access to the presence of God, indicating that the issue is not one of spatial proximity but of *personal relationship*. The Holy Spirit and demons are in close proximity when *outside* the human body, so why could they not be in close proximity while *inside* one? Finally, the Holy Spirit indwells the Christian even though the latter still has a sinful nature or sinful flesh. In other words, if the *Holy* Spirit can inhabit the same body with *unholy* human sin, why could he not inhabit the same body with an *unholy* demon?

It strikes me that the force of this argument appears to be

more emotional than biblical. The idea of the Holy Spirit and a demon living inside a believer is *too close, too intimate* contact. The thought of it is emotionally provocative and scandalous; it violates one's sense of spiritual propriety. The *feeling* is that God simply wouldn't allow it. His love for his own is too great to let demonic influence get that far. But we must always keep in mind that the only criterion for making a decision on an issue such as this is not what *seems* or *feels* proper to us, but what the Scripture explicitly asserts.

There are a number of other, miscellaneous arguments that I should mention. For example, I've been asked, How can a Christian who is *possessed* by Christ be *possessed* by a demon? But in this question, the word "possessed" is being used in two entirely different senses. To say that one is "possessed" by a demon (although that in itself is an unbiblical term) is to say that he or she is severely influenced by the evil spirit. To say that one is "possessed" by Christ is to say he or she is owned by the Lord because purchased with his blood (1 Corinthians 6).

Another argument goes like this: How can a Christian who is *in Christ* have a demon *in him or her*? Again, words are here being used in a way that provokes an emotional response but lacks theological substance. To be "in Christ" refers to eternal salvation, whereas to say a demon is "in a believer" refers to influence or powers of persuasion.

Perhaps you've heard it said that "the internal struggle of the Christian is portrayed in the New Testament as between the Holy Spirit and the flesh, not the Holy Spirit and a demon." However, in the first place, this is an argument from silence. Or to put it another way, what biblical text *denies* or *precludes* the Holy Spirit from fighting against an indwelling demon? Also, if a Christian yields to the flesh and grieves the Holy Spirit, wouldn't this open the door to demonic presence? Finally, Ephesians 6 says that our primary struggle *is* against the demonic. Although there is no explicit reference to this being an *internal* battle, there is nothing here that precludes it being such, especially if we fail to employ the full armor.

Arguments Supporting the
Demonization of Christians

We've looked closely at most, if not all, of the arguments used to prove that a Christian cannot be demonized. My conclusion is that none of these texts or the inferences drawn from them conclusively makes the case. We now turn our attention to texts that may suggest a Christian can be indwelt by a demonic spirit.

We begin with those passages that describe *the reality of demonic activity and attack*. Most of these texts fail to prove the thesis that a Christian can be demonized because they fail to say anything about the *location* of the activity relative to the individual. For example, 2 Corinthians 2:11 asserts that Satan has a strategy to bring division to the body of Christ. No one would deny that Satan seeks to divide and disrupt, to exploit disagreements, or to intensify unforgiveness, and the like. But nothing explicitly is said here about demonization.

Second Corinthians 11:3–4 speaks of the danger that the Corinthian believers might "receive" a "different spirit" from the one they had earlier accepted. What does "spirit" mean? Is this a demonic being, or could it be an attitude, an influence, or a principle? And what does "receive" mean? Is it invasion and subsequent inhabitation, or perhaps tolerance, attentiveness, and similar influence? The most likely explanation is that the Corinthians were tolerating the presence and influence of false teachers who were energized by demons.

We are all familiar with 2 Corinthians 12:7–8, where Paul's thorn in the flesh came to him through a "messenger of Satan." Although God used a demonic being to keep Paul humble, no one would wish to conclude that he was demonized! If he were, would he have rejoiced in its effects (vv. 9–10)?

Ephesians 4:26–27 is a far more important passage, for here we see what might happen should the Devil exploit the relational strains and tension that develop in the Christian community. Page is correct to point out "that the devil is not credited with producing anger; that is, its source is apparently to be found within the person himself or herself. Nevertheless, anger can provide the devil with an opportunity to wreak havoc in the life of the individual and the community."[5] It seems reasonable that Satan's activity in this regard would extend to the other sins mentioned in the immediately subsequent context: stealing, unwholesome speech, bitterness, wrath, clamor, slander, malice, and unforgiveness (see vv. 28–32).

Arnold points to Paul's use of the term *topos*, translated "foothold" or "opportunity" (v. 27). He argues that this word is often used in the New Testament for "inhabited space" (cf. Luke 2:7; 4:37; 14:9; John 14:2–3). Even more to the point, says Arnold, are passages that illustrate the use of *topos* to refer to the inhabiting space of an evil spirit, such as Luke 11:24 and Revelation 12:7–8. Thus he concludes that "the most natural way to interpret the use of *topos* in Ephesians 4:27 is the idea of inhabitable space. Paul is thus calling these believers to vigilance and moral purity so that they do not relinquish a base of operations to demonic spirits."[6]

Everyone is familiar with Ephesians 6:10–18 and Paul's passionate exhortation that we put on the full armor of God to prepare ourselves for the onslaught of demonic attack. What happens to the believer who does *not* stand in the strength of Christ, who does *not* put on the full armor of God, who does *not* therefore "stand firm" (v. 13)?

There are a handful of passages that speak of Satanic and demonic attack. First Thessalonians 2:18 says that "Satan hindered" Paul from making a desired visit to Thessalonica. The apostle describes the danger of a believer falling into "a snare of the devil" (1 Tim. 3:7). Does this entail demonization? There's no way to know. The language itself neither implies nor precludes the possibility. Characteristic of "later times" is that people will come under the influence of demonic doctrine, perhaps even a form of mind control. Paul speaks of them as "devoting themselves to deceitful spirits and teachings of demons" (1 Tim. 4:1). But does this entail or require inhabitation? And does he have in mind born-again

---

[5] Sydney H. T. Page, *Powers of Evil: A Biblical Study of Satan and Demons* (Grand Rapids: Baker, 1995), 188–89.
[6] Arnold, *Three Crucial Questions*, 88.

Christians or only professing believers who in fact know nothing of the saving grace of Jesus?

Paul describes some as escaping from "the snare of the devil, after being captured by him to do his will" (2 Tim. 2:26). But these would appear to be unbelievers who Paul hopes and prays will come to saving faith through Timothy's ministry. It does raise the question, of course, about what happens when a demonized person comes to saving faith. Does the Holy Spirit's activity in regenerating such a person automatically result in deliverance or exorcism of the indwelling demon? No text of which I am aware ever answers that question.

James refers to a form of "wisdom" that is "earthly, unspiritual, demonic" (James 3:15), and he evidently envisions the possibility that a believer might act on the basis of it. But does this entail demonization? More explicit still is Peter's exhortation that we be watchful in view of the fact that "your adversary the devil prowls around like a roaring lion, seeking someone to devour" (1 Pet. 5:8). His counsel is that we humble ourselves (v. 6) and cast all our anxieties on God and remain sober and alert. It seems reasonable to conclude that if we do *not* humble ourselves, if we do *not* cast our cares on him, if we are *not* sober and alert, we may well be devoured by the Devil. "Devour" means to swallow up (Matt. 23:24; 1 Cor. 15:54; 2 Cor. 2:7; 5:4; Heb. 11:29; Rev. 12:16). Nothing, however, is said explicitly about how or from where this "devouring" takes place. I would think that if given the opportunity, Satan or demons can make a serious encroachment on the life of a believer; simply being a Christian does not automatically insulate you from this sort of potentially devastating attack. On the other hand, if we "resist" the Devil (1 Pet. 5:9), we are assured of victory.

And a passage we looked at earlier, 1 John 4:1–4, would be relevant to this debate only if some of the false teachers in whom the spirit of antichrist operated were Christians. This, however, is highly unlikely.

We turn next to texts where the experience of particular individuals is described. *Balaam* (Numbers 22–24) is often mentioned. But was Balaam a believer? Whatever answer we come to, nothing is said about an indwelling demonic presence in his life. The case of *Saul* is more intriguing. Was he a believer? Probably so (1 Sam. 10:9). Because of his rebellion and sin he came under demonic attack (1 Sam. 16:14–23; 18:10–11; 19:9). However, the evil spirit is said to come "upon/on" him, not "into/in" him. Does the fact that this happened prior to Pentecost have any bearing on how we interpret it?

Most helpful of all is the story of *the woman bent double* (Luke 13:10–17). Her condition has been identified by some as "spondylitis ankylopoetica" (which produces fusion of the vertebrae). But again we ask, was she a believer? She "glorified" God immediately on being delivered (v. 13) and is called "a daughter of Abraham" (v. 16; cf. Luke 19:9). The latter may simply mean she was Jewish. Was she demonized? The NASB reads, "had a sickness caused by a spirit" (13:11), whereas a literal reading would be, "she had a spirit of sickness [or of infirmity]," which is similar to the language of demonization ("to have a spirit"; see also v. 16); thus the ESV reads, "had a disabling spirit." Others have argued, however, that this narrative reads more like a simple healing than an exorcism. But even if true, that doesn't answer the question of whether the demon indwelt her.

I would be remiss if I didn't mention the story of *Ananias and Sapphira* (Acts 5). Certainly they were both believers. It seems unlikely that the example of their deaths would have any relevance for the church if they were not (cf. v. 11). Were they demonized? Satan is said to have "filled" their heart (v. 3). This verb "filled" is the same one used in Ephesians 5:18 for being "filled" with the Holy Spirit. But with what did Satan fill them? Did he fill them with himself, so as to indwell them? Or did Satan fill their heart with the temptation or idea or notion to hold back the money? At minimum, this is the case of a believer coming under powerful Satanic influence. Notwithstanding Satan's influence, *they* were responsible for their sin. *They* were disciplined with death (see Acts 5:4b, 9—"you"). The point is that they could have said *no* to Satan's influence.

The case of the man in 1 Corinthians 5 who was discovered having sexual relations with his stepmother is often mentioned in this debate. Paul counseled that he be delivered "to Satan for the destruction of the flesh" (1 Cor. 5:5). This probably refers to his excommunication or expulsion from the fellowship of the church. To "deliver to Satan" refers to turning him out into the world, back into the domain of Satan. "Destruction of the flesh" refers not to physical death but to the anticipated effect of his expulsion, namely, the mortification or crucifixion of his carnal appetites so that he may be saved on the day of Christ. So here we see yet another example of Satan intending one thing in a particular action (no doubt he wanted only to ruin this man) while God intended something entirely different (salvation).

First Corinthians 10:14–22 is a special case that probably comes as close as any text to providing us with the explicit evidence we need to draw a firm conclusion on this debate. There Paul urgently warns the Corinthians against participating in pagan feasts and then turning to the fellowship of the Lord's Supper in the meeting of the local church. Clearly, the apostle thought it possible for a Christian to become a "participant" (ESV) or "sharer" or "partner" with demons. The word he uses here is *koinōnia*, typically used to describe fellowship or communion with a person or thing. It is the same word used in verse 16 for our sharing in or participating with or entering into fellowship with Christ at his table! What does this mean? Is he referring merely to "agreement with" or the "holding of a common purpose with" Christ versus a demon? Is it merely a description of external attendance at a pagan feast? Or does Paul have in mind a more active sharing of an internal spiritual bond or link or fellowship with a demon? His point seems to be that when you sit to worship at the table of the Lord, or conversely, in the presence of idols, you open yourself to the power and influence of one or the other. There is a sharing of an intimate spiritual experience, an association of sorts, a relationship that is personal and powerful. But does it entail inhabitation by a demon?

Conclusion

Clinton Arnold responds to those who think it is significant that no text explicitly describes a case of a Christian being demonized:

Although the Epistles do not use the terms *demonization* or *have a demon* to describe the experience of a Christian, the concept is nevertheless present. The ideas of demonic inhabitation and control are clearly a part of the biblical teaching on what demons can do to saints. To limit ourselves to the same Greek words that the Gospels use to describe the phenomena of demonic influence could cause us to miss the same concept expressed in different terms. No one, for instance, questions the validity of making disciples as part of the church's mission. Yet the term *disciple* (*mathetes*) never appears in the New Testament after the Book of Acts. It would be quite erroneous to conclude that the concept of discipleship died out early in the history of the church. What has happened is that Paul, Peter, John, and other New Testament authors have made use of a variety of other terms to describe the same reality.[7]

It would seem, then, that the debate reduces to the question of the *location* of demonic spirits relative to the believer, rather than to their *influence*. In other words, all must concede that Christians can be attacked, tempted, oppressed, devoured, and led into grievous sin. Satan can fill our hearts to lie, he can exploit our anger, he can deceive our minds with false doctrine. The question, then, is this: Does all this take place from outside our minds, spirits, bodies, or could it arise from a demon who is indwelling us?

The New Testament does not supply an unequivocal, indisputable answer to our question. Nothing precludes the demonization of a believer. Nor does any text explicitly affirm it or provide us with an undeniable example of a believer who was indwelt by a demon. So of what *practical* significance is the question? In other words, will the location of the demonic spirit affect how I pray for and minister to the person who is under attack? Will I use different words, different prayers, or different texts of Scripture? I'm inclined to agree with Thomas White when he says, "Whether a demon buffets me from a mile away, the corner of the room, sitting on my shoulder, whispering in my ear, or clinging to my corruptible flesh, the result is the same."[8]

---

[7] Ibid., 92–93.
[8] Thomas B. White, *The Believer's Guide to Spiritual Warfare* (Ann Arbor, MI: Servant, 1990), 44.

Or is it, in fact, the same? Is it necessary for a demon to be spatially "inside" a person's mind to infuse or to suggest words, thoughts, or for that person to "hear voices" not his or her own? In the case of Peter (Matthew 16), Satan put the thought into his mind without indwelling him. People often report "hearing voices" inside their heads, not audibly, but ideas, words, images springing into mind involuntarily. They have the sense that the source is not themselves. Must a demon be *inside* for this to happen?

If I were to tell you that a Christian can be demonized, you might be frightened. But if I tell you that a Christian can be hit by a passing car, you don't get scared; you simply take steps to stay out of traffic! You don't walk into the middle of a busy street. You don't live in constant worry or fear simply because it is possible to get hit by a car. Likewise, if it is possible for a Christian to be demonized, do not be afraid. Rather, follow the steps outlined in Scripture, employ the protection made available by the Holy Spirit, and if you are attacked anyway, seek refuge and protection in Christ Jesus!

There is one final question to be asked: What place or level of authority should we give to the testimony and experience of other Christians in deciding this issue? In other words, what am I to conclude, if anything, from personal experience in having prayed for and ministered to people who I have great confidence are Christians and who give every indication of being demonized? Those who are dogmatically assured that a Christian cannot be demonized would not be impressed by any examples I might describe. For them, in each case there are two options, not three. Either the person is self-deluded and has deceived others into thinking he or she is born again, or the demonic activity was not from within but from without. The possibility that the person is both born again and inhabited by a demonic spirit is simply not entertained.

So I will simply end with this tentative, guarded conclusion: yes, in the final analysis, my opinion is that a Christian can be demonized.

Recommended Reading

Arnold, Clinton E. *Three Crucial Questions about Spiritual Warfare.* Grand Rapids: Baker, 1997.

Dickason, C. Fred. *Demon Possession and the Christian.* Chicago: Moody, 1987.

Powlison, David. *Power Encounters: Reclaiming Spiritual Warfare.* Grand Rapids: Baker, 1995.

14

Does Satan Assign Demons to Specific Geopolitical Regions? Are There Territorial Spirits?

Has Satan assigned specific demons responsibility, authority, and power over specific geographical and political areas? Could the entrenched resistance to the gospel in some nations and cultures be due to the ruling presence of a demonic spirit (or spirits) placed there by Satan? If so, what is the responsibility of the Christian? Is there a unique form of spiritual warfare calling for special tactics when it comes to dealing with so-called territorial spirits?

Biblical Evidence for Territorial Spirits[1]

Several lines of evidence lead me to conclude that there *may* well be territorial spirits.[2] We know, for example, that Satan has orga-

---

[1] The best overall treatment of this issue, albeit a critical and somewhat negative one, is provided by Chuck Lowe in his book *Territorial Spirits and World Evangelisation: A Biblical, Historical and Missiological Critique of Strategic-Level Spiritual Warfare* (Ross-Shire: Christian Focus, 2001).
[2] A close examination of the literature advocating the reality of territorial spirits, notes Lowe, indicates that "territorial demons are purportedly assigned not only to geographical regions, but also

nized his demonic forces into a hierarchy. There is some form of rank, as indicated by the sixfold description in Paul's letters: *principalities, authorities, powers, dominions, thrones, world rulers.* Jesus himself indicated that demons differ both in their degree or depth of wickedness (Matt. 12:45) and in their strength or power (Mark 9:29). Could this possibly be what determines their organizational position? We should also remember that Satan does not operate haphazardly. He has a plan, schemes, tactics, a cosmic agenda (Eph. 6:11; 2 Cor. 2:11; 1 John 5:18–19).

The scenario described in Daniel 10 is perhaps the most explicit support for the idea of territorial or "nationalistic" spirits. The events of this chapter occur in "the third year of Cyrus king of Persia" (v. 1). This would have been 535 BC, two years after the appearance of Gabriel in Daniel 9. Daniel himself would have been approximately eighty-five years old.

It was in this year that "a word was revealed to Daniel," a word that "was true" regarding "a great conflict" (10:1). Daniel did not take this lightly but immediately began a season of personal preparation that entailed three weeks of "mourning" and a fast in which he "ate no delicacies, no meat or wine" (v. 3). Our best estimate is that he began his partial fast on the third day of Nisan (March–April, the first month) and experienced his angelic visitation on the twenty-fourth day.

There is no explanation given why Daniel himself had not returned to Palestine with the first wave of former captives. Perhaps his age was a hindrance. Perhaps he was too important in government affairs to be spared. He may even have voluntarily chosen to remain behind, thinking that he could do more for the Jewish effort from his power base in Babylon. In any case, he took three weeks off from his duties and sought the Lord in prayer and fasting, somewhere in the vicinity of the Tigris River, which originated several hundred miles north of Babylon and flowed to the Persian Gulf (passing within twenty miles of the capital city).

---

to geopolitical institutions, such as nations or states; to topographical features, such as valleys, mountains or rivers; to ecological features, such as trees, streams and rocks; or to smaller physical objects, such as houses, temples or idols" (ibid., 19).

The angelic visitation that followed is described in Daniel 10:5–9. Several things should be noted concerning the characteristics of this "angel"(?). In Daniel 12:6 an angel is portrayed as being in the air above the Tigris; perhaps the same is true here (notice that Daniel "lifted up" his eyes and looked, 10:5). This "angel" took on the form and appearance of a man (v. 5) and was clothed in "linen" (v. 5). Both priests (Ex. 28:42; Lev. 6:10) and angels (Ezek. 9:2–3, 11; 10:2, 6–7; Luke 24:4) wore white linen, a symbol of purity (cf. Isa. 1:18; Dan. 11:35; 12:10). The angel's waist was girded with a belt of the "gold from Uphaz" (Dan. 10:5). This may have been a linen belt embroidered with gold, or perhaps even gold chain links, indicating royalty or the power to judge. His body was like "beryl" (v. 6), also identified as "chrysolite," some form of gold-colored precious stone. His face looked like "lightning" (v. 6), a reference either to lightning bolts or simply the brilliance of his face (after all, how does a face look like lightning?). His eyes were like "flaming torches" (v. 6; cf. Rev. 1:14). Pause for a moment and try to envision a face of "lightning" surrounding eyes that look like torches on fire! His arms and feet were like "burnished bronze" (Dan. 10:6). The "sound of his words" were "like the sound of a multitude" (v. 6; cf. Rev. 10:3).

Who was this being? Some say it was once again the preincarnate Son of God, the same divine person who appeared in the furnace (Daniel 3) and in the lion's den (Daniel 6). If so, we must differentiate between this being and the "angel" who appears in Daniel 10:10ff. (see the similar descriptions in Ezek. 1:26–28 and Rev. 1:12–16). But we face a slight problem, for if this is God the Son, we must ask about the purpose of his appearance. Why would he appear only then to be replaced on the scene by an angel? It makes better sense if the being who terrifies Daniel in Daniel 10:5–9 is the same one who touches and teaches him in verses 10ff. Therefore, others insist that this was Gabriel, who had earlier appeared to Daniel in chapter 9. One argument used against this view is that in chapter 9 Daniel was not afraid of Gabriel, but here in chapter 10 he is terrified. But that may well be due to the form of his appearance (perhaps the description in vv. 5–6 is designed precisely to explain why Daniel reacted differently). Or this may be yet another angel, similar to Gabriel and Michael in power and majesty (see esp. Rev. 10:1).

The explanation for this unfolding scenario comes in verses 10–17 of Daniel 10. The simple answer is that in response to his humility and prayer (v. 12), God sent this angel to Daniel. His arrival was delayed twenty-one days because he had been hindered by "the prince of the kingdom of Persia" (v. 13). Who or what was this "prince"? Several factors suggest that he was not a human prince. In the first place, he was able to resist this exalted angelic being, something no human could reasonably be said to do. Second, he was able to resist with such force that Michael had to be summoned for help (v. 13b). We should also note that the word "prince" is applied equally to Michael (the archangel). It would seem, then, that we are dealing here with a demonic spirit who engaged in direct conflict with another angelic being. Since he sustained an ongoing relationship to the nation of Persia (v. 20), I conclude that "the prince of the kingdom of Persia" was a demonic being assigned by Satan to this nation as his special area of activity. His purpose was to provoke hindrance to God's will and kingdom there, especially among God's people under Persian rule.

We read in verse 13 that Gabriel was "left there with the kings of Persia." One view is that the "kings" of Persia refers to the future rulers of that nation and that Gabriel successfully gained a position of influence over them in the place of the "prince" (demon) "of Persia" mentioned in verse 13a. Others contend that the "kings of Persia" were additional demonic spirits assigned by Satan to influence this nation, which currently ruled the world. We read in verse 20 that, after his encounter with Daniel, Gabriel was to return to resume his battle with the prince of Persia. This indicates that whatever the nature of the fight in verse 13, Gabriel was not able to forever destroy or banish that "prince." In verse 20 we also read of the "prince of Greece." Might this indicate that there is *at least* one high ranking demon assigned to each country or nation, perhaps with lesser demons assigned to assist? Note well that, according to Daniel 10:13, 21; 12:1, Michael is portrayed as the special guardian or protector over Israel.

There are several conclusions to be drawn from this. First, it is important to note that Daniel is nowhere portrayed as praying to or commanding angels. His prayer is directed to God alone, who in turn, it would appear, commissioned his angelic hosts to engage in the conflict. Second, we clearly see that the demonic hosts engaged in warfare with the angelic hosts of heaven, the prize being the opportunity to manipulate earthly kings, nations, and peoples. Page explains:

> These rebellious angels oppose the forces that support Israel, and the conflict between these two groups affects relationships between the nations with which they are allied. That is, the situation on earth reflects the situation in heaven. Presumably, the antagonism of the prince of Persia in the extraterrestrial realm manifested itself in the human opposition Israel encountered as she sought to rebuild the walls and temple of Jerusalem (Ezra 4). Later, Israel would find herself under the control of another foreign power, Greece, and the mention of the prince of Greece alludes to this.[3]

Third, Daniel's prayer did, in fact, provoke a heavenly conflict. The fact that Daniel's three-week fast coincided with the three-week struggle between the "prince of Persia" and the unnamed angel "demonstrates a relationship between human intercession and what happens on a higher plane. Daniel's prayers appear to influence angels who play a significant role in shaping the destinies of nations."[4] Does this suggest that the outcome of the heavenly conflict is *dependent* on the frequency or fervency of one's prayers on earth? Whatever answer one gives to that question, it is important to remember, as Arnold points out, that

> Daniel had no idea of what was happening in the spiritual realm as he prayed. *There is no indication that Daniel was attempting to discern territorial spirits, pray against them, or cast them down.* In fact, Daniel only learned about what had happened in the angelic realm *after* the warring in heaven.[5]

---

[3] Sydney H. T. Page, *Powers of Evil: A Biblical Study of Satan and Demons* (Grand Rapids: Baker, 1995), 64.

[4] Ibid.

[5] Clinton E. Arnold, *Three Crucial Questions about Spiritual Warfare* (Grand Rapids: Baker, 1997), 162 (emphasis his).

Fourth, the outcome of battles and struggles on earth clearly reflects the involvement of heaven. "The purposes of kings and nations," observes John Goldingay, "are more than merely the decisions of particular human beings. Something in the realm of the spirit lies behind them."[6] In other words, the unfolding events in human history are not determined solely by the will of man. Page explains:

> In particular, there are malevolent forces in the universe that exercise a baneful influence in the sociopolitical realm, especially where the people of God are concerned. Nevertheless, the power of these evil agencies is limited, for transcendent powers of goodness oppose them, and the faithful prayers of believers are also effective against them. However antagonistic the forces of evil may be towards the will of God, they cannot prevent it from being accomplished.[7]

In short, there is more to historical conflict than meets the eye (see 2 Kings 6:15–17)!

Fifth, Arnold makes this important observation:

> The events of Daniel 10 took place in 535 BC. On the human plane, the Greek Empire did not surface to prominence until the rise of Alexander the Great, almost exactly two hundred years later. For the next two centuries, the Persian Empire remained the dominant power in the Ancient Near East. It is important, then, to observe that the text does not teach that Daniel, by his prayer, was able to bind, cast down, or evict the Persian prince— he remains powerfully influential for two hundred years. Of course, casting down a territorial ruler was not the objective of Daniel's prayer anyway.[8]

Sixth, whereas in Daniel 10:13, 21 we see that Michael came to assist Gabriel, two years earlier (c. 538 BC) Gabriel had to assist Michael! Why? Perhaps this is related to the return of the Jewish exiles to Palestine following the decree of Cyrus. If indeed

---

[6] John E. Goldingay, *Daniel*, Word Biblical Commentary (Dallas: Word, 1989), 312.
[7] Page, *Powers of Evil*, 64.
[8] Arnold, *Three Crucial Questions*, 155.

this was a necessary prelude to the eventual appearance of the Messiah, Satan would be especially concerned to do everything in his power to undermine the return and renewal of Israel. It was a little more than fifty years later that another attempt was made to exterminate God's people when Haman secured the approval of King Ahasuerus to wipe out the Jewish race. Although we read nothing in the book of Esther of a cosmic battle between angels and demonic forces, it seems likely that her success was the result of angelic support and strength.

Additional Biblical Support for Territorial Spirits

Several other texts implicitly hint at a territorial dimension among the demonic hosts. The first to be noted is Deuteronomy 32:7–8. Here we are told that the Lord apportioned humanity into groupings ("fixed the borders of the peoples") according to the number of "the sons of God." The ESV marginal reading says "the sons of Israel." However, the Septuagint (LXX) and a scroll of Deuteronomy from Qumran support the ESV primary reading, "the sons of God," an obvious reference to the angelic hosts. If this is correct, as many Old Testament scholars believe, the implication would be that "the number of the nations of the earth is directly proportional to the number of angels. Certain groupings of angels are associated with particular countries and peoples."[9] Thus, administration over the various nations has been, in a manner of speaking, parceled out among a corresponding number of angelic powers.[10] If God originally made this assignment among the holy angels, it would not be out of keeping with Satan's character to copy and combat it (but this is admittedly only speculative and by itself a weak foundation on which to build a case for territorial spirits).

Yet another text that hints at the notion of territorial demonic spirits is Mark 5:10. Here we have the strange request by "Legion" that Jesus not "send them out of the country." Why did they fear (and resist) being driven from that specific geographical locale? Could it be that they had been assigned to that region by Satan

---

[9] Ibid., 151.
[10] Some believe the idea of nations having "patron angels" is found in Psalm 82 as well.

and feared his reprisal for failing to "keep their post" so to speak? Others argue that, based on Luke's version of this story, the only reason the demons did not want to be sent "out of the country" was that they did not want Jesus to send them "into the abyss" (Luke 8:31).

Although 2 Corinthians 4:4 does not directly address our subject, we read there that "the god of this world [i.e., Satan] has blinded the minds of the unbelievers, to keep them from seeing the light of the gospel of the glory of Christ, who is the image of God." Why would not the blinding of individuals by Satan extend to nations, states, and cities as well?

In Revelation 2:13 Pergamum is described as "where Satan's throne is" and "where Satan dwells." This city was infamous for its paganism, and several things may account for this description. Pergamum was the center for the imperial cult where a temple had been erected in honor of "the divine Augustus and the goddess Roma." There was also a temple in Pergamum for Zeus, king of the Greek gods. The citizens of Pergamum worshiped Asclepius, the god of healing (portrayed or symbolized by the serpent, Satan). Perhaps Pergamum was the focal point of Satan's activity at this time, the home base, as it were, from which he directed his demonic hosts. The point is that some places, and hence people, are more intensely under the control or rule of demonic power than others because of an unusual concentration or presence of demonic activity.

My conclusion, though tentative, is that I see nothing in the Bible that precludes the possibility of territorial spirits, and I see numerous texts that certainly imply their reality.

What Do We Do Now?

If a good case can be made for the existence of territorial spirits, the question everyone asks next is, What should we do? Is there a special strategy for spiritual warfare that we should embrace and pursue? There is not the slightest indication anywhere in Scripture that our responsibility in the presence of a territorial spirit would be any different from what it is in dealing with a routine demonic influence elsewhere. We are never instructed to identify and aggressively engage a territorial spirit. We are never commanded to confront or rebuke a territorial spirit, as if by that alone we can break whatever power or authority it might have over a geopolitical region.

Some argue that an appropriate strategy is what is called *spiritual mapping*. This is an attempt to look beyond and behind the natural, material, and cultural features of a city to the spiritual forces that give it shape and influence its character. I once heard George Otis say that it involves "superimposing our understanding of forces and events in the spiritual domain onto places and circumstances in the material world." In other words, it is an attempt to discover the doors through which Satan and his demonic hosts gained access into and influence over a geographical locale, a city, or a nation. This will supposedly reveal the moral or legal grounds on which the stronghold is built, as well as the demonic spirits who energize it. I've heard spiritual mapping compared to what an X-ray accomplishes in the effort to diagnose a physical problem. That is to say, spiritual mapping provides a supernatural image or photograph, so to speak, of Satan's strategy, location, and authority, as well as the most effective way to defeat him. With this knowledge, intercessors are, supposedly, better equipped to pray for the dismantling of the spiritual stronghold and to pursue other courses of action that will break the demonic influence and thereby open opportunities for evangelization of the lost.[11]

I see nothing in Scripture that explicitly endorses spiritual mapping, but neither do I see anything that would necessarily rule it out as altogether illegitimate. Perhaps the best and most biblical response to what we have learned about territorial spirits is simply to follow Paul's counsel in Ephesians 6 and adorn ourselves daily with the armor of God, and having done so, to stand firm!

---

[11] Spiritual mapping is often, but not always, based on an active and aggressive approach to spiritual warfare known as *strategic level spiritual warfare*. According to this view, the church is called to do more than simply stand firm, resist, and defend. The church is called to actively seek out, uncover, and confront the demonic powers that influence our corporate existence. If you are looking for a persuasive response to this perspective and a proposal for a biblically grounded approach to the issue, I can do no better than refer you to Lowe, *Territorial Spirits and World Evangelisation*, esp. 46–73, 130–51.

Recommended Reading

Arnold, Clinton E. *Powers of Darkness: Principalities and Powers in Paul's Letters*. Downers Grove, IL: InterVarsity, 1992.

————. *Three Crucial Questions about Spiritual Warfare*. Grand Rapids: Baker, 1997.

Lowe, Chuck. *Territorial Spirits and World Evangelisation: A Biblical, Historical and Missiological Critique of Strategic-Level Spiritual Warfare*. Ross-Shire: Christian Focus, 2001.

15

Can Christians Lose Their Salvation?

Why do people doubt or deny the doctrine of eternal security? Why do so many insist that they've known friends or family members who once were genuinely born again, but through some sin or backslidden rebellion have lost their salvation? There are several reasons.

Often the culprit is tradition: "That's what I was raised to believe. I can't bring myself to believe that Mom and Dad and the preacher and all my friends were wrong." This is a far more powerful influence, subtle and unconscious though it be, than most of us realize. To be open to another view seems as if we are saying, "The past was all for naught. It meant nothing." To some it feels as if they must question the integrity or value of people and pastors they love and respect and who've been a powerful influence in their lives. That is difficult for many to cope with.

Undoubtedly a major contributing factor is the presence of several so-called problem passages in the New Testament. Two such texts are found in Hebrews 6 and 10, both of which I attempt to explain in chapter 16 in this book.

I also suspect many fear that if people are told they can't lose their salvation, they will take advantage of this to indulge in gross immorality: "If I can't lose my salvation, I'll do whatever I please" (cf. Rom. 6:1ff.). In other words, the *legitimate* concern for holiness leads some to an *illegitimate* rejection of security. As noted, others have known people who, they are convinced, were Christians but later fell away. Assuming they had truly been born again, the only explanation is that they lost their salvation.

Part of the blame for denials of eternal security can also be laid at the feet of certain religious leaders who need people to be insecure in their salvation in order to remain under the leaders' control. Fear is a powerful means of keeping people under one's religious thumb. Many believe that eternal security diminishes a person's moral responsibility. It places too much emphasis on God's sovereignty and not enough on human free will. Finally, for some the exhortations in Scripture to be holy, to persevere, to endure, make sense only if the possibility exists that one may choose not to do so.

Entire books have been written on this subject, so I have no illusions of being able to address every point and answer every question. I'm going to limit myself by noting what the possibility of apostasy would mean for each of the three members of the Trinity. In other words, should it be possible for a Christian to fall fully and finally from salvation, what would this entail for Father, Son, and Holy Spirit?

What It Would Mean for God the Father

If a genuine believer could fully and finally fall from saving grace and fail to enter into the inheritance of eternal life, God the Father would not be deserving of our ascription of glory or our praise and worship. I say this because of what we read in Jude 24–25. There God is deemed worthy of adoration precisely because he "is able to keep you from stumbling and to present you blameless before the presence of his glory with great joy" (v. 24).

God is keenly aware of the perils and pitfalls his people face in trying to remain faithful in this world. He knows how difficult spiritual fidelity can be. He is not ignorant of what you encounter, whether temptations or trials. He sees and knows the power of the world and its allure, its appeal, and the power of its promises. He is cognizant of every stone over which you might stumble, every cliff off which you might fall, every dark alley down which you may wander. And he is more than able to keep you safe in the midst of it all!

The background to this language may well come from numerous instances in the Psalms where God is portrayed as delivering his people from stumbling.

> For you have delivered up my soul from death,
>> yes, my feet from falling,
> that I may walk before God
>> in the light of life. (Ps. 56:13)

> For you have delivered my soul from death,
>> my eyes from tears,
> [you have delivered] my feet from stumbling. (Ps. 116:8)

Psalm 121:3–8 is especially relevant here:

> He will not let your foot be moved;
>> he who keeps you will not slumber.
> Behold, he who keeps Israel
>> will neither slumber nor sleep.

> The LORD is your keeper;
>> the LORD is your shade on your right hand.
> The sun shall not strike you by day,
>> nor the moon by night.

> The LORD will keep you from all evil;
>> he will keep your life.
> The LORD will keep
>> your going out and your coming in
>> from this time forth and forevermore.

The word *guard* would be a more literal translation than "keep." To properly understand this idea, we must note 2 Thessalonians

3:3: "But the Lord is faithful. He will establish you and *guard* you against the evil one." Note that this is an issue of God's faithfulness as much as his power. It's a matter of character. His integrity is at stake in his guarding and keeping of you. If he were to lose so much as one blood-bought child, both his faithfulness and his power would be suspect (see also John 17:11, 15; 1 Pet. 1:5). The reason why we don't stumble isn't that we are especially noble or strong or committed, but that God is! Left to ourselves, we are hopeless and helpless!

According to 1 Corinthians 1:8, God "will sustain you to the end, guiltless in the day of our Lord Jesus Christ" (cf. 1 Thess. 5:23). Even here in the book of Jude, verse 1, we see this emphasis: "Jude, a servant of Jesus Christ and brother of James, to those who are called, beloved in God the Father and *kept for Jesus Christ.*"

But don't we have a responsibility to keep ourselves? Yes, as Jude 21 makes clear: "Keep yourselves in the love of God." The promise of verse 24 does not cancel out the command of verse 21. Rather, verse 24 is the explanation of how we do it. God keeps us and equips and empowers us to fulfill the command he issues (see Phil. 2:12–13; Heb. 13:20–21).

This statement in Jude 24–25 isn't a promise of sinless perfection, but an assurance that God will never permit us to apostatize or fail to attain that eternal and joyful standing in his presence. Jude's emphasis is less on the ability of the saint to persevere than on the ability of God to preserve. Yes, we must remain committed to him, and we shall remain committed because he remains committed to us.

Okay, you say, I'll concede that God is able. But is he willing? The answer is found in the relation between Jude 24 and 25. Would God be deserving of such praise and honor if he were merely a God of power and not of purpose? If he were merely a God who *can* but *won't* keep his people from stumbling, would he be deserving of worship? What if he were merely a God of ability but lacked affection for his people? What possible good is it if God can preserve us but declines to do so? Is that kind of God worthy of the praise we read about in verse 25? No! Can you imagine God saying, "Well, yes, of course I'm able to keep you from stumbling and able to present you before me with joy, but I have no intention of doing so. In fact, I'm not in the least inclined to help you. As far as I'm concerned, you're on your own. Good luck. But don't look to me for help." Is that kind of God worthy of praise? Hardly.

Another group of texts that highlight the purpose and power of God in preserving his people is found in Romans, chapters 5 and 8. In each of these texts we see the unbreakable and reassuring logic of heaven.

> Since, therefore, we have now been justified by his blood, much more shall we be saved by him from the wrath of God. For if while we were enemies we were reconciled to God by the death of his Son, much more, now that we are reconciled, shall we be saved by his life. (Rom. 5:9–10)

> He who did not spare his own Son but gave him up for us all, how will he not also with him graciously give us all things? (Rom. 8:32)

The technical name for this argument is *a fortiori*, reasoning from *the greater to the lesser*. If the greater task was for God to send his Son to die for us while we were his enemies, how much easier is it for him to save us now that we are his friends! If Christ died for us when we hated him, how much more shall he live for us now that we are his friends! If God loved us as much as he did while we were helpless, sinful, and ungodly, how much more shall he love us now that by his grace we are justified, righteous in Christ, adopted as children, reconciled to his heart!

If ever there were a time for God not to love you or a time for him to forsake and abandon and desert you, it would be while you were an alien, unreconciled, and at enmity with him. But now you are no longer an alien but a member of God's household; no longer unreconciled but a child; no longer at enmity but in love with the Lord of your life. It is logically and theologically impossible that God should love you less now, now that you are his child, than he loved you then, when you were his enemy!

Consider again Romans 8:32. If Paul had merely asked, Will God give us all things? we might have wondered. We might have said: "Well, you know, I need so many things, great and difficult things, so how can I be certain God will provide them?" But note how Paul asks the question: *"He who did not spare his own Son . . . !"* In other words, the God whom we ask to give us all things is the God who has already given us his own Son! God has already done the immeasurably greater and more costly thing by giving up his Son for us, which is the ground of our confidence that he will easily and joyfully do what is by comparison far, far less.

Let's think for a moment about Paul's use of the word translated "spare." Parents spare their children when they refrain from inflicting the full measure of discipline. Judges spare criminals when they reduce or suspend a sentence. But this is precisely what the Father did *not* do with Jesus. He did not withhold or diminish or lighten in any degree the full weight of judgment imposed on his one and only Son. Instead, he "gave him up for us all" (v. 32).

If, then, God has done the greater thing in sacrificing his beloved Son on our behalf, he will surely do the lesser thing and provide us with every resource and gift and power necessary for us to persevere in the saving faith that is ours. Paul's assertion is designed to drive home the unshakeable assurance that *whatever is necessary to guarantee the ultimate glorification* of those whom God justified, called, predestined, and foreknew (Rom. 8:29–30), God will do it. If God spared not his own Son, the most precious and costly gift, how could he possibly fail to do all lesser things to guarantee that we receive *everything essential for salvation*? John Piper explains:

> Suppose two tasks are motivated by the same desire, but one is very improbable because the cost is so high, and one is more probable because the cost is less. If I have the desire for both tasks, and somehow manage to accomplish the costly one, then it is virtually assured the less costly one will be accomplished. Overcoming the greater obstacles assures you that I will overcome the lesser ones.[1]

---

[1] John Piper, *Future Grace* (Sisters, OR: Multnomah, 1995), 114. This is the same logic Jesus used in Matt. 6:30 when he said, "But if God so clothes the grass of the field, which today is alive and

Paul's reasoning in Romans 8:32, therefore, is from the hard to the easy, from the greater to the lesser. Again, listen to Piper's explanation:

> The reason [God's sparing not his own Son is] the greater thing is that God loved his Son infinitely. His Son did not deserve to be killed. His Son was worthy of worship by every creature, not spitting and whipping and scorn and torture. To hand over his beloved son (Colossians 1:13) was the incomparably great thing. The reason for this is the immensity of God's love for his Son. This is what made it so unlikely that God would hand him over. Yet God did it. And in doing it he showed that he most certainly would do all other things—all of which would be easy by comparison—to give all things to the people for whom he gave his Son.[2]

There are yet other consequences for the Father, should any of his beloved children fail to inherit salvation. For one thing, his purpose in redemption would fail and unravel. That purpose is unpacked in Romans 8:29–30. There we see that God's intent was for those whom he foreknew to be predestined to be conformed to the image of Jesus, and that those predestined should be called, and those called should be justified, and those justified should be glorified.

Notice also that each link is coextensive with every other link. Paul makes it clear that the objects of God's saving activity are the same from start to finish. Those whom he foreknew, not one more or one less, these he predestined. And those whom he predestined, not one more or one less, these he called. And those whom he called, not one more or one less, these he justified. And those whom he justified, not one more or one less, these he glorified. So, how many did God lose in the process? Not one! All whom he foreknew in eternity past will ultimately be glorified in eternity future. Not

tomorrow is thrown into the oven, will he not much more clothe you, O you of little faith?" The point of his argument, says Piper, is that "it is highly improbable that God Almighty would waste his time clothing field flowers which last only a day. This high improbability is the 'greater thing' in his argument from greater to lesser. On the other hand, there is a *small amount of improbability* that God would neglect his Son's disciples and not clothe them. This small improbability is the 'lesser thing' in his argument. So when God overcomes the high improbability and clothes field flowers, he proves that he can and will overcome the small improbability and clothe the disciples" (ibid.).
[2] Ibid., 114–15.

one is lost. Not one! No one who is foreknown fails to be predestined. And no one who is predestined fails to be called. And no one who is called fails to be justified. And no one who is justified fails to be glorified! This is simply another way of saying, as Paul does, that "he who began a good work in you will bring it to completion at the day of Jesus Christ" (Phil. 1:6).

We must also reckon with the fact that, should the Father lose any whom he determined to save, his will would be frustrated and unfulfilled. Jesus tells us explicitly what the will of the Father is, namely, that he (Jesus) "should lose nothing of all that he [the Father] has given me, but raise it up on the last day. For this is the will of my Father, that everyone who looks on the Son and believes in him should have eternal life, and I will raise him up on the last day" (John 6:39–40).

The argument of Jesus in these verses must be carefully noted. On several occasions in John's Gospel divine election is described in terms of God the Father giving certain persons to God the Son (6:37, 39; 10:29; 17:1–2, 6, 9, 24). In each of these cases the giving of men to Christ precedes and is the cause of their receiving eternal life. Those who are given to the Son include not only the present company of disciples who believe in Jesus but also the elect of future ages who will come to faith through the gospel. Jesus looks upon them as already his (John 17:20–21; see also John 10:16; Acts 18:10), even though they have not yet believed in his name. They are his because they were given to him by the Father in eternity past.

What is of special importance to us is what Jesus says about how those whom the Father has given to him come to him and whether or not those who come can ever lose their salvation. It will prove helpful to look at this in terms of *three impossibilities*. First, Jesus says that it is morally and spiritually impossible for a person to come to Christ apart from the "drawing" of that person by God the Father (John 6:44, 65). Second, Jesus also says that it is *impossible* for someone whom the Father "draws" *not* to come to him. He says in verse 37, "All that the Father gives me will come to me." In other words, just as it is impossible for a person to come to Christ apart from the Father drawing him or her, so also is it impossible for a person not to come to Christ if the Father does draw him or her.

To the previous two impossibilities Jesus adds a third. He has already said it is impossible to come to him *unless* the Father draws. He has also said it is impossible *not* to come if the Father *does* draw. Now he says that when a man does come through the drawing of the Father, it is impossible for him to be cast out. Look again at verse 37: "and whoever comes to me I will never cast out." The point is that those whom the Father gives to the Son, who therefore come to the Son, will be received by the Son and shall never perish. The verb translated "cast out" in verse 37 is used several times in John (2:15; 6:37; 9:34f.; 10:4; 12:31) and always means to cast out someone or something already in. Thus the emphasis here is not so much on receiving the one who comes (although that is true enough in itself) but on preserving him.

Who would suggest that Jesus Christ would refuse to accept what his Father has given him? If the Father was pleased to make a gift of certain sinners to his most blessed Son, you may rest assured that the Son will neither despise nor deny his Father's gracious generosity. The certainty of ultimate and absolute salvation for those who come to the Son is reaffirmed in verses 38–40 of John 6. Their life in Christ is eternal and irrevocable because that is the will of the Father; a will or a purpose that the whole of Christ's person and work was designed to secure, a will or purpose that shall ultimately be (Pss. 115:3; 135:6; Dan. 4:34–35; Acts 4:28; Eph. 1:11). What did Jesus come to do? He came to do the Father's will (John 6:38). What is the Father's will? The Father's will is that all those he has given to the Son be fully and finally saved (v. 39).

If any of God's chosen should finally fail to inherit salvation, it would mean that the Father has refused to answer the prayers of his Son! Jesus prayed, saying, "Holy Father, keep them in your name, which you have given me, that they may be one, even as we are one" (John 17:11). And again, a few verses later, he prays that the Father would "keep" us "from the evil one" (i.e., from Satan; John 17:15).

If God should lose even one of his elect, he would be exposed as weak and impotent and helpless to accomplish his purposes or fulfill his promises. Consider Jesus's words concerning his sheep in John 10:28–30: "I give them eternal life, and they will never perish, and no one will snatch them out of my hand. My Father, who has given them to me, is greater than all, and no one is able to snatch them out of the Father's hand. I and the Father are one."

Jesus grounds his confidence concerning the safety of his sheep in the incomparable omnipotence of his Father. It is because there is no one greater or more powerful than God the Father that the sheep are secure. Was Jesus mistaken in his assessment of the Father's power and purpose?

What will you do with his declaration that his sheep "will never perish" (John 10:28)? A more literal translation would be, "they shall not, by no means ever, perish." This is an absolute, unequivocal, unassailable negative. Would Jesus have said this if in fact many of his sheep *shall* perish? If so much as one true child of God can ever perish, Jesus has deceived us.

"And no one will snatch them out of my hand" (v. 28). Not the attacking wolf (v. 12), not the thieves and robbers (vv. 1, 8), not anyone else. "No one" means *no one*. "My Father, who has given them to me, is greater than all, and no one is able to snatch them out of the Father's hand" (v. 29). God the Father himself stands behind God the Son in keeping the sheep in the fold. Jesus holds us tightly. God holds us tightly. Who can steal from God? Who has the cunning or the power to outwit and outmuscle almighty God?

In verse 28 Jesus says "no one *will* snatch them," whereas in verse 29 he says "no one *is able* to snatch them." Some may attempt to snatch them. But they cannot succeed because the Son and the Father are united in purpose and power to keep them secure. "Okay, perhaps no one *else* can snatch me from God's hand. But what if *I myself* wriggle free and jump out of my own accord?" Is *your* power of choice greater than God's? Is *your* will more powerful than his? Look again at Jesus's words: "No one" rules out everyone: me, others, you! If eternal security is false, then Jesus is saying, "No one can snatch them out of my Father's hand—except, that is, for every one of the sheep themselves." But if you mean *everyone*, you don't say "no one"! Jesus doesn't say, "No one *except* for the person himself." In Romans 8:38–39 all creatures are excluded as threats to loss of salvation. In John 10 the Creator himself is excluded as well.

If Jesus wanted to teach eternal security, how could he have done it better or more explicitly than the way he does it here? If *you* wanted to assert eternal security, how could you do it better than by using the words of Jesus in John 10? Someone might object by saying, "They won't perish so long as they remain sheep." But the text doesn't say that. The assertion of the text is precisely that sheep always *do* remain sheep! The point of the text is, "Once a sheep, always a sheep." If Jesus wanted us to believe that some of his sheep could cease being sheep and suffer eternal death, why did he say his sheep will never suffer eternal death and no one can snatch them from him or from his Father? Surely Jesus is not guilty of the crassest form of double-talk. In other words, "they will never perish" means "they shall always stay sheep"!

"But what if some sin or failure or weakness or lapse of faith occurs repeatedly?" How repeatedly? How much sin does it take to lose one's salvation? What does a *good* shepherd do with wandering sheep? He wouldn't be a good shepherd if he didn't restore them when they wandered. Our security is ultimately dependent on God's character, not ours. People say, "If we change, we lose our salvation." No. We can't lose it, not because we can't change, but because *God* can't.

If any of God's elect should fail to attain final salvation, God himself, whom Scripture reveals as righteous, would be exposed as a liar and an impostor. I say this because God has declared, "I will never leave you nor forsake you" (Heb. 13:5). God would also prove to be faithless, for his promise to the Corinthians (and to us) is that he "will sustain you to the end, guiltless in the day of our Lord Jesus Christ" (1 Cor. 1:8). We also have the promise that "God is faithful, and he will not let you be tempted beyond your ability, but with the temptation he will also provide the way of escape, that you may be able to endure it" (1 Cor. 10:13). Some argue that salvation is tenuous because of the potential for a believer to succumb to temptation, the ultimate fruit of which may be loss of spiritual life. But Paul's point in this text is that the elect will in fact endure to the end precisely because God will not allow the temptation they face to exceed their power to resist and will not permit the test to overcome their ability to persevere.

What It Would Mean for God the Son

Having spent considerable space outlining what the loss of salvation would mean for God the Father, I will only briefly list a few consequences for God the Son and the Spirit.

To begin, should any of those given by the Father to the Son fail to be saved, Christ would have failed in the purpose for which he died (John 6:37–40; 10:14–18, 27–30). He also would have failed in the purpose for which he was raised from the dead (Rom. 4:24–25). He would also have failed in the purpose for which he now intercedes in the presence of the Father (Rom. 8:31–34; Heb. 7:25; 1 John 2:1–2). Add to these that Christ would fail to accomplish the goal for which he is to return to this earth (John 6:40b). And Jesus would prove to have been a liar (John 6:37; 10:27–28), his word and promise having failed to come true.

What It Would Mean for God the Holy Spirit

Finally, we should note just a few of the consequences this would bring to bear upon the person of the Holy Spirit.

First, the Holy Spirit would have failed in his work of sealing the saints (2 Cor. 1:21–22; Eph. 1:13–14; 4:30). The literal use of the term "seal" was of a stamped impression in wax pointing to ownership and protection. "As Eph. 1:13 and 4:30 make certain, the 'seal' is the Spirit, by whom God has marked believers and claimed them for his own."[3] Likewise, the Holy Spirit would have failed in his ministry as a pledge of the future consummation of our redemption (2 Cor. 1:21–22; 5:5). God the Holy Spirit would have broken and violated a promise, having declared that he is a

---

[3] Gordon Fee, *God's Empowering Presence: The Holy Spirit in the Letters of Paul* (Peabody, MA: Hendrickson, 1994), 807.

down payment in pledge of the complete and consummate gift yet to come. But if the complete and consummate gift would *not* come, he would have reneged on his word. Judith Gundry-Volf offers this explanation:

> The Spirit given to believers . . . functions as a divine promise and guarantee that the redemptive process will be completed. Final salvation is as certain to follow the gift of the Spirit as full payment must by law succeed the deposit for a purchase. Paul drives home the message of God's faithfulness in the work of salvation by using the familiar language of legally binding business transactions which alludes to the practice of the handing over of an *arrabon* with its ensuing financial obligations. Believers have in the indwelling Spirit, then, a sign that God is committed to their full redemption. This outcome is entirely dependent on God's faithfulness, as the metaphor implies.[4]

Gordon Fee agrees, pointing out that the term variously translated "guarantee" or "pledge" or "down payment" (*arrabōn*) was used in commercial transactions to refer to the first installment of the total amount due. The down payment effectively guaranteed the fulfillment of whatever contractual obligations were assumed. "The Spirit, therefore," says Fee, "serves as God's down payment in our present lives, the certain evidence that the future has come into the present, the sure guarantee that the future will be realized in full measure."[5]

Finally, if a true child of God could fully and finally apostatize from the faith, the Spirit would have failed in his ministry as firstfruits (Rom. 8:23). This metaphor is also used of Christ's resurrection as the guarantee of ours (1 Cor. 15:20, 23). Similar to the idea of the Spirit as the down payment or guarantee, the Holy Spirit as "the first sheaf is God's pledge to us of the final harvest. Thus . . . the Spirit plays the essential role in our present existence, as both evidence and guarantee that the future is now and yet to be."[6]

---

[4] Judith M. Gundry-Volf, *Paul and Perseverance: Staying In and Falling Away* (Louisville: Westminster/John Knox, 1990), 30.
[5] Fee, *God's Empowering Presence*, 807.
[6] Ibid.

Conclusion

The basis for our security in salvation is not ultimately our righteousness or obedience but God's promise, God's power, God's purpose, and most of all God's passionate love for us in Christ. God is committed to preserving us in faith, for if we were to stumble so as to fully and finally fall away, God would stand to lose more than we do.

Do you tend to think that your salvation hangs suspended on the thin thread of your own willpower and commitment to righteousness? I know my own soul all too well. Were it not for God's preserving grace I would have lost my salvation the day after I was born again. If you do not believe in the security of your soul in Christ, tomorrow should hold little but fear and misery and perhaps despair for you. For it may well be the day you commit that sin that forever severs you from the Savior's love. I can face tomorrow, and the day after, and the day after that with confidence because I know his promise, "I will never leave you nor forsake you" (Heb. 13:5).

Recommended Reading

Peterson, Robert A. *Our Secure Salvation: Preservation and Apostasy.* Phillipsburg, NJ: P&R, 2009.

Pinson, J. Matthew, ed. *Four Views on Eternal Security.* Grand Rapids: Zondervan, 2002.

Schreiner, Thomas R., and Ardel B. Caneday. *The Race Set before Us: A Biblical Theology of Perseverance and Assurance.* Downers Grove, IL: InterVarsity, 2001.

16

Does Hebrews Teach that Christians Can Apostatize?

Hebrews 6 and 10 are undoubtedly two of the most controversial and frequently debated chapters in all of Scripture. It would not be going too far to say that those who believe a genuine believer can forfeit (or lose) his or her salvation appeal to these texts more often than any other. Here is how the specific passages read:

> For it is impossible, in the case of those who have once been enlightened, who have tasted the heavenly gift, and have shared in the Holy Spirit, and have tasted the goodness of the word of God and the powers of the age to come, and then have fallen away, to restore them again to repentance, since they are crucifying once again the Son of God to their own harm and holding him up to contempt. For land that has drunk the rain that often falls on it, and produces a crop useful to those for whose sake it is cultivated, receives a blessing from God. But if it bears thorns and thistles, it is worthless and near to being cursed, and its end is to be burned.
>
> Though we speak in this way, yet in your case, beloved, we feel sure of better things—things that belong to salvation. For

God is not unjust so as to overlook your work and the love that you have shown for his name in serving the saints, as you still do. (Heb. 6:4–10)

For if we go on sinning deliberately after receiving the knowledge of the truth, there no longer remains a sacrifice for sins, but a fearful expectation of judgment, and a fury of fire that will consume the adversaries. Anyone who has set aside the law of Moses dies without mercy on the evidence of two or three witnesses. How much worse punishment, do you think, will be deserved by the one who has trampled underfoot the Son of God, and has profaned the blood of the covenant by which he was sanctified, and has outraged the Spirit of grace? (Heb. 10:26–29)

Let's look at each passage.

Hebrews 6:4–10

Who are the people who "have once been enlightened, who have tasted the heavenly gift, and have shared in the Holy Spirit, and have tasted the goodness of the word of God and the powers of the age to come, and then have fallen away" (Heb. 6:4–6)? It is important for us to know because it is impossible "to restore them again to repentance, since they are crucifying once again the Son of God to their own harm and holding him up to contempt." There are probably a dozen or more interpretive options of this passage that may be found in the commentaries and journal literature. It isn't my purpose to interact with them here. Rather, I am focusing solely on whether the terminology in verses 4–5 would lead us to conclude that these individuals are born-again, justified, believers.[1]

Are they born-again Christian men and women? If so, the doctrine of eternal security is shattered. Or is it possible for a person to somehow have been spiritually "enlightened" and to have "tasted" spiritual blessings and to have "shared in" the Holy Spirit and yet never know Jesus in a saving way? I believe the answer to

---

[1] I have been greatly helped in this chapter by the article by Wayne Grudem, "Perseverance of the Saints: A Case Study from Hebrews 6:4–6 and the Other Warning Passages in Hebrews," in *The Grace of God, the Bondage of the Will: Biblical and Practical Perspectives on Calvinism*, ed. Thomas R. Schreiner and Bruce A. Ware (Grand Rapids: Baker, 1995), 133–82.

this latter question is yes. Let me begin by giving six reasons from the book of Hebrews itself why these people are *not* born-again believers who have apostatized.

First, the situation described in verses 4–6 is illustrated in verses 7–8. There we read,

> For land that has drunk the rain that often falls on it [this drink-ing of frequent rains refers to the blessings of verses 4–5: enlight-enment, partaking of the Holy Spirit, tasting spiritual blessings, etc.], and produces a crop useful to those for whose sake it is cultivated, receives a blessing from God. But if it bears thorns and thistles [this corresponds to the "falling away" of v. 6a], it is worthless and near to being cursed, and its end is to be burned.

Rain falls on all kinds of ground, but one cannot tell from that alone what kind of vegetation, if any, will appear. The picture here is not of ground that receives frequent rain, yields life and veg-etation, and then loses it. The picture is of two different kinds of ground altogether. One responds to the rain (spiritual blessings and opportunities) by producing bountiful vegetation, while the other is barren, lifeless, and thus condemned. Likewise, people who hear the gospel and respond with saving faith bring forth life. Oth-ers, however, who sit in church and hear the truth and are blessed by the ministry of the Holy Spirit but eventually turn their back on it all are like a field that never yields vegetation and thus comes into judgment. As Wayne Grudem notes:

> The idea of land that once bore good fruit and now bears thorns is not compatible with this picture. The implication is this: While the positive experiences listed in verses 4–6 do not provide us enough information to know whether the people were truly saved or not, the committing of apostasy and holding Christ up to con-tempt do reveal the true nature of those who fall away: all along they have been like bad ground that can only bear bad fruit. If the metaphor of the thorn-bearing land explains verses 4–6 (as it surely does), then their falling away shows that they were never saved in the first place.[2]

---

[2] Ibid., 156–57.

Second, in 6:9 we read of a significant contrast: "Though we speak in this way, yet in your case, beloved, we feel sure of better things—things that belong to salvation." The "better things" in view are stated in verses 10–12, things like "work" and "love" and "serving" and "earnestness" and "full assurance of hope" and "faith" and "patience" and "inherit[ing] the promises." These "things" are "better" than the experiences of verses 4–6 precisely because they "belong to" or "accompany" *salvation*. In other words, Grudem explains, "the author says he is confident that most of his readers have better things than the people he described in verses 4–6, and *these things are better in that his readers also have things that belong to salvation*. This implies that the blessings in verses 4–6 were not things that belong to salvation."[3] Grudem summarizes verses 7–12:

> Verses 7–8 describe the people in verses 4–6 as unfruitful land that repeatedly bears thorns and thistles, and thus indicate that they were never saved. Verses 9–12 say that the readers, in general, have better things than the temporary experiences of verses 4–6, and that those better things include salvation. Therefore both verses 7–8 and verse 9 indicate that the people in verses 4–6 who fell away never had salvation.[4]

Third, according to Hebrews 3:14 (see also 3:6), "we have come to share in Christ, if indeed we hold our original confidence firm to the end." Note well: he says we *"have come"* to share in Christ, not "will come" to share, if we persevere in faith. In other words, holding fast in faith—that is, persevering—proves that you *became* a partaker of Christ in the past. Failing to hold fast—apostatizing from the faith—proves that you *never were* a partaker of Christ. Apostasy or falling away (6:6a) doesn't mean you once were in and have now fallen out of partaking in Christ. It means you never were or never became a partaker in the first place.

Fourth, we read in Hebrews 10:14 that "he has perfected for all time those who are being sanctified." As Piper notes, here we

---

[3] Ibid., 159.
[4] Ibid., 160.

are told that for those who are now being sanctified (i.e., indwelt by the Holy Spirit, growing in holiness by faith),

> the offering of Christ on the cross *has perfected that person for all time*. For all time! In other words to become a beneficiary of the perfecting, justifying work of Christ on the cross is to be perfected in the sight of God forever. This suggests that Hebrews 6:6 does not mean that those who re-crucify Christ were once really justified by the blood of Jesus and were really being sanctified in an inward spiritual sense.[5]

Fifth, our author concludes this letter with a prayer relating to the fulfillment in us of the blessings of the new covenant. He prays that God would "equip you with everything good that you may do his will, working in us that which is pleasing in his sight, through Jesus Christ" (13:21). The promise of the new and "eternal" covenant is that God will put in his people a new heart and cause them to walk in his ways and not turn away from doing them good (see Jer. 24:7; 32:40; Ezek. 11:19; 36:27). Thus, Piper concludes that

> in [Heb. 13] verse 21 he says that it is not finally dependent on us whether we persevere in faith and bear fruit. It is finally dependent on God: He is working in us that which is pleasing in his sight. He is fulfilling the new covenant promise to preserve us. This means that Hebrews 6:6 would contradict the new covenant if it meant that people could be truly justified members of the new covenant and then commit apostasy and be rejected. That would mean that God did not fulfill his promise to "work in them what is pleasing in his sight." He would have broken his new covenant promise.[6]

Sixth, we must take note not just of what is said of these people in 6:4–6 but also of what is *not* said of them that is usually said of Christians. Typical terms used to describe believers, such as *regeneration*, *conversion*, *justified*, *adopted*, *elect*, and *faith* in Jesus, are conspicuous by their absence. This is more than merely an

---

[5] John Piper, "When Is Saving Repentance Impossible?," accessed October 13, 1996, http://www
.desiringgod.org (emphasis mine).
[6] Ibid.

argument from silence when we consider the way Christians are described in the book of Hebrews itself. Here is a listing of things that are true of the genuine believer, all of which are absent from the description of those who apostatize in 6:4–6:

1. God has forgiven their sins (8:12; 10:17).
2. God has cleansed their consciences (9:14; 10:22).
3. God has written his laws on their hearts (8:10; 10:16).
4. God is producing holiness of life in them (2:11; 10:14; 13:21).
5. God has given them an unshakable kingdom (12:28).
6. God is pleased with them (11:5–6; 13:16, 21).
7. They have faith (4:3; 6:12; 10:22, 38–39; 12:2; 13:7; etc.).
8. They have hope (6:11, 18; 7:19; 10:23).
9. They have love (6:10; 10:33–34; 13:1).
10. They worship and pray (4:16; 10:22; 12:28; 13:15).
11. They obey God (5:9; 10:36; 12:10, 11, 14).
12. They persevere (3:6, 14; 6:11; 10:23).
13. They enter God's rest (4:3, 11).
14. They know God (8:11).
15. They are God's house, his children, his people (2:10, 13; 3:6; 8:10).
16. They share in Christ (3:14).
17. They will receive future salvation (1:14; 5:9; 7:25; 9:28).

Someone might object by saying, "Okay, typical descriptions of the saved are not found in 6:4–6, but neither are typical descriptions of the lost found there!" Grudem responds:

> I agree that the phrases [in 6:4–6] alone do not match the author's descriptions of the lost, and they do not indicate that these people are lost (before they commit apostasy). But that is just the point: *Before they commit apostasy their spiritual status is uncertain.* It remains to be seen whether they are among the saved or the lost. They have not yet given decisive indications either way. That is the reason the author warns them not to turn away—they are still at a point where a decision to be among the saved or the lost must be made.[7]

What about the terms used in 6:4–5 ("enlightened," "tasted,"

---

[7] Grudem, "Perseverance of the Saints," 171.

"shared in," etc.)? On the one hand, it is certain that all Christians experience these realities. But do *only* Christians experience them? Or is it possible for these experiences also to be true of people who have been repeatedly exposed to the gospel and the benefits it brings, yet without personally embracing Christ as Lord and Savior? Let's look at each one in turn.

They have "once been enlightened." Have true Christians been "enlightened"? Yes. But this term need mean no more than to hear the gospel, to learn, or to understand. "Certainly such intellectual understanding of the facts of the gospel is an important step toward saving faith, but it does not itself constitute the element of personal trust in Christ that is essential to faith."[8] All of us know people, perhaps family members, who have been repeatedly exposed to the truth of the gospel, understand what it means, can articulate the claims of Christ with incredible precision, yet refuse to put their trust in him as Lord and Savior. Thus, whereas all true Christians have been enlightened, not all those who are enlightened are true Christians.

They have "tasted the heavenly gift" and "the goodness of the word of God" and "the powers of the age to come." This certainly points to a genuine spiritual experience. But must we conclude that it was a genuine *saving* experience? These are not strangers to the gospel or to the church. These are people who have come under conviction of the Holy Spirit, who have experienced some degree of blessing both through common grace and through their close, intimate contact with genuine believers. Perhaps they have been healed. Perhaps a demon has been cast out. They have heard the Word of God and have come to taste and feel and enjoy something of its power and beauty and truth. They have felt the "wooing" of the Spirit and have seen great and wonderful things in the body of Christ. Those in Matthew 7:22–23 preached, prophesied, performed miracles, and cast out demons in Christ's name—*but were not saved*. Jesus said to them: "I never knew you; depart from me, you workers of lawlessness" (v. 23). These, then, "have tasted" the power and blessings of the new covenant, but *they have not per-*

---

[8] Ibid., 142–43.

sonally prized, cherished, embraced, loved, trusted, treasured, or savored the atoning death of Jesus as their only hope for eternal life.

They have "shared in the Holy Spirit." Whereas the word translated "shared" or "partaker" can certainly refer to a saving participation in Christ (cf. Heb. 3:14), it can also refer to a looser association or participation (see Luke 5:7; Heb. 1:9, "comrades" or "companions"). These people have in some way come to share in some aspect of the Holy Spirit and his ministry. But in what way? Must we conclude that it is a "saving" way? Why does our author *not* use terminology that would put the question of their spiritual status to rest, such as "filled with" or "baptized in" or "indwelt by" the Holy Spirit?

They have in some sense "repented." There is a sorrow for sins and a turning from them that even nonbelievers can experience. This is clear from Hebrews 12:17 and the reference to Esau, as well as the "repentance" of Judas Iscariot in Matthew 27:3. Paul refers to a repentance that "leads to salvation" (2 Cor. 7:10), the implication being that there is a repentance that does *not* lead to salvation. As with "belief" and "faith," so too with "repentance," we must always distinguish between what is substantial and saving, on the one hand, and what is spurious, on the other. Grudem provides this helpful summation:

> What has happened to these people? They are at least people who have been affiliated closely with the fellowship of the church. They have had some sorrow for sin and a decision to forsake their sin (*repentance*). They have clearly understood the gospel and given some assent to it (they have been *enlightened*). They have come to appreciate the attractiveness of the Christian life and the change that comes about in people's lives because of becoming a Christian, and they have probably had answers to prayers in their own lives and felt the power of the Holy Spirit at work, perhaps even using some spiritual gifts (they have become "associated with" the work of the Holy Spirit or have become *partakers* of the Holy Spirit and have tasted the heavenly gift and the powers of the age to come). They have been exposed to the true preaching of the Word and have appreciated much of its teachings (they have *tasted* the goodness of the Word of God). These factors are all positive, and people who have experienced these things may

be genuine Christians. But these factors alone are not enough to give conclusive evidence of any of the decisive beginning stages of the Christian life (regeneration, saving faith and repentance unto life, justification, adoption, initial sanctification). In fact, *these experiences are all preliminary to those decisive beginning stages of the Christian life*. The actual spiritual status of those who have experienced these things is still unclear.[9]

I conclude that the people described in Hebrews 6:4–5, who, according to verse 6, fall away, are not now and never were born-again believers. They are not Christians who have "lost" their salvation. I believe the spiritual state and experience of those described in verses 4–6 is virtually identical to that of the first three soils in the parable of the sower (see Matt. 13:3–23; Mark 4:1–9; Luke 8:4–15). In that parable, only the fourth soil is called "good" and subsequently bears fruit. The other three represent those who hear the gospel and respond with varying degrees of understanding, interest, and joy, none of which, however, bears fruit that testifies of genuine spiritual life. That is to say, they are "enlightened" and "have tasted" the goodness and power of the ministry of the Spirit and the blessings of the kingdom, yet turn their back on the truth when trials, troubles, or temptations come their way. Their apostasy is proof of the falsity of their initial "faith" (see esp. John 8:31; Heb. 3:6, 14; 1 John 2:19).

Hebrews 10:26–31

But we must also take note of Hebrews 10:26–31. Here our author describes someone as continuing in willful sin after "receiving the knowledge of the truth." This phrase implies no more than that they have heard and understood the gospel and have given mental assent or agreement to it. Tragically, many people hear the good news and commit themselves to shape their lives by the ethics of Jesus and in accordance with the standards and life of a local church while never experiencing regeneration and placing their personal trust in Christ for salvation. They then turn from what

[9] Ibid., 153 (emphasis his).

they have heard and understood and openly and defiantly repudiate it as false. There are unsaved theologians and biblical commentators whose "knowledge of the truth" of Christianity, at least in terms of objective data, is more extensive and insightful than that held by some true believers (in this regard, see 2 Pet. 2:20–21).

But the troubling phrase in this passage is in Hebrews 10:29, where the person in question is said to have regarded as unclean "the blood of the covenant by which he was sanctified." Does this mean a genuine Christian is in view? Those who affirm eternal security have pointed to one of two possible interpretations.

First, some have suggested that the "he" who is sanctified is actually Jesus Christ, not the apostate. This is grammatically possible. It is also theologically possible, as John 17:19 speaks of Jesus "sanctifying" himself. We must remember that "to sanctify" can mean "to set apart for a special purpose or use" without the notion of sin being involved (see also similar language and thought in Heb. 2:10; 5:7, 9; 9:11–12). Thus, according to this view, a parallel exists between the consecration of Aaron as high priest by the blood of the sacrifice (see Exodus 29) and the consecration of Jesus as High Priest through the shedding of his own blood.

Second, and more likely still, Wayne Grudem and others contend that "the word *sanctified* need not refer to the internal moral purification that comes with salvation, for the term *hagiazo* has a broader range than that, both in Hebrews and in the New Testament generally."[10] Grudem points to Hebrews 9:13 as an example where the word refers to rendering someone ceremonially clean but not necessarily spiritually (or savingly) clean (see also Matt. 23:17, 19; 1 Cor. 7:14; 1 Tim. 4:5). The context in Hebrews 10 appears to support this view, as our author is concerned with parallels between the Old Testament Levitical sacrifice and the better new covenant sacrifice of Christ. Says Grudem:

> The author of Hebrews knows that some may fall away, even though *they assemble with the congregation of believers* and so

---

[10] Ibid., 177.

share in this great privilege of coming before God [see 10:19–22]. So he says, "not neglecting to meet together, as is the habit of some, but encouraging one another" (10:25). The reason to encourage one another is the warning in 10:26, "For if we sin deliberately after receiving the knowledge of the truth." In such a context, it is appropriate to understand "profaned the blood of the covenant by which he was *sanctified*" to mean *"by which he was given the privilege of coming before God with the congregation of God's people."* In this sense, the blood of Christ opened up a new way of access to God for the congregation—it "sanctified" them in a parallel to the Old Testament ceremonial sense—and this person, by associating with the congregation, was also "sanctified" in that sense: He or she had the privilege of coming before God in worship.[11]

Someone who has experienced that awesome opportunity and privilege and then willfully repudiates the person and work of Christ through whom it was made possible can expect only judgment. Consistent with this, our author proceeds to distinguish between two groups in 10:39. There are, on the one hand, those who do not have saving faith and thus eventually fall away ("shrink back") into destruction. On the other hand, there are those who have saving faith and thus persevere to the preserving of the soul. The author of Hebrews doesn't envision a third group: those who have saving faith and later fall away. And for this we can only give thanks and praise to the grace of God that preserves his people from falling.

Conclusion

This chapter and the one preceding have addressed what is undoubtedly one of the more controversial and undeniably "tough topics" that we encounter in Scripture. Although I have taken a definitive stance on the question of whether genuine Christians can fully and finally apostatize from the faith ("No! They cannot!"), it would be irresponsible of me to suggest that the New Testament texts on this issue are unambiguous in each case. These are indeed

---

[11] Ibid., 178 (emphasis his).

hard texts to interpret. My hope is that, at minimum, I may challenge in a humble and healthy way those who insist that a Christian can indeed apostatize from the faith. I also pray that what I've written will be a source of encouragement and a cause for praise as we thank God for his amazing, sustaining, preserving grace!

Recommended Reading

Bateman, Herbert W., IV, ed. *Four Views on the Warning Passages in Hebrews*. Grand Rapids: Kregel, 2007.

Grudem, Wayne. "Perseverance of the Saints: A Case Study from Hebrews 6:4–6 and the Other Warning Passages in Hebrews." In *The Grace of God, the Bondage of the Will: Biblical and Practical Perspectives on Calvinism*, edited by Thomas R. Schreiner and Bruce A. Ware, 133–82. Grand Rapids: Baker, 1995.

17

Will There Be Sex in Heaven?

My guess is that when you first picked up this book, scanned the table of contents to see what tough topics I planned on addressing, and saw the title to this chapter, you turned here first, ignoring questions about blasphemy of the Holy Spirit and whether you should tithe! I know human nature well enough (including myself!) to realize that the question of whether there will be sex in heaven is of far more interest than any or all of the other topics this book examines. So don't feel bad or guilty if this is the first chapter you read. Trust me, you're in good company!

The Context of the Question

If we are going to answer this question with any degree of accuracy (assuming it *can* be answered), we must set it within the context of Jesus's interaction with the Sadducees and the question they posed to him in Mark 12:18–23. As you'll see in a moment, the Sadducees of our Lord's day didn't believe in an afterlife, which puts them greatly at odds with the vast majority of Americans in our day. A recent poll conducted by the Barna Institute indicates that in spite of the increasingly materialistic and naturalistic mood of our society, most people still believe in some form of life after death. The statistics are actually quite stunning. More than 80 percent of Americans believe in an afterlife of some sort (whether resurrection or reincarnation or some other expression). Another 9 percent say that life after death may exist, but they aren't certain. In other words, only about one in ten Americans contends that there is no life after death. Of those responding, 76 percent believe that heaven exists, and 71 percent say the same thing about hell.

Undoubtedly the most eye-opening statistic is that only half of 1 percent actually think they will go to hell following their death. In other words, the vast majority of those who believe in life after death are convinced that they will end up in heaven, however heaven may be defined for them.

The ancient world didn't have the luxury of conducting public opinion polls, but if they had they would have discovered that nearly everyone in every culture affirmed some concept of life beyond the grave. For example, it was true of the Egyptians. In the tomb of the Pharaoh Cheops, who died some five thousand years ago, archaeologists have discovered a "solar boat" designed for sailing through the heavens during the next life. The Greeks would often bury a person with a coin between his teeth to pay for his fare across the river Styx on his way to hades. Some American Indians buried a horse along with bow and arrows so the dead warrior could ride and hunt in the happy hunting grounds.

Of course, as the Barna poll reveals, not everyone today believes in life after death. And that was true even in the ancient world. As I've noted, one group that denied any notion of immortality or resurrection of the body was the Sadducees. The Sadducees and Pharisees were what we might call the Democrats and Republicans of the ancient world. They were two groups of deeply religious people who differed greatly on issues of both lifestyle and doctrine. Though the Sadducees were few in number, they constituted the wealthy, aristocratic, ruling class. Most of the chief priests were Sadducees. They often collaborated with the Roman government when it served their purposes. They were a little like

Washington politicians who ignore their state and their party and strike backroom deals with the other side if it serves their cause.

The Sadducees had an interesting view of the Old Testament. They refused to accept the oral traditions of the Pharisees and acknowledged only the Pentateuch, the first five books of the Old Testament, as inspired Scripture: that is, Genesis, Exodus, Leviticus, Numbers, and Deuteronomy. They rejected all the historical books, the Prophets, and the poetic literature such as the Psalms. The one thing that most set them apart, however, was their adamant denial of life after death. More on that in a moment.

Prior to our Lord's triumphal entry into Jerusalem, the Sadducees had not shown a great deal of interest in Jesus or his message. In fact, they were probably quite happy to hear about his repeated denunciations of the Pharisees, their rivals. They watched and listened from a distance, giggling under their breath, "Boy, that guy from Nazareth just nailed them again!"

But everything changed when Jesus entered the temple and began to disrupt the merchants by turning over the tables and declaring God's judgment on those who were trying to make a profit from selling sacrificial animals. The reason is simple: the Sadducees were in charge of the temple concessions! This was their party. The temple was their gig. Jesus was cutting into their profits. Their wealth was largely obtained from the commissions they charged on the sale of animals and other items associated with Passover. So Jesus was now invading their territory. Jesus was little more than a blip on their radar screen until he hit them where it mattered most: their bank accounts! They could tolerate, and perhaps even enjoy, Jesus's volatile encounters with the Pharisees. But when he disrupted their operations during Passover, the most lucrative time of the year, they launched a counterassault.

They had no doubt watched and listened as Jesus repeatedly made fools of the Pharisees. They were determined to succeed where their religious rivals had failed. So they conjured up what they thought was a trick question, hoping to publicly humiliate Jesus and dispose of him for good.

Mark 12:18–23

Let's look at the account closely:

> And Sadducees came to him, who say that there is no resurrection. And they asked him a question, saying, "Teacher, Moses wrote for us that if a man's brother dies and leaves a wife, but leaves no child, the man must take the widow and raise up offspring for his brother. There were seven brothers; the first took a wife, and when he died left no offspring. And the second took her, and died, leaving no offspring. And the third likewise. And the seven left no offspring. Last of all the woman also died. In the resurrection, when they rise again, whose wife will she be? For the seven had her as wife." (Mark 12:18–23)

Their question was based on the Old Testament custom known as levirate law. According to levirate law, if a man were to die without having any children, his brother was obligated to marry the widow, his sister-in-law, and raise up children in his deceased brother's name.

> If brothers dwell together, and one of them dies and has no son, the wife of the dead man shall not be married outside the family to a stranger. Her husband's brother shall go in to her and take her as his wife and perform the duty of a husband's brother to her. And the first son whom she bears shall succeed to the name of his dead brother, that his name may not be blotted out of Israel. And if the man does not wish to take his brother's wife, then his brother's wife shall go up to the gate to the elders and say, "My husband's brother refuses to perpetuate his brother's name in Israel; he will not perform the duty of a husband's brother to me." Then the elders of his city shall call him and speak to him, and if he persists, saying, "I do not wish to take her," then his brother's wife shall go up to him in the presence of the elders and pull his sandal off his foot and spit in his face. And she shall answer and say, "So shall it be done to the man who does not build up his brother's house." And the name of his house shall be called in Israel, "The house of him who had his sandal pulled off." (Deut. 25:5–10)

The Sadducees concocted an obviously hypothetical scenario

in which the law of the levirate is followed six times. No doubt smirking and laughing under their breath, probably with a gleam of revenge in their eyes, they put forth the question, "In the resurrection, when they rise again, whose wife will she be? For the seven had her as wife" (Mark 12:23). You can almost hear them saying to themselves, "Jesus may have confounded the Pharisees when they asked him about his authority, and he may have tied them in knots and silenced them following their question about paying taxes to Caesar, but we've really got him now!"

They were no doubt thinking, "If all eight of these people appear in the afterlife in the same condition or circumstances as on earth, how can their marriage relationships ever be reconciled?" In other words, if the woman is to be the wife of all seven men simultaneously, that would violate numerous biblical laws and especially the one against incest. And if only one of the men is arbitrarily designated as her husband in heaven, which one will it be, and why? They were trying to make the point that the entire notion of resurrection and the afterlife is absurd.

Our Lord's response is painfully pointed: "Is this not the reason you are wrong, because you know neither the Scriptures nor the power of God?" (v. 24). In other words: "You dummies! You chowderheads! In the first place, you've denied the clear teaching of Scripture concerning the resurrection. You claim to be scholars of the Word but are utterly ignorant of what it says. And if you really understood the Scriptures, you would know that God is infinite in power and perfectly capable of raising the dead to an existence quite unlike this present one. You have wrongly assumed that if there is an afterlife, it will be identical to the here-and-now. Don't you realize that God is omnipotent and will radically transform and transfigure the conditions of our existence in the age to come?"

"For when they rise from the dead," says Jesus, assuring them that all humanity will, "they neither marry nor are given in marriage, but are like angels in heaven" (v. 25). Let's be sure we take note of what Jesus is not saying. He is not saying that there will be no memory of earthly existence and our relationships here. Much of heavenly life will be spent reflecting on the life we are now living as we will be enabled by God to see the beauty of his redemptive and gracious work.

Don't think for a moment that Jesus is suggesting that we will lack bodies in heaven. One of the great and lingering misconceptions many Christians have of the afterlife is that the redeemed of God will spend eternity in some bodiless, ghost-like existence (but see Rom. 8:11; 1 Cor. 15:35–49; Phil. 3:20–21; yes, the body we will receive will be "transformed" and "glorious" but it will still be a body!). When Jesus says we will be "like angels in heaven," he does not mean we will be ephemeral spirits without physical bodies, but that we will not experience death or marriage there. The angels don't die, and the angels don't get married. When we get to heaven, neither will we (cf. Luke 20:36).

Neither is Jesus saying that in heaven we will lose our sexual identity as male and female. If you are a male now, you will be a male forever. If you are a female now, you will be a female forever. When we receive our resurrection bodies, we don't get *de-sexed* or *neutered*! Remember that Jesus was still a man after his resurrection. On Easter morning he was mistaken for a gardener or groundskeeper, a distinctly male occupation in the first century. And when Moses and Elijah appeared with Jesus on the Mount of Transfiguration, they were still men.

Some mistakenly point to Romans 8:29, where Paul says that we will be conformed to the image of Christ, and argue that everyone will therefore be male in heaven. But don't worry, ladies! The conformity to Christ in view here is *moral*, not physiological, and refers to the fact that our nature or character will be like him and thus lacking in sin or corruption.

Sexual identity as male and female is foundational to our personality as created in the image of God (Gen. 1:27). There is no such thing as a *neuter* human being. So, when the question is asked, Will there be sex in heaven? we must define the word "sex." If you mean sex as a point of identity, the answer is yes. I will always be a male and retain those characteristics of personality associated with maleness, and my wife, Ann, will always be female and retain for eternity all the characteristics of personality associated with her being a female.

What Jesus Meant

So what, then, did Jesus mean by his response to the question? As we seek an answer, we need to remember that marriage has primarily a twofold purpose: procreation and partnership, or fruitfulness and fellowship, or children and companionship. This is what Jesus says will end in heaven. In other words, marriage as an institution around which human life is organized will cease in heaven. Marriage as the social fabric or foundational unit of a society will end. Marriage as the means for procreation and the propagation of the human species will end. In heaven we will be like the angels, which is to say that we will be immortal and incapable of dying. There is no need to procreate. And marriage as the primary context for fellowship, intimacy, and love will end. Now, on earth, it is in marriage that we experience to the highest degree the joy of interpersonal fellowship, love, sharing, growth, nurturing, and spiritual fellowship.

In heaven all these things will continue: in fact they will be expanded and intensified beyond our wildest imagination. Jesus isn't saying that love will end in heaven. Quite the opposite. The love that on earth could best be achieved in a marriage relationship between husband and wife will be so marvelously magnified that all of God's people will experience it jointly. That woman in the hypothetical story the Sadducees told will be able to love her seven husbands perfectly, as they in turn will all love her perfectly, but none of them will live or love in the state of marriage.

Jesus is not saying you will love your earthly husband or wife less once you get to heaven, or that the relationships you *now* have will be obliterated or annulled *then*, but that what you experience now with one person you will experience then to an infinitely higher degree with all of God's people.

"Okay, Sam, but get to the point! Will there be sex in heaven?"

Some of you may think that even to ask such a question is inappropriate and in poor taste. You may suspect that I raised the question just to get a few laughs. But you would be wrong. If you are bothered by the question, I submit that you have a less-than-biblical perspective on the subject. Let's not forget that this is in essence what the Sadducees were asking. But if we are going to answer it, as I said above, we must define what we mean by the word "sex."

The Meaning of "Sex"

First, as I've already made clear, sex as identity or gender will always remain, for eternity. Second, sex as an attitude, or sexuality, will always remain. We will always recognize and appreciate and enjoy the beauty of the differences between male and female. Sexual passion, per se, is not sinful. Adam and Eve experienced sexual passion and desire before the fall into sin. There is no reason to think that sexual attraction will be absent from heaven, but it will most certainly not be characterized by lust or perversion or desire for illicit activity. But sexual intercourse is meant only for this life.

Let me be even more specific.

Most, perhaps all, of us simply cannot envision what life would be like in the absence of those sexual impulses we now experience as a normal, though often sinful, part of being human. One thing I believe we can know for certain is that in the new heaven and new earth we will remain *anatomically* male and female. I don't want to be unnecessarily crude in making this point, but at least so far as men are concerned, the resurrection and glorification of the body does not entail some form of celestial castration. Men will remain anatomically and genitally male forever. Women will remain anatomically and genitally female forever. And both men and women will be aware of this not only in their own bodies but also in the other. It would be a grotesque and unbiblical reversal of God's original creative design if the redeemed in heaven lived as genderless beings.

This raises the obvious question of the function of such genitalia in the eternal state. Only a gnostic and overly spiritualized view of human nature would suggest that this dimension of our physical frame ceases to exist altogether, or if it does exist, it no longer functions at all.

So, if in fact our glorified bodies will remain anatomically male and female forever, to what end? Will men and women be susceptible to sexual arousal? If the answer is yes, then why? What would be the purpose of these sexual sensations if not intercourse? As already noted, although it exceeds our present capacity to understand, we know for certain that such arousal would by no means be sinful or caused by ungodly lust or perversion or in any way lead to inappropriate fantasies or actions inconsistent with the pure love that will obtain among all of the redeemed.

I know what some of you are thinking: "If there won't be sex in heaven, I'm not going!" Or, "No sex in heaven? Sounds more like *hell* to me!" Allow me to put your fears and disappointment to rest. I can assure you that whatever physical or sensual pleasures one experiences in this life through sexual intimacy will be magnified and intensified apart from sexual intercourse in the next life. I don't know how God will do it, but I'm convinced that the joys of heaven, the happiness and pleasures of heaven, will infinitely exceed those on earth.

No one put this better or more provocatively than did Jonathan Edwards (1703–1758). One may be surprised to discover such language coming from the pen of America's most famous Puritan pastor. But we would do well to ponder deeply the implications of what he says. In a brief meditation on the *Happiness of Heaven*, he writes:

> [In heaven] the glorified spiritual bodies of the saints shall be filled with pleasures of the most exquisite kind that such refined bodies are capable of. . . . The sweetness and pleasure that shall be in the mind, shall put the spirits of the body into such a motion as shall cause a sweet sensation throughout the body, infinitely excelling any sensual pleasure here.[1]

What is this "sweet sensation" of which Edwards speaks? What-

---

[1] Jonathan Edwards, *The Works of Jonathan Edwards*, vol. 13, *The "Miscellanies": Entry Nos. a–z, aa–zz, 1–500*, ed. Thomas A. Schafer (New Haven, CT: Yale University Press, 1994), 351.

ever it is, rest assured that you won't be disappointed when you get there! You will be deprived of nothing in heaven that is essential to your optimum happiness. The problem is that you and I are very much like the Sadducees: we think heaven is going to be like earth, we think the next life is going to be precisely like this one. We mistakenly assume that the way in which we experience both physical and spiritual pleasures now is the limit for how we will experience them then. And Jesus says to you and me, "You are ignorant, and know neither the Scriptures nor the power of God!"

The Real Question

But before we close this discussion, let's not lose sight of what the Sadducees' real question is. The real question isn't whether or not there will be sex after death, but whether or not there will be *life* after death. Is there a resurrection to life? Yes, says Jesus, and here is his proof: "And as for the dead being raised, have you not read in the book of Moses, in the passage about the bush, how God spoke to him, saying, 'I am the God of Abraham, and the God of Isaac, and the God of Jacob'? He is not God of the dead, but of the living. You are quite wrong" (Mark 12:26–27). Jesus quotes directly from Exodus 3:6 and the account of the burning bush. Note that Jesus uses for his proof text a passage from the Pentateuch, the one portion of the Old Testament the Sadducees recognized as inspired and authoritative! Many believe the emphasis should be placed on the present tense verb, "I *am* the God of Abraham." The point would then be that if God *is* the God of Abraham, Isaac, and Jacob even when addressing Moses hundreds of years after those three patriarchs died, then they must be alive to him. In other words, the living God is the God of living men!

But perhaps the key word here isn't "is" but the preposition "of." "I am the God *of* Abraham, Isaac, and Jacob." That is to say, I have committed myself to them and they are mine. God is essentially saying: "I established a relationship with Abraham, Isaac, and Jacob, a covenant to which I pledged myself. I promised these men and their believing posterity blessings that are eternal. I promised to love them and care for them and provide for them forever. I am, therefore, the God *of* Abraham, Isaac, and Jacob, even as I declared to Moses." The fact of God's covenant commitment to these men (and to all believers) requires that they live in resurrection power beyond death in order to receive what was promised. Could the living, saving, covenant-keeping God establish a relationship with these men only to allow it to be terminated by their deaths? No.

To be "the God of" such men implies an ongoing, caring, protecting, helping, saving relationship that is as permanent as the loving God who makes it. If Abraham or Isaac or Jacob did not continue to exist after their earthly deaths, then the promises of God to them are empty and void, and God is a liar. God's fidelity to the covenant requires that he raise the dead. God will raise the dead because he cannot fail to keep his promises to them that he will be their God and they will be his people.

Conclusion

The question is not whether sex will be in heaven, but whether *you* will be in heaven! All mankind will be raised from the dead to live eternally (John 5:25–29). The only question is whether that eternal existence will be in heaven, in the presence of God, or in hell, utterly separated and alone and isolated from everyone and everything.

The Sadducees were very religious people who didn't believe in an afterlife, which makes absolutely no sense to me whatsoever. The question I would love to have asked them is simply this: *If there is no afterlife, why be religious?* If there is no afterlife, why not live like Charlie Sheen or Lady Gaga or Tiger Woods? If the Sadducees are right, if there's no resurrection, then why not fornicate as much as you can, do as many drugs as you can, steal as much money as you can get away with, make self-gratification and the pursuit of power your ambition? If the Sadducees are right, you might as well eat, drink, and be merry, for after you die there is *nothing*! If there is nothing beyond the grave, then nothing in this life ultimately matters. If there is nothing beyond the grave, then "good" and "evil" are little more than personal preferences, the likes and dislikes of utterly autonomous minds. If there is no afterlife, the only thing that matters is whatever feels good. So, if the Sadducees are right, sleep with as many as you can, steal as much as you can, exploit everyone for monetary gain and glory, lie whenever it advances your cause, live solely for yourself, and immerse yourself in every imaginable sinful activity, because when you die, that's it! You might as well indulge while you can, because this is all there is.

But if Jesus is right, and there is a heaven of infinite beauty and bliss and joy, trust him to get you there. If Jesus is right, and the Sadducees are wrong, cast your hope on his death for sinners and his resurrection from the dead. Put aside your concerns for the question in my title and ask yourself an infinitely more important one: Am I prepared for death? Have I, by faith, laid hold of Jesus Christ and his work on the cross in dying for my sins as the only hope for my eternal forgiveness and eternal joy?

Recommended Reading

Alcorn, Randy C. *Heaven*. Wheaton, IL: Tyndale, 2004.

Tada, Joni Eareckson. *Heaven*. Grand Rapids: Zondervan, 1995.

Wright, N. T. *Surprised by Hope: Rethinking Heaven, the Resurrection, and the Mission of the Church*. New York: Harper One, 2008.

18

Are Miraculous
Gifts for Today?

The question addressed in this chapter actually deserves a book-length response. Although I obviously cannot do that here, it has been done elsewhere, and I encourage you to investigate this matter in far greater detail than I provide in these few pages.[1]

In order to bring this massive subject down to manageable proportions, I'm going to give what I believe are twelve bad reasons for being a cessationist, followed by twelve good reasons for being a continuationist. But I should begin by defining those terms.

A *cessationist* is not a person who believes the South had a right to secede from the Union in the middle of the nineteenth century! That would be a *secessionist*. A *cessationist* is someone who believes that certain spiritual gifts, typically those of a more overtly supernatural nature, *ceased* in the church sometime late in the first century AD. A *continuationist* is a person who believes that all the gifts of the Spirit *continue* to be given by God and are

---

[1]Among the many books on this topic, I'll recommend only two. The first, and truly the best, is Jack Deere, *Surprised by the Power of the Spirit* (Grand Rapids: Zondervan, 1996). Another helpful book, to which I contributed, is *Are Miraculous Gifts for Today? Four Views*, ed. Wayne A. Grudem (Grand Rapids: Zondervan, 1996). Much of what I write in this chapter has been adapted from my much longer discussion in the four-views book.

therefore operative in the church today and should be prayed for and sought after. In case you haven't guessed it, I'm a continuationist. Here is why.

Twelve Bad Reasons for Being a Cessationist

1. The first bad reason for being a cessationist is an appeal to 1 Corinthians 13:8–12 on the assumption that the "perfect," the coming of which will mark the end of "prophecies," "tongues," and "knowledge," is something other or less than the fullness of the eternal state ushered in at the second coming of Jesus Christ. Even most cessationists now agree that the "perfect" cannot be a reference to the canon of Scripture or the alleged maturity of the church in the first century. The "perfect" is that glorious state of final consummation when, as Paul says, we will see "face to face" and "know fully" (v. 12), as over against the limitations imposed by our life now, in which we see as "in a mirror dimly" and know only "in part" (v. 12).

There is simply no evidence that even Paul anticipated the formation of a "canon" of Scripture following the death of the apostles. In fact, Paul seems to have expected that he himself might survive until the coming of the Lord (1 Cor. 15:51; 1 Thess. 4:15–16). Furthermore, there is no reason to think that Paul could have expected the Corinthians to figure out that he meant the "canon" when he used the term *to teleion*, "the perfect." "In any case," notes Max Turner,

> the completed canon of Scripture would hardly signify for the Corinthians the *passing away of merely "partial" knowledge* (and prophecy and tongues with it), and the arrival of "full knowledge," for the Corinthians already had the Old Testament, the gospel tradition (presumably), and (almost certainly) more Pauline teaching than finally got into the canon.[2]

We must also take note of verse 12b, where Paul says that with the coming of the "perfect" our knowing "in part" will give way to a depth of knowledge that is matched only by the way we are known

---

[2] Max Turner, *The Holy Spirit and Spiritual Gifts, Then and Now* (Carlisle, UK: Paternoster, 1996), 294.

by God. That is to say, when the perfect comes, we will then see "face to face" and will know even as we are now known by God. Few people any longer dispute that this language describes our experience in the eternal state subsequent to the return of Christ. As Turner says, "However much we respect the New Testament canon, Paul can only be accused of the wildest exaggeration in verse 12 if that is what he was talking about."[3] That view rests on the assumption that prophecy was a form of divine revelation designed to serve the church in the interim, until such time as the canon was formed. But a careful examination of the New Testament reveals that prophecy had a much broader purpose that would not in the least be affected by the completion of the canon.

2. Another illegitimate reason for being a cessationist is the belief that signs and wonders as well as certain spiritual gifts served only to confirm or authenticate the original company of apostles, and that when the apostles passed away, so also did the gifts. The fact is, no biblical text (not even Heb. 2:4) ever says that signs and wonders or spiritual gifts of a particular sort authenticated the apostles. Signs and wonders authenticated Jesus and the apostolic message about him. If signs and wonders were designed exclusively to authenticate apostles, we have no explanation why nonapostolic believers (such as Philip and Stephen) were empowered to perform them.

Therefore, this is a good reason for being a cessationist only if you can demonstrate that authentication or attestation of the apostolic message was the *sole and exclusive purpose* of such displays of divine power. However, *nowhere in the New Testament is the purpose or function of the miraculous or the charismata reduced to that of attestation.* The miraculous, in whatever form in which it appeared, served several other distinct purposes: *doxological* (to glorify God—Matt. 15:29–31; John 2:11; 9:3; 11:4, 40); *evangelistic* (to prepare the way for the gospel to be made known—see Acts 9:32–43); *pastoral* (as an expression of compassion and love and care for the sheep—Matt. 14:14; Mark 1:40–41); and *edification* (that is, to build up and strengthen believers, for the common good—1 Cor. 12:7; 1 Cor. 14:3–5, 26).

---

[3] Ibid., 295.

My point is this: *all* the gifts of the Spirit—whether tongues or teaching, whether prophecy or mercy, whether healing or helps—were given, among other reasons, for the edification and building up and encouraging and instructing and consoling and sanctifying of the body of Christ. Therefore, even if the ministry of the miraculous gifts to attest and authenticate has ceased, a point I concede only for the sake of argument, such gifts would continue to function in the church for the other reasons cited.

Someone might object to this by asking, Weren't miraculous gifts "signs of an apostle" such that when apostleship ceased, so too did the signs? No; in fact 2 Corinthians 12:12 says no such thing. Paul does *not* say the insignia or marks of an apostle *are* signs, wonders and miracles. Rather, as the NASB accurately translates, he asserts that "the signs of a true apostle were performed among you with all perseverance, *by* [or better still, *accompanied by*, or according to the ESV, *with*] signs and wonders and miracles." Paul's point is that miraculous phenomena accompanied his ministry in Corinth. Signs, wonders, and miracles were attendant elements in his apostolic work. But they were not themselves the "signs of an apostle."

3. Another poor reason for being a cessationist is the belief that since we now have the completed canon of Scripture, we no longer need the operation of so-called miraculous gifts. However, the Bible itself quite simply never says this. In fact, as will become evident below, it says precisely the opposite. It is the Bible itself that gives us warrant for believing that all spiritual gifts are designed by God for the church in the present age.

No biblical author ever claims that written Scripture has replaced or in some sense supplanted the need for signs, wonders, and the like. Why would the presence of the completed canon preclude the need for miraculous phenomena? If signs, wonders, and the power of the Holy Spirit were essential in bearing witness to the truth of the gospel *then*, why not *now*? In other words, it seems reasonable to assume that the miracles that confirmed the gospel in the first century, wherever it was preached, would serve no less to confirm the gospel in subsequent centuries, even our own.

If signs, wonders, and miracles were essential in the physical presence of the Son of God, how much more so now in his absence. Surely we are not prepared to suggest that the Bible, for all its glory, is sufficient to do what Jesus couldn't do. Jesus thought it necessary to utilize the miraculous phenomena of the Holy Spirit to attest and confirm his ministry. If it was essential for him, how much more so for us? In other words, if the glorious presence of the Son of God himself did not preclude the need for miraculous phenomena, how can we suggest that our possession of the Bible does?

4. A fourth inadequate cessationist argument is the belief that to embrace the validity of all spiritual gifts today requires that one embrace classical Pentecostalism and its belief in Spirit baptism as separate from and subsequent to conversion, as well as the doctrine that speaking in tongues is the initial physical evidence of having experienced this Spirit baptism. However, one can be a continuationist, as I am, and affirm that Spirit baptism happens for all believers at the moment of their faith and conversion to Christ, as well as affirm that speaking in tongues is a gift for some, but not all, believers.

5. Another bad reason for being a cessationist is the idea that if one spiritual gift, such as apostleship, has ceased to be operative in the church that other, and perhaps all, miraculous gifts have ceased to be operative in the church. But is "apostleship" a spiritual gift? I doubt it. Even if it is, there is nothing inconsistent about acknowledging that one gift might have ceased while others continue. If you can make an exegetical case for the cessation of apostleship, fine. But then you must make an equally persuasive exegetical case for the cessation of other gifts. That is what I contend you cannot do. I'm more than happy to concede that *every* spiritual gift has ceased and is no longer operative if you can provide me with biblical evidence to that effect. In the meantime, the mere potential for one or more gifts to have ceased is no argument that others definitely have.

6. A sixth bad argument for cessationism is the fear that to acknowledge the validity today of revelatory gifts such as prophecy and word of knowledge would necessarily undermine the finality

and sufficiency of Holy Scripture. But this argument is based on the false assumption that revelatory gifts such as prophecy and word of knowledge provide us with infallible truths that are equal in authority to the biblical text itself.

7. Cessationism is poorly served by appeals to Ephesians 2:20 on the assumption that revelatory gifts such as prophecy were uniquely linked to the apostles and therefore designed to function only during the so-called foundational period in the early church.

A closer look at Scripture indicates that there are numerous instances where prophecy was not linked to the apostles and never functioned foundationally. Not everyone who ministered prophetically was apostolic! In other words, Ephesians 2:20 clearly does not have in view all prophetic ministry. Consider, for example, Acts 2 (where men and women, young and old, from all walks of life are expected to prophesy in the new covenant age); Acts 21:9 (the four daughters of Philip who prophesied); Acts 21:10–11 (the ministry of Agabus); as well as Romans 12; 1 Corinthians 12:7–10; 14:1, 39 (in these two texts all believers are exhorted to earnestly desire to prophesy); 1 Corinthians 14:26; and 1 Thessalonians 5:19ff.

In summary, both the nature of the prophetic gift and its widespread distribution among Christians clearly indicate that there was far more to this gift than simply the apostles laying the foundation of the church. Therefore, neither the passing of the apostles nor the movement of the church beyond its foundational years has any bearing whatsoever on the validity of prophecy today.

8. Another faulty argument for cessationism is that since we typically don't see miracles or gifts today equal in quality or intensity to those in the ministries of Jesus and the apostles, God doesn't intend for *any* miraculous gifts of a lesser quality or intensity to operate in the church among ordinary Christians (but see Romans 12; 1 Corinthians 12–14; 1 Thess. 5:19–22; James 5).

However, no one denies that Jesus and the apostles operated at a far superior level of the supernatural than others. But why should that be an argument against the validity of the spiritual gifts listed in 1 Corinthians 12? If we are going to insist that the apostles set the standard by which we are to judge the validity of all spiritual gifts, such as those in 1 Corinthians 12 and Romans 12, then we might be forced to conclude that no spiritual gift of any sort is valid today, for who would claim to teach like Paul or evangelize like Paul? No one measures up to the apostles in any respect.

The most that we may conclude from our not seeing apostolic healing or apostolic miracles is that we are not seeing healing or miracles at the level and frequency that they occurred in the ministry of the apostles. It does not mean that God has withdrawn gifts of healing or the gift of working miracles from the church at large.

9. The so-called "cluster" argument is another inadequate reason for being a cessationist. According to this argument, miracles and supernatural phenomena were concentrated or "clustered" at specific times in biblical history and therefore should not be expected to appear as regular or normal phenomena in other periods of history. But Jack Deere's book, *Surprised by the Power of the Spirit*, referenced in an earlier footnote, provides an extensive and detailed refutation of this argument. I only wish space allowed me to reproduce his findings here.

Also, the cluster argument, even if true, demonstrates only that miracles, signs, and wonders were especially prevalent in some seasons, but not that they were nonexistent during other seasons or that we shouldn't pray for them today. One must also explain not only why miraculous phenomena were prevalent in those three periods (assuming they were) but also why they were, allegedly, infrequent or isolated in all other periods (see Pss. 74:9–11; 77:7–14; Mark 6:5).

We must also not forget that there were no cessationists in the Old Testament! No one during the time of the old covenant appealed to the alleged "clustering" of supernatural phenomena as grounds for arguing that such had altogether ceased. And, of course, as I hinted at above, the cluster argument is simply unbiblical and false. Miracles, signs, and wonders occur consistently throughout the Old Testament (as Deere demonstrates in his extensive survey of the Old Testament; see especially Jer. 32:20, as well as the miraculous and supernatural activity during the Babylonian captivity as recorded in the book of Daniel). Prophecy in particular was prevalent through most of the Old Testament, being absent or comparatively less active only because of the idolatry of Israel.

10. A spurious argument for cessationism is the appeal to the alleged absence of miraculous gifts in church history subsequent to the first century. I'll say more about this below.

11. An additional bad reason to be a cessationist is the absence of good experiences with spiritual gifts in one's own life, combined with the often fanatical excesses of certain TV evangelists and some involved in the Word of Faith or "prosperity gospel" movements (as well as the anti-intellectualism often found in those movements).

12. Finally, a poor reason for being a cessationist is the fear of what embracing continuationism might entail for your life personally and the well-being of your church corporately. Whereas it is certainly true that embracing the reality of these gifts for today will alter your prayer life, your approach to ministry, and your expectations of what God might do in your midst, so long as each of these is guided by Scripture and held accountable to the authority of God's Word, such changes should be welcomed, not shunned.

Twelve Good Reasons for Being a Continuationist

1. This may sound strange, but the first good reason for being a continuationist is the set of twelve bad reasons for being a cessationist! In other words, there simply is no convincing biblical, theological, historical, or experiential argument that either in isolation or in conjunction with other arguments gives reason to believe that what God did in the first century he will not do in the twenty-first.

2. Another good reason for being a continuationist is the consistent, indeed pervasive and altogether positive presence throughout the New Testament of all spiritual gifts.[4] Beginning with Pentecost and continuing throughout the book of Acts, whenever the Spirit is poured out on new believers, they experience the manifestation of his charismata. There is nothing to indicate that this phenomenon

---

[4] The problems that emerged in the church at Corinth were not due to spiritual gifts, but due to unspiritual people. It was not the gifts of God but the immature, ambitious, and prideful distortion of gifts on the part of some in that church that prompted Paul's corrective comments. Let's not forget that whatever else one may think or say about spiritual gifts, they were God's idea!

was restricted to them and then. The gifts appear to be both widespread and common in the New Testament church. Christians in Rome (Romans 12), Corinth (1 Corinthians 12–14), Samaria (Acts 8), Caesarea (Acts 10), Antioch (Acts 13), Ephesus (Acts 19; 1 Timothy 1), Thessalonica (1 Thessalonians 5), and Galatia (Galatians 3) experience the miraculous and revelatory gifts. It is difficult to imagine how the New Testament authors could have said any more clearly than *this* what new covenant Christianity is supposed to look like. In other words, the burden of proof rests with the cessationist. If certain gifts of a special class have ceased, the responsibility is his to prove it.

3. Also supporting continuationism is the extensive New Testament evidence of the operation of so-called miraculous gifts among Christians who are not apostles. In other words, numerous nonapostolic men and women, young and old, across the breadth of the Roman Empire consistently exercised these gifts of the Spirit (and Stephen and Philip ministered in the power of signs and wonders).

Others, aside from the apostles, who exercised miraculous gifts include (1) the seventy who were commissioned in Luke 10:9, 19–20; (2) at least 108 people among the 120 who were gathered in the upper room on the day of Pentecost; (3) Stephen (Acts 6–7); (4) Phillip (Acts 8); (5) Ananias (Acts 9); (6) church members in Antioch (Acts 13:1); (7) new converts in Ephesus (Acts 19:6); (8) women at Caesarea (Acts 21:8–9); (9) the unnamed brethren of Galatians 3:5; (10) believers in Rome (Rom. 12:6–8); (11) believers in Corinth (1 Corinthians 12–14); and (12) Christians in Thessalonica (1 Thess. 5:19–20). See also 1 Corinthians 12:7–10.

4. A fourth good factor in favor of continuationism is the explicit and oft-repeated purpose of the charismata: namely, the edification of the body of Christ (1 Cor. 12:7; 14:3, 26). Nothing that I read in the New Testament or see in the condition of the church in any age, past or present, leads me to believe we have progressed beyond the need for edification and therefore beyond the need for the contribution of the charismata. I freely admit that spiritual gifts were essential for the birth of the church, but why would they be any less important or needful for its continued growth and maturation?

5. The fifth good reason for being a continuationist is the fundamental continuity or spiritually organic relationship between the church in Acts and the church in subsequent centuries. No one denies that there was an era in the early church that we might call "apostolic." We must acknowledge the significance of the personal physical presence of the apostles and their unique role in laying the foundation for the early church. But nowhere does the New Testament ever suggest that certain spiritual gifts were uniquely and exclusively tied to them or that with their passing is the passing of such gifts. The universal church or body of Christ that was established and gifted through the ministry of the apostles is the same universal church and body of Christ that exists today (something that only the most extreme of hyper-dispensationalists would deny). We are, together with Paul and Peter and Silas and Lydia and Priscilla and Luke, members of the same one body of Christ.

6. Very much related to the fifth point, continuationism finds support in what Peter (through Luke) says in Acts 2 concerning the operation of so-called miraculous gifts as characteristic of the new covenant age of the church. As D. A. Carson has said, "The coming of the Spirit is not associated merely with the *dawning* of the new age but with its *presence*, not merely with Pentecost but with the entire period from Pentecost to the return of Jesus the Messiah."[5] Or again, the gifts of prophecy and tongues (Acts 2) are portrayed not merely as *inaugurating* the new covenant age but also as *characterizing* it (and let us not forget that the present church age is the latter days).

7. A good reason for being a continuationist is what Paul says in 1 Corinthians 13:8–12. As noted above, here Paul asserts that spiritual gifts will not "pass away" (vv. 8–10) until the coming of the "perfect." If the "perfect" is indeed the consummation of God's redemptive purposes as expressed in the new heaven and new earth, following Christ's return, we can confidently expect him to continue to bless and empower his church with the gifts until that time.

---

[5] D. A. Carson, *Showing the Spirit: A Theological Exposition of 1 Corinthians 12–14* (Grand Rapids: Baker, 1987), 155.

8. Another good reason for being a continuationist is what Paul says in Ephesians 4:11–13. There he speaks of the bestowal of spiritual gifts (together with the office of apostle)—and in particular the gifts of prophecy, evangelism, pastor, and teacher—as functioning in the building up of the church "*until* we all attain to the unity of the faith and of the knowledge of the Son of God, to mature manhood, to the measure of the stature of the fullness of Christ" (v. 13). Since that fullness most assuredly has not yet been attained by the church, we can confidently anticipate the presence and power of such gifts until that day arrives.

9. A ninth good argument for continuationism is that the Holy Spirit in Christ is the Holy Spirit in Christians. We are indwelt, anointed, filled, and empowered by the same Spirit as was Jesus. His ministry is (with certain obvious limitations) the model for our ministry (cf. Acts 10:38).

10. Vital to continuationism is the absence of any explicit or implicit notion that we should view spiritual gifts any differently than we do other New Testament practices and ministries that are portrayed as essential for the life and well-being of the church. When we read the New Testament, it seems evident on the surface of things that church discipline is to be practiced in our assemblies today, that we are to celebrate the Lord's Table and water baptism, and that the requirements for the office of elder as set forth in the pastoral epistles are still guidelines for how life in the church is to be pursued, just to mention a few. What good exegetical or theological reasons are there for treating the presence and operation of spiritual gifts any differently? None, so far as I can see.

11. Also lending support for continuationism is the testimony throughout most of church history concerning the operation of the miraculous gifts of the Spirit. Contrary to what many cessationists have suggested, the gifts did not cease or disappear from early church life following the death of the last apostle.[6] Indeed, before

---

[6]After studying the documentation for claims to the presence of these gifts, D. A. Carson concludes that "there is enough evidence that some form of 'charismatic' gifts continued sporadically across the centuries of church history that it is futile to insist on doctrinaire grounds that every report is spurious or the fruit of demonic activity or psychological aberration" (ibid., 166). Among the many helpful resources that document the presence of the gifts throughout church history, see especially Ronald Kydd, *Charismatic Gifts in the Early Church* (Peabody, MA: Hendrickson, 1984); Richard

Chrysostom in the East (347–407) and Augustine in the West (354–430), no church father ever suggested that any or all of the charismata had ceased in the first century. And even Augustine later retracted his earlier cessationism (see below). Among the numerous early church fathers who explicitly testify to the existence of the charismata in their day, we cite the following.

The Epistle of Barnabas (written sometime between AD 70 and 132), *The Shepherd of Hermas* (mid–second century AD), Justin Martyr (c. 100–165), Irenaeus (c. 120–202), and Tertullian (d. 225; he first coined the term *Trinity*) all provide explicit documentation of the gifts in their day. We also have extensive evidence of revelatory visions in operation in the life of the martyrs Perpetua and her handmaiden Felicitas (AD 202). Likewise bearing witness to the operation of the gifts are Theodotus (late second century), Clement of Alexandria (d. 215), Origen (d. 254), Hippolytus (d. 236), Novatian (c. 245), Cyprian (bishop of Carthage, 248–258), Gregory Thaumaturgus (213–270), Eusebius of Caesarea (260–339), Cyril of Jerusalem (d. 386), Hilary of Poitiers (356), and each of the Cappadocian fathers, Basil of Caesarea (b. 330), Gregory of Nyssa (b. 336; Basil's younger brother), and Gregory of Nazianzen (b. 330).

By the late fourth century the gifts of the Spirit were increasingly found among ascetics and those involved in the monastic movements. The various compromises and accommodations to the wider culture that infiltrated the church subsequent to the formal legalization of Christianity under Constantine drove many of the more spiritually minded leaders into the desert.

Something must be said about Augustine (354–430), who early in his ministry espoused cessationism. However, in his later writings he retracted his denial of the ongoing reality of the miracu-

---

Riss, "Tongues and Other Miraculous Gifts in the Second Through Nineteenth Centuries," *Basileia* (1985); Kilian McDonnell and George T. Montague, *Christian Initiation and Baptism in the Holy Spirit: Evidence from the First Eight Centuries* (Collegeville, MN: Liturgical Press, 1991); Cecil Robuck, *Prophecy in Carthage: Perpetua, Tertullian, and Cyprian* (Cleveland: Pilgrim, 1992); Stanley M. Burgess, "Proclaiming the Gospel with Miraculous Gifts in the Postbiblical Early Church," in *The Kingdom and the Power*, ed. Gary S. Greig and Kevin N. Springer (Ventura, CA: Regal, 1993), 277–88; Greig and Springer, *The Spirit and the Church: Antiquity* (Peabody, MA: Hendrickson, 1984); Greig and Springer, *The Holy Spirit: Eastern Christian Traditions* (Peabody, MA: Hendrickson, 1989); Greig and Springer, *The Holy Spirit: Medieval Roman Catholic and Reformation Traditions (Sixth–Sixteenth Centuries)* (Peabody, MA: Hendrickson, 1997); and Paul Thigpen, "Did the Power of the Spirit Ever Leave the Church?" *Charisma* (September 1992: 20–29.

lous and carefully documented no fewer than seventy instances of divine healing in his own diocese during a two-year span (see his *City of God*, 22.8–10). After describing numerous miracles of healing and even resurrections from the dead, Augustine writes:

> What am I to do? I am so pressed by the promise of finishing this work, that I cannot record all the miracles I know; and doubtless several of our adherents, when they read what I have narrated, will regret that I have omitted so many which they, as well as I, certainly know. Even now I beg these persons to excuse me, and to consider how long it would take me to relate all those miracles, which the necessity of finishing the work I have undertaken forces me to omit. (22.8)

Even during the medieval period, we find evidence for the operation of the charismata among figures such as Leo the Great (400–461), who served as bishop of Rome (440–461); Genevieve of Paris (422–500); Gregory the Great (540–604); Gregory of Tours (538–594); the Venerable Bede (673–735), whose *Ecclesiastical History of the English People*, written in 731, contains numerous accounts of miraculous gifts in operation; Aidan, bishop of Lindisfarne (d. 651) and his successor Cuthbert (d. 687), both of whom served as missionaries in Britain; Bernard of Clairvaux (1090–1153) and Bernard's treatise on the *Life and Death of Saint Malachy the Irishman* (1094–1148); Richard of St. Victor (d. 1173); Anthony of Padua (1195–1231); Bonaventure (1217–1274); Francis of Assisi (1182–1226), documented in Bonaventure's *Life of St. Francis*; Thomas Aquinas (1225–1274), together with virtually all of the medieval mystics, among whom are several women: Hildegard of Bingen (1098–1179), Gertrude of Helfta (1256–1301), Bergitta of Sweden (1302–1373), St. Clare of Montefalco (d. 1308), Catherine of Siena (1347–1380), Julian of Norwich (1342–1416), Margery Kempe (1373–1433); Dominican preacher Vincent Ferrer (1350–1419); and Teresa of Avila (1515–1582).

Those who insist that spiritual gifts such as prophecy, discerning of spirits, and word of knowledge ceased to function beyond the first century also have a difficult time accounting for the operation of these gifts in the lives of many who were involved in the Scottish Reformation, as well as several who ministered in its aftermath. Jack Deere, in his book *Surprised by the Voice of God*,[7] has provided extensive documentation of the gift of prophecy at work in and through such men as George Wishart (1513–1546), mentor of John Knox; John Knox himself (1514–1572); John Welsh (1570–1622); Robert Bruce (1554–1631); and Alexander Peden (1626–1686). Deere also draws our attention to one of the historians of the seventeenth century, Robert Fleming (1630–1694), as well as one of the major architects of the Westminster Confession of Faith, Samuel Rutherford (1600–1661), both of whom acknowledged the operation of the gifts in their day.

It may surprise some to discover that we have extensive knowledge of but a small fraction of what happened in the history of the church. It is presumptuous to conclude that the gifts of the Spirit were absent from the lives of people about whom we know virtually nothing. In other words, the absence of evidence is not necessarily the evidence of absence! We simply don't know what was happening in the thousands upon thousands of churches and home meetings of Christians in centuries past. I cannot say with confidence that believers regularly prayed for the sick and saw them healed any more than others can say they didn't. One cannot say they never prophesied to the comfort, exhortation, and consolation (1 Cor. 14:3) of the church any more than I can say they did. No one can say with any confidence whether countless thousands of Christians throughout the inhabited earth prayed in tongues in their private devotions. That is hardly the sort of thing for which we could expect extensive documentation. We must remember that printing with movable type did not exist until the work of Johann Gutenberg (c. 1398–1468). The absence of documented evidence for spiritual gifts in a time when documented evidence for most of church life was, at best, sparse is hardly good grounds for concluding that such gifts did not exist.

If the gifts were sporadic, there may be an explanation other than the theory that they were restricted to the first century. We

---

[7] Jack Deere, *Surprised by the Voice of God* (Grand Rapids: Zondervan, 1996), 64–93.

must remember that prior to the Protestant Reformation in the sixteenth century the average Christian did not have access to the Bible in his own language. Biblical ignorance was rampant. That is hardly the sort of atmosphere in which people would be aware of spiritual gifts (their name, nature, function, and the believer's responsibility to pursue them) and thus hardly the sort of atmosphere in which we would expect them to seek and pray for such phenomena or to recognize them were they to be manifest. If the gifts were sparse, and this again is highly debatable (as the list of names in this chapter would demonstrate), it was as likely due as much to ignorance and the spiritual lethargy it breeds as to any theological principle that limits the gifts to the lifetime of the apostles.

Especially important in this regard is the concentration of spiritual authority and ministry in the office of bishop and priest in the emerging Church of Rome. By the early fourth century AD (much earlier, according to some), there was already a move to limit to the ordained clergy the opportunity to speak, serve, and minister in the life of the church. Lay folk were silenced and marginalized and left almost entirely dependent on the contribution of the local priest or monarchical bishop.

Although Cyprian (bishop of Carthage, 248–258) was a continuationist, he was also responsible for the gradual disappearance of such charismata from the life of the church. He, among others, insisted that only the bishop and priest of the church should be permitted to exercise these revelatory gifts. In the words of James Ash, "The charisma of prophecy was captured by the monarchical episcopate, used in its defense, and left to die an unnoticed death when true episcopate stability rendered it a superfluous tool."[8]

If we concede, for the sake of argument, that certain spiritual gifts were less prevalent than others in certain seasons of the church, their absence may well be due to unbelief, apostasy, and other sins that serve only to quench and grieve the Holy Spirit. If Israel experienced the loss of power because of repeated rebellion,

---

[8]James Ash, "The Decline of Ecstatic Prophecy in the Early Church," *Theological Studies* 36 (June 1976): 252.

if Jesus himself "could do no miracle there except that He laid His hands on a few sick people and healed them" (Mark 6:5, NASB), all because of their "unbelief" (v. 6), we should hardly be surprised at the infrequency of the miraculous in periods of church history marked by theological ignorance and both personal and clerical immorality.

We must also remember that God mercifully blesses us both with what we don't deserve and what we refuse or are unable to recognize. I am persuaded that numerous churches today who advocate cessationism experience these gifts but dismiss them as something less than the miraculous manifestation of the Holy Spirit.

For example, someone with the gift of discerning spirits may be described as possessing remarkable sensitivity and insight. Someone with the gift of word of knowledge is rather said to have deep understanding of spiritual truths. Someone who prophesies is said to have spoken with timely encouragement to the needs of the congregation. Someone who lays hands on the sick and prays successfully for healing is told that God still answers prayer but that gifts of healing are no longer operative. These churches wouldn't be caught dead labeling such phenomena by the names given them in 1 Corinthians 12:7–10 because they are committed to the theory that such phenomena don't exist.

If this experience of the New Testament gifts described in different terminology occurs today (and it does, as it did in a church in which I ministered for several years), there is every reason to think it has occurred repeatedly throughout the course of history subsequent to the first century.

Consider this hypothetical example. Suppose a man in, say, AD 845 is assigned to write a descriptive history of church life in what is now southern France. How might he label what he sees and hears? If he is ignorant of spiritual gifts, being untaught or perhaps a well-educated cessationist, his record will make no reference to prophecy, healing, miracles, word of knowledge, and the like. Such phenomena might well exist, perhaps even flourish, but will be identified and explained in other terms by our hypothetical historian.

Centuries later we discover his manuscript. Would it be fair to conclude from his observations that certain spiritual gifts ceased subsequent to the apostolic age? Of course not! My point is simply that in both the distant past and the present the Holy Spirit can empower God's people with gifts for ministry they either do not recognize or, for whatever reason, explain in terms other than those of 1 Corinthians 12:7–10. The absence of explicit reference to certain charismata is therefore a weak basis on which to argue for their permanent withdrawal from church life.

Or consider this illustration from the ministry of Charles Spurgeon (1834–1892), who tells of an incident in the middle of his sermon in which he paused and pointed at a man whom he accused of taking an unjust profit on Sunday, of all days! The culprit later described the event to a friend:

> Mr. Spurgeon looked at me as if he knew me, and in his sermon he pointed to me, and told the congregation that I was a shoemaker, and that I kept my shop open on Sundays; and I did, sir. I should not have minded that; but he also said that I took ninepence the Sunday before, and that there was fourpence profit out of it. I did take ninepence that day, and fourpence was just the profit; but how he should know that, I could not tell. Then it struck me that it was God who had spoken to my soul through him, so I shut up my shop the next Sunday. At first, I was afraid to go again to hear him, lest he should tell the people more about me; but afterwards I went, and the Lord met with me, and saved my soul.[9]

Spurgeon adds this comment:

> I could tell as many as a *dozen* similar cases in which I pointed at somebody in the hall without having the slightest knowledge of the person, or any idea that what I said was right, except that I believed I was moved by the Spirit to say it; and so striking has been my description, that the persons have gone away, and said to their friends, "Come, see a man that told me all things that ever I did; beyond a doubt, he must have been sent of God to my soul, or else he could not have described me so exactly." And not only so,

---

[9] Charles H. Spurgeon, *The Autobiography of Charles H. Spurgeon*, vol. 2 (Cincinnati: Curtis & Jennings, 1899), 226–27.

but I have known many instances in which the thoughts of men have been revealed from the pulpit. I have sometimes seen persons nudge their neighbours with their elbow, because they had got a smart hit, and they have been heard to say, when they were going out, *"The preacher told us just what we said to one another when we went in at the door."*[10]

On another occasion, Spurgeon broke off his sermon and pointed at a young man, declaring, "Young man, those gloves you are wearing have not been paid for: you have stolen them from your employer."[11] After the service the man brought the gloves to Spurgeon and asked that he not tell his mother, who would be heartbroken to discover that her son was a thief!

My opinion is that this is a not uncommon example of what the apostle Paul described in 1 Corinthians 14:24–25. Spurgeon exercised the gift of *prophecy* (or some might say the *word of knowledge*, 1 Cor. 12:8). He did not label it as such, but that does not alter the reality of what the Holy Spirit accomplished through him. If one were to examine Spurgeon's theology and ministry, as well as recorded accounts of it by his contemporaries and subsequent biographers, most would conclude from the absence of explicit reference to miraculous charismata such as prophecy and the word of knowledge that such gifts had been withdrawn from church life. But Spurgeon's own testimony inadvertently says otherwise!

The question we are considering is this: If the Holy Spirit wanted the church to experience the miraculous charismata, would they not have been more visible and prevalent in church history (and I'm only conceding for the sake of argument that they were not)? Let's take the principle underlying that argument and apply it to several other issues.

We all believe that the Holy Spirit is the *teacher* of the church. We all believe that the New Testament describes his ministry of *enlightening* our hearts and *illuminating* our minds to understand the truths of Scripture (see 2 Tim. 2:7; 1 John 2:20, 27; etc.).

---

[10] Ibid. (emphasis mine).
[11] Charles H. Spurgeon, *Autobiography: The Full Harvest, 1860–1892*, vol. 2 (Edinburgh: Banner of Truth, 1973), 60.

Yet within the first generation after the death of the apostles the doctrine of justification by faith was being compromised. Salvation by faith plus works soon became standard doctrine and was not successfully challenged (with a few notable exceptions) until Martin Luther's courageous stand in the sixteenth century. My question, then, is this: If God intended for the Holy Spirit to continue to teach and enlighten Christians concerning vital biblical truths beyond the death of the apostles, why did the church languish in ignorance of this most fundamental truth for more than thirteen hundred years? Why did Christians suffer from the absence of those experiential blessings this vital truth might otherwise have brought to their church life?

Undoubtedly your response will be that none of this proves the Holy Spirit ceased his ministry of teaching and illumination. None of this proves that God ceased to want his people to understand such vital doctrinal principles. Precisely! And the relative infrequency or absence of certain spiritual gifts during the same period of church history does not prove that God was opposed to their use or had negated their validity for the remainder of the present age.

Both theological ignorance of certain biblical truths and a loss of experiential blessings provided by spiritual gifts can be, and should be, attributed to factors other than the suggestion that God intended such knowledge and power only for believers in the early church.

Finally, and most important of all, is the fact that what has or has not occurred in church history is ultimately irrelevant to what *we* should pursue, pray for, and expect in the life of our churches today. The final criterion for deciding whether God wants to bestow certain spiritual gifts on his people today is the Word of God. I'm disappointed to hear people cite the alleged absence of a particular experience in the life of an admired saint from the church's past as reason for doubting its present validity. As much as I respect the giants of the Reformation and of other periods in church history, I intend to emulate the giants of the New Testament who wrote under the inspiration of the Holy Spirit. I admire John Calvin, but I obey the apostle Paul.

In sum, neither the failure nor the success of Christians in days past is the ultimate standard by which we determine what God wants for us today. We can learn from their mistakes as well as their achievements. But the only question of ultimate relevance for us and for this issue is, "What saith the Scripture?"

12. Finally, although it is technically not a *reason* or argument for being a continuationist like the previous eleven, personal experience should not be ignored. The fact is that I've seen all spiritual gifts in operation, tested and confirmed them, and experienced them firsthand on countless occasions. As stated, this is less a *reason* to become a continuationist and more a *confirmation* (although not an infallible one) of the validity of that decision. Experience, in isolation from the biblical text, proves little. But experience must be noted, especially if it illustrates or embodies what we see in the text.[12]

Conclusion

To sum up as briefly as I can, are miraculous gifts for today? Yes, I believe they are. But let us keep one thing in mind as we continue to search the Scriptures regarding this matter. This is not an issue, in my opinion, over which Christians should part company. Disagree? Yes. Divide? No. As we continue to dialogue on this matter, let's commit ourselves to remain "eager to maintain the unity of the Spirit in the bond of peace" (Eph. 4:3).

Recommended Reading

Deere, Jack. *Surprised by the Power of the Spirit*. Grand Rapids: Zondervan, 1996.

Grudem, Wayne, ed. *Are Miraculous Gifts for Today? Four Views*. Grand Rapids: Zondervan, 1996.

Storms, Sam. *The Beginner's Guide to Spiritual Gifts*. 2nd ed. Ventura, CA: Gospel Light, 2013.

Turner, Max. *The Holy Spirit and Spiritual Gifts, Then and Now*. Carlisle, UK: Paternoster, 1996.

---

[12] In this regard, I would recommend my book *Convergence: Spiritual Journeys of a Charismatic Calvinist* (Kansas City: Enjoying God Ministries, 2005), where I describe in detail several of these personal experiences.

19

What Is Baptism in the Spirit, and When Does It Happen?

Paula was raised in a Christian home where church attendance was commonplace. But it wasn't until she was eleven years old that she began to take a serious interest in who Jesus is. That summer she attended a church camp and for the very first time consciously repented of her sins and put her faith in the atoning death of Jesus as her only hope for eternal life. It was a wonderful experience that brought both joy and a sense of relief. She never doubted from that moment on that she was a child of God.

The next few years proved difficult for Paula. She was not especially attractive, and boys never seemed to pay her much attention. Her grades were average, at best, and she had few friends. When she turned sixteen, Paula was invited to an overnight party where she took her first drink of beer. She won instant acceptance with a small group of classmates who before would hardly give her the time of day. She soon discovered that as long as she joined in on whatever they were doing, they included and affirmed her. Her heart was often troubled as she recognized how her behavior was contrary to what she had been taught in church, but the fear of rejection was too powerful to overcome.

It wasn't until Paula was in her second year of college that things began to change. She accepted the invitation of a sorority sister to attend a Bible study that met each Wednesday night. It was here that she began to awaken to how far she had wandered from the Lord. She was brokenhearted and grieved that she had lived in such indifference to the Lord's faithful appeal that she return to her first love.

One Wednesday night she asked that some of the girls in her Bible study group pray for her. Paula knew that they believed in spiritual gifts, but the church she grew up in had always warned against such things. As they laid hands on her, Paula cried out to Jesus to forgive her for those many years of spiritual apathy. One of the girls praying for Paula then said, "Oh, Lord Jesus, we ask that you would pour out your Spirit on Paula and empower her to live and witness for you as she never has before."

Suddenly Paula felt a strange warmth envelop her like a blanket. She sensed what she later described as a geyser erupting from deep within her soul. Not really knowing what was happening, she then began to cry out to Jesus her praise and gratitude. The unfamiliarity of her experience was exceeded only by the joy and peace that it brought. From that day to the present, Paula has sought by God's grace to live passionately for the Son of God.

What happened to Paula? If she were to ask you to open the Bible and explain her experience, what texts would you use? What would you call it? Was she *baptized in the Holy Spirit*? Was she *filled with the Holy Spirit*? Was she *anointed with the Holy Spirit*? Or did she simply experience a renewal of faith and the profound assurance of salvation that the apostle Paul had in mind in Romans 8:16 when he spoke of the Spirit bearing witness with our spirit "that we are children of God"? Or was her experience nothing more than the emotional fruit of manipulation by her friends who wanted to win her over to their strange brand of Christianity?

In this chapter I want to answer these questions. There is

much confusion today about "spiritual experiences" like Paula's. Christians divide over it. Churches divide over it. As for Paula, she's just happy it happened!

What's at Stake?

The debate over Spirit baptism has often been summarized by the question, Is the Christian life characterized by one or two stages? Or again, Is Spirit baptism an *initiatory* experience for *all* Christians or a *second-stage* experience that only *some* receive?[1] Although it may be a bit simplistic to phrase it in those terms, the issue is still this: Are all Christians automatically baptized in the Spirit at the moment they first trust in Christ for salvation? Or are some, if not most, baptized in the Spirit at some point in life *subsequent* to their initial conversion? Was Paula baptized in the Spirit at the age of eleven when she trusted Jesus at church camp, or did it happen nine years later during that mid-week Bible study?

The most common view among evangelical Christians is that Spirit baptism is *simultaneous* with and essentially the *same* as regeneration and conversion. Spirit baptism is understood as a phenomenon that comes to *all* Christians at the moment of the new birth. The only significant division among the proponents of this view concerns whether Spirit baptism is a "felt" experience or happens beneath the level of our consciousness.

Others contend that Spirit baptism is *subsequent* to and *distinct* from regeneration and conversion. There are a number of variations to this view. Some, such as the late Martyn Lloyd-Jones,[2] who served as pastor for many years at Westminster Chapel in London, identify Spirit baptism with the "sealing" of the Holy Spirit described in Ephesians 1:13. It is an *experiential* event subsequent to regeneration (and therefore to be sought) that brings a profound, inner, *direct*, assurance of salvation. It also produces power for ministry and witness, joy, and a sense of

---

[1] The most exhaustive treatment of these issues is found in H. I. Lederle, *Treasures Old and New: Interpretations of "Spirit-Baptism" in the Charismatic Renewal Movement* (Peabody, MA: Hendrickson, 1988).
[2] See Martyn Lloyd-Jones, *Joy Unspeakable: Power and Renewal in the Holy Spirit* (Wheaton, IL: Shaw, 1984).

God's glorious presence. Those who advocate this position typically make no connection between baptism in the Spirit and the charismatic gifts.

The Methodist evangelist John Wesley taught a second transforming work of grace, distinct from and subsequent to the new birth, in which the Spirit roots out of the Christian's heart all sinful motivation. The result is that "the whole of his [the Christian's] mental and emotional energy is henceforth channeled into love for God and others: love that is Christlike and supernatural, strong and steady, purposeful and passionate, and free from any contrary or competing affection whatsoever."[3] This state of "perfection," according to Wesley, occurs instantaneously through the same insistent, expectant, empty-handed faith through which we received the grace of justification. One may still lack knowledge and act foolishly. But such "mistakes," said Wesley, are not to be regarded as "moral transgressions." Perfection, then, is primarily a matter of love for God and men being the constant driving force in one's life. On occasion, both Wesley and his followers would refer to this experience as the "baptism in the Holy Spirit."

We also need to take note of the Keswick movement and those associated with its teachings, such as Hannah Whithall Smith, F. B. Meyer, Andrew Murray, R. A. Torrey, A. J. Gordon, and A. B. Simpson. According to H. I. Lederle, the Keswick view "preserves the Wesleyan two-stage grid, but it rejects the view that believers' hearts may become perfect in love. The second work of grace was not an eradicating of inbred sin but rather living a life of victory in which a perfection of deeds is achieved."[4] This second work of grace was seen as an impartation of power rather than a purification from sin.

The key to Keswick theology is a *passive* view of faith in which one confesses one's inability, reckons oneself dead to sin (much emphasis is placed on Rom. 6:1–14), and "rests" in Jesus. This occurs as a crisis event and issues in the "higher life" wherein the believer experiences victory over all known sin. The emphasis is

---

[3] J. I. Packer, *Keep in Step with the Spirit* (Old Tappan, NJ: Revell, 1984), 132.
[4] Lederle, *Treasures Old and New*, 11.

not on eradication of sin from the heart but on an impartation of power for obedience and ministry.[5]

Perhaps the most well known of those who embrace a two-stage view are classical Pentecostals such as members of the Assemblies of God. The classical Pentecostal view is clearly articulated in points 7 and 8 of the "Statement of Fundamental Truths" of the Assemblies of God:

> 7. The Promise of the Father. All believers are entitled to, and should ardently expect and earnestly seek, the promise of the Father, the Baptism in the Holy Ghost and fire, according to the command of our Lord Jesus Christ. This was the normal experience of all the early Christian Church. With it comes the enduement of power for life and service, the bestowment of the gifts and their uses in the work of the ministry (Luke 24:49; Acts 1:4, 8; 1 Cor. 12:1–31). This wonderful experience is *distinct from and subsequent to* the experience of the new birth (Acts 10:44–46; 11:14–16; 15:7–9).

> 8. The Evidence of the Baptism in the Holy Ghost. The Baptism of believers in the Holy Ghost is witnessed by the initial physical sign of speaking with other tongues as the Spirit of God gives them utterance (Acts 2:4). The speaking in tongues in this instance is the same in essence as the gift of tongues (1 Cor. 12:4–10, 28) but different in purpose and use.

There are three crucial elements in the classical view. First, there is the doctrine of *subsequence*. Spirit baptism is always subsequent to and therefore distinct from conversion. The time intervening between the two events may be momentary or conceivably years (nine years, for example, in the case of Paula). Second, there is an emphasis on *conditions*. Depending on whom you read, the conditions on which Spirit baptism is suspended may include repentance, confession, faith, prayers, waiting ("tarrying"), seeking, yielding, and so on. The obvious danger here is in dividing the Christian life in such a way that *salvation* becomes a *gift* to the

---

[5] The best critique of the Keswick theology is found in Andy Naselli, *Let Go and Let God? A Survey and Analysis of Keswick Theology* (Logos Research Systems, 2010).

sinner whereas the *fullness of the Spirit* becomes a *reward* to the *saint*. Third, and most controversial of all, adherents emphasize the doctrine of *initial evidence*. The initial and physical evidence of having been baptized in the Spirit is speaking in tongues. If one has not spoken in tongues, one has not been baptized in the Spirit. Those in the Assemblies do not deny that a person may be saved without speaking in tongues. But tongues is itself the evidence that one has also been baptized in the Spirit.[6]

We must also take note of what is often referred to as the *sacramental view*, found most often in Roman Catholicism. The original Catholic view of Spirit baptism is that it is "a 'release' of the Spirit—a revitalization or flowering of the sacramental grace received in Christian initiation, breaking through into the personal conscious experience of the believer."[7] Catholic theologian Kilian McDonnell argues that every member of the church who receives the sacrament of water baptism is baptized in the Spirit at that same time. This "grace" has, as it were, "lain dormant, and at a particular moment in time or over a longer period it breaks through into the awareness of the individual. It is this conscious experience which is generally called 'the baptism in the Holy Spirit' in charismatic circles."[8]

We now come to the contemporary *charismatic* view. Generally speaking, most charismatics endorse the two-stage doctrine of subsequence (although an increasing number are beginning to question this). Many, however, reject any conditions on which Spirit baptism is suspended and do not believe all Spirit-baptized Christians necessarily speak in tongues.

The *third wave* is a term used to identify evangelicals who not only believe in but also consistently practice and minister in the full range of the Spirit's gifts. According to this view, Spirit baptism describes what happens when one becomes a Christian. There-

---

[6] I should point out that not all "classical Pentecostals" affirm the doctrine of initial evidence. Well-known New Testament scholar Gordon Fee has rejected all three of these doctrines relating to Spirit baptism while yet remaining within the Assemblies of God denomination. See Fee, "Baptism in the Holy Spirit: The Issue of Separability and Subsequence," *Pneuma: The Journal of the Society for Pentecostal Studies* 7, no. 2 (Fall 1985): 87–99.

[7] Lederle, *Treasures Old and New*, 105–6.

[8] Ibid., 108.

fore, all Christians, by definition, have been baptized in the Holy Spirit. However, there are also multiple, *subsequent* experiences of the Spirit's activity. After conversion the Spirit may yet "come" with varying degrees of intensity, wherein the Christian is "overwhelmed," "empowered," "anointed," or in some sense "endued." This "release" of new power, this "manifestation" of the Spirit's intimate presence, is most likely to be identified with what the New Testament calls the "filling" of the Spirit. This is the view that I believe is biblical and I will defend in what follows.[9]

The Apostle Paul on Spirit Baptism

Paul's statement in 1 Corinthians 12:13 is the principal text for this topic: "For in one Spirit we were all baptized into one body— Jews or Greeks, slaves or free—and all were made to drink of one Spirit." Not all agree on what the apostle is teaching. Some argue that Paul is describing a baptism *by* the Holy Spirit into Christ for salvation (which all Christians experience at conversion), whereas elsewhere in the New Testament it is Jesus who baptizes *in* the Holy Spirit for power (which only some Christians receive, though it is available to all). This may be diagrammed in table 1.

Table 1

At conversion	Holy Spirit	baptizes *all*	"into" Jesus Christ	salvation
After conversion	Jesus Christ	baptizes *some*	"in" Holy Spirit	power

Part of the motivation for this view is the seemingly awkward phrase "*in* one Spirit *into* one body" (hence, the alternative rendering, "*by* one Spirit *into* one body"). But what sounds harsh in

---

[9] Some of what you are about to read is adapted from my contribution to the book *Are Miraculous Gifts for Today? Four Views*, ed. Wayne A. Grudem (Grand Rapids: Zondervan, 1996), esp. 176–85, in which this issue is examined from a variety of differing perspectives. Among the texts that should encourage us to expect postconversion encounters with and experiences of the Holy Spirit are Luke 11:13; Rom. 5:5; 8:15–17; Gal. 3:1–5; Eph. 1:15–23; 3:16–19; 5:18; Phil. 1:19; 1 Thess. 4:8; 1 Pet. 1:8; as well as the many passages in Acts that speak of believers being "filled" with the Spirit for ministry and life. These texts would appear to dispel the concept of a singular, once-for-all deposit of the Spirit that would supposedly render superfluous the need for subsequent, postconversion anointing. The Spirit who was once given and now indwells each believer is continually given to enhance and intensify our relationship with Christ and to empower our efforts in ministry. But we need not label any one such experience as Spirit baptism.

English is not at all so in Greek. Indeed, as D. A. Carson points out, "the combination of Greek phrases nicely stresses exactly the point that Paul is trying to make: *all* Christians have been baptized in *one* Spirit; *all* Christians have been baptized into *one* body."[10]

Wayne Grudem also points to the same terminology in 1 Corinthians 10:2: "All were baptized *into* Moses *in* the cloud and *in* the sea." Here the *cloud* and the *sea* are the "elements" that surrounded or overwhelmed the people, and *Moses* points to the new life of participation in the Mosaic covenant and the fellowship of God's people, of which he was the leader. Grudem explains:

> It is not that there were two locations for the same baptism, but one was the element in which they were baptized and the other was the location in which they found themselves after the baptism. This is very similar to 1 Corinthians 12:13—the Holy Spirit was the *element* in which they were baptized, and the body of Christ, the church, was the *location* in which they found themselves after that baptism.[11]

In all of the other texts referring to Spirit baptism, the preposition *en* means "in," describing the element in which one is, as it were, immersed. In no text is the Holy Spirit ever said to be the agent by which one is baptized. Jesus is the baptizer. The Holy Spirit is he in whom we are engulfed or the "element" with which we are saturated.[12]

Another variation is to argue that whereas verse 13a refers to conversion, verse 13b describes a second, postconversion work of the Holy Spirit. But parallelism is a common literary device employed by the biblical authors. Here Paul employs two different metaphors that describe the same reality. Furthermore, whatever occurs to those in verse 13a occurs to those in verse 13b. In other

---

[10] D. A. Carson, *Showing the Spirit: A Theological Exposition of 1 Corinthians 12–14* (Grand Rapids: Baker, 1987), 47.

[11] Wayne Grudem, *Systematic Theology: An Introduction to Biblical Doctrine* (Grand Rapids: Zondervan, 2000), 768.

[12] It should be noted that in the New Testament to be baptized "by" someone is always expressed by the preposition *hypo* followed by a genitive noun. People were baptized "by" John the Baptist in the Jordan River (Matt. 3:6; Mark 1:5; Luke 3:7). Jesus was baptized "by" John (Matt. 3:13; Mark 1:9). The Pharisees were not baptized "by" John (Luke 7:30), etc. Most likely, then, if Paul had wanted to say that the Corinthians had all been baptized "by" the Holy Spirit, he would have used *hypo* with the genitive, not *en* with the dative.

words, the same "we all" who were baptized in one Spirit into one body were also made to drink of the same Spirit. The activity in the two phrases is coextensive.

Paul is probably using two vivid metaphors to describe our experience of the Holy Spirit at the time of conversion, the time when we became members of the body of Christ, the church:

> *baptism*, or immersion in the Holy Spirit, and
> *drinking* to the fill of the Holy Spirit,
> the purpose or goal of which is to unite us all in one body.

Thus, our "saturation" with the Spirit, our experience of being "engulfed" in and "deluged" and "inundated" by the Holy Spirit, results in our participation in the spiritual organism of the body of Christ, the church. It may even be that in verse 13b Paul is referring to the Old Testament imagery of the golden age to come, in which the land and its people have the Spirit poured out on them:

> until the Spirit is poured upon us from on high,
>   and the wilderness becomes a fruitful field,
>   and the fruitful field is deemed a forest. (Isa. 32:15)

> For I will pour water on the thirsty land,
>   and streams on the dry ground;
> I will pour my Spirit upon your offspring,
>   and my blessing on your descendants. (Isa. 44:3)

> And I will not hide my face anymore from them, when I pour out my Spirit upon the house of Israel, declares the Lord GOD. (Ezek. 39:29)

Thus, conversion is an experience of the Holy Spirit analogous to the outpouring of a sudden flood or rainstorm on parched ground, transforming dry and barren earth into a well-watered garden (cf. Jer. 31:12). Fee points out that

> such expressive metaphors (immersion in the Spirit and drinking to the fill of the Spirit) . . . imply a much greater experiential and visibly manifest reception of the Spirit than many have tended to experience in subsequent church history. Paul may appeal to their

common experience of Spirit as the presupposition for the unity of the body precisely because, as in Gal. 3:2–5, the Spirit was a dynamically experienced reality, which had happened to all.[13]

In view of Paul's statement in 1 Corinthians 12:13, I'm led to draw the following conclusions. First, baptism in the Spirit is a metaphor that describes our experience of the Spirit at *conversion*: we are immersed and submerged in him and forever enjoy his presence and power. Second, *all* Christians are baptized in the Spirit at the moment of the new birth, not subsequent to it. Third, biblical usage demands that we apply the terminology of "Spirit baptism" to the conversion experience of all believers. However, this *in no way restricts* the activity of the Spirit to conversion! The New Testament endorses and encourages multiple, subsequent experiences of the Spirit's power and presence. Thus, evangelicals are *right* in affirming that all Christians have experienced Spirit baptism at conversion. They are *wrong* in minimizing (sometimes even denying) the reality of subsequent, additional experiences of the Spirit in the course of the Christian life. Charismatics are *right* in affirming the reality and importance of postconversion encounters with the Spirit that empower, enlighten, and transform. They are *wrong* in calling this experience "Spirit baptism."

Distinguishing between Baptism in the Holy Spirit and the Filling of the Holy Spirit

What we've seen thus far also helps us differentiate between Spirit baptism and Spirit filling. Spirit baptism is a metaphor that describes our reception of the Spirit at the moment of our conversion to Jesus in faith and repentance. When we believe and are justified, we are, as it were, deluged and engulfed by the Holy Spirit; we are, as it were, immersed in and saturated by the Spirit. The result of this is that we are made members of the body of Christ, incorporated into the spiritual organism called the church, and permanently indwelt by the Holy Spirit.

---

[13] Gordon D. Fee, *God's Empowering Presence: The Holy Spirit in the Letters of Paul* (Peabody, MA: Hendrickson, 1994), 181.

Spirit baptism is therefore *instantaneous* (i.e., it is not a process), *coincident* with conversion, *universal* (i.e., all Christians are recipients), *unrepeatable*, and *permanent*. Spirit filling is also a metaphor describing our continuous, ongoing experience and appropriation of the Holy Spirit. To be filled with the Spirit is to come under progressively more intense and intimate influence of the Spirit. Spirit filling can be forfeited and subsequently experienced yet again, on multiple occasions, throughout the course of the Christian life.

There are *two senses* in which one may be filled with the Holy Spirit. First, there are biblical texts that describe people as being *"full of* the Holy Spirit,"* as if it were a *condition* or consistent *quality* of Christian character, a moral *disposition* possessing and reflecting a maturity in Christ (see Luke 4:1; Acts 6:3, 5; 7:55; 11:24; 13:52, lit., "they continued to be full"). This is the ideal condition of every Christian. It emphasizes the *abiding state* of being filled. Second, there are also texts that describe people as being *"filled with* the Holy Spirit"* to enable them to fulfill or perform a special task or to equip them for service or lifelong ministry (see Luke 1:15–17; Acts 9:17). On certain occasions, perhaps a spiritual emergency of sorts, a person may be "filled" with an immediate and special endowment of power for an especially important and urgent task. Thus, someone who is already filled with the Holy Spirit may experience an additional filling. That is to say, no matter how much of the Holy Spirit one may have, there's always room for more![14] I should also point out that there is no indication that these people ask to be filled or empowered. It is a sovereign work of God: as they walk in obedience and make themselves available, God "fills" them in accordance with their need.[15]

In sum, to be filled with the Spirit is different from being baptized in the Spirit. There is one baptism, but there are multiple fillings. In no New Testament text are we commanded to be bap-

---

[14] See Luke 1:41, 67; Acts 4:8, 31; 13:9. Also, in Acts 7:55 Stephen, though "full of the Holy Spirit," is again "filled" with the Spirit to prepare him to endure persecution and eventual martyrdom, as well as to "see" the vision of Jesus.

[15] Consider these Old Testament instances: Ex. 31:3; 35:31; Num. 24:2 (Balaam); Judg. 6:34; 14:6, 19; 15:14; 1 Sam. 10:6; 16:13.

tized in the Holy Spirit. There is no appeal to do something in order to be baptized; there is no exhortation or imperative. On the other hand, we *are* commanded to be filled with the Holy Spirit (Eph. 5:18). Thus it is possible to be baptized in the Holy Spirit, to experience the permanent indwelling of the Holy Spirit, and yet *not* be filled with the Holy Spirit. Finally, to be "full of the Holy Spirit" is to reflect a maturity of character; it is the ideal condition of every believer. To be "filled with the Holy Spirit" is to experience an anointing for power, purity, proclamation, and praise.

The Doctrine of Subsequence

The question is frequently asked, How and why did Spirit baptism come to be viewed by those in the Pentecostal and charismatic traditions as an event separate from and subsequent to salvation or conversion? Gordon Fee suggests the following scenario to account for this development.[16]

First, it probably began with dissatisfaction with the lethargy and lifelessness of their own Christian experience and that of the church corporately. The coldness, cowardice, and routine of religion sparked in them a passion, thirst, and hunger for more of God, for more of what they saw New Testament Christians experience. Second, this passion for more led to a genuine, biblical, life-changing experience. They were undeniably touched by the presence of God. A transforming encounter with God brought new power, renewed commitment, a zealous rededication to holiness of life, and deepened love. Third, this experience was clearly subsequent to their conversion (often years after they were saved). Therefore, it was something different from the new birth or justification or anything else associated with their initial saving encounter with Christ. Fourth, as has often been said, these were a people with an experience in search of a theology. Turning to the Bible to identify and justify what had occurred, they found what they believed was a threefold precedent for what had happened to them (see below). The final step was simply to identify what happened to them as the "baptism in the Holy Spirit."

---

[16] Fee, "Baptism in the Holy Spirit," 87–99.

Biblical support for the doctrine of subsequence is allegedly found by appealing to the experience of Jesus, the experience of the first disciples, and certain texts in the book of Acts that appear to portray Christians receiving the fullness of the Spirit separate from and subsequent to their initial experience of saving faith in Christ. We need to briefly examine each of these in turn.

The Analogy Based on the Experience of Jesus

The argument based on Jesus's experience goes as follows: Jesus is conceived by the Holy Spirit and born of the Virgin Mary, an event said to correspond with *our* regeneration or new birth by the Holy Spirit. Approximately thirty years later, Jesus is anointed with the power of the Spirit for public ministry (Acts 10:38). This event is interpreted as his "baptism in the Holy Spirit." So, if the Son of God needed this extra enduement of power, how much more do we, his disciples?

Whereas I certainly believe that Jesus was anointed with the Holy Spirit at his baptism in the river Jordan, all for the purpose of empowering him for ministry (Acts 10:38), I do not believe this experience is a valid parallel or pattern for us when it comes to our baptism in the Spirit. The text does not say Jesus was "baptized" in the Spirit. It says he was "anointed" (Acts 10:38; see also Luke 4:18). Indeed, far from being "baptized in the Spirit," *Jesus is himself the one who does the baptizing!* John the Baptist clearly asserts of Jesus, "He will baptize you with the Holy Spirit and fire" (Matt. 3:11; see also Mark 1:8; Luke 3:16; John 1:33). The analogy also breaks down when we observe that Jesus didn't need to get saved. Unlike all of us, Jesus was not unregenerate. There was no time at which he was an unbeliever and thus no time at which he experienced conversion. Therefore, it makes no sense to speak of any particular incident in his life as being *separate from and subsequent to conversion.* The Holy Spirit anointed Jesus with power at the age of thirty simply because that was the point at which Jesus began his public ministry as God's Messiah. There is no biblical evidence to suggest that this event reflects a normative, God-ordained will for "subsequence" in either his life or the lives of his followers. There certainly *is* an analogy between the experience of Jesus and the experience of the Christian: we *do* need the power of the Holy Spirit to do the works of Jesus. But there is no biblical justification for identifying this with Spirit baptism. In Acts, it is more appropriately called the filling of the Spirit.

The Analogy Based on the Experience of the First Disciples

The argument for subsequence also appeals to the first disciples' "two-stage" experience: they were regenerated and converted in John 20:22, at which time they received the Holy Spirit, but they did not experience Spirit baptism until the day of Pentecost. Their baptism in the Spirit, therefore, was obviously separate from and subsequent to their conversion (this would be the case even if we don't regard John 20:22 as their conversion experience).

However, John 20:22 does not describe their regeneration or new birth. The disciples were already "clean" (John 13:10); their names were already written down in heaven (Luke 10:20). Peter had openly testified that Jesus was the Christ (Matt. 16:16–17; John 16:30; see also John 17:8–19, where Jesus refers to them as already belonging to the Father). Moreover, this impartation of the Spirit was related not to their conversion but to their *commission* ("even so I am sending you," John 20:21).

So what was going on in John 20:22? Some argue that this constituted a *preliminary* impartation of the Spirit, in anticipation of the complete gift that would come at Pentecost. Since Luke 24:49 clearly teaches that at Pentecost the followers of Jesus would receive the fullness of divine power (i.e., the Holy Spirit), whatever occurred in John 20:22 was at most a taste of Pentecost, not the "full meal." It was at most a *transitional empowering* of the disciples to get them from Easter to Pentecost. Others insist that there was no actual impartation of the Holy Spirit. Rather, John 20:22 is an *acted parable*, a symbolic promise of the coming power of the Holy Spirit that is not fulfilled until the day of Pentecost.

In the final analysis it matters little if this was a partial enduement of power in anticipation of Pentecost or simply a symbolic act or prophetic parable pointing forward to Pentecost. The fact remains that the principal concern of the Son after his resurrection is the gift of the Holy Spirit to the church for the perpetuation of the divine mission he initiated.

But does the experience of the disciples provide a pattern for us regarding Spirit baptism? I don't think so. It is unwise to argue that their experience is a pattern for ours when we realize that *their experience could not have been otherwise than it was*. In other words, it was *impossible* for them to be baptized in the Spirit when they believed, simply because they believed long before Spirit baptism was even possible. Lederle puts it this way:

> This conclusion is . . . underscored by the fact that the apostles began believing in Jesus (in some or other form at least) before the Spirit was poured out on the church on the day of Pentecost. This places them in a situation different to every Christian living after Pentecost. It was thus necessary that the apostles experience the new freedom and life in the Spirit which came with Pentecost in a unique way because they could not experience it before it had come (prior to Acts 2).[17]

Whereas the results of Pentecost (the presence and power of the Holy Spirit) extend to the church as a whole, that day was in a very real sense unique and unrepeatable in redemptive history. The Spirit "came" on that day in a way that could occur but once. The Spirit, therefore, is now "here" in a way that prior to Pentecost he was not. Pentecost was the inauguration of a new phase or age in the redemptive plan of God. Thus, it is unwise to assume that the sequence in the experience of those who were alive and believing when it occurred is normative for the experience of those who were not. Wayne Grudem explains it this way:

> They [the first disciples] received this remarkable new empowering from the Holy Spirit *because they were living at the time of the transition between the old covenant work of the Holy Spirit and the new covenant work of the Holy Spirit*. Though it was a "second experience" of the Holy Spirit, coming as it did long after their

[17] Lederle, *Treasures Old and New*, 60.

conversion, it is not to be taken as a pattern for us, for we are not living at a time of transition in the work of the Holy Spirit. In their case, believers with an old covenant empowering from the Holy Spirit became believers with a new covenant empowering from the Holy Spirit. But we today do not first become believers with a weaker, old covenant work of the Holy Spirit in our hearts and wait until some later time to receive a new covenant work of the Holy Spirit. Rather, we are in the same position as those who became Christians in the church at Corinth: when we become Christians we are all *"baptized in one Spirit* into one body" (1 Cor. 12:13)—just as the Corinthians were, and just as were the new believers in many churches who were converted when Paul traveled on his missionary journeys.[18]

The Argument Based on the Experience of Individuals in Acts

If a persuasive case is going to be made for the doctrine of subsequence as normative for all Christians in every age, it is going to come from the experience of believers as recorded in the book of Acts. Three groups of people are typically singled out.

We begin with the *Samaritans* in Acts 8:4–24. Most are familiar with the story of how Philip the evangelist traveled to Samaria and preached the gospel with amazing results. Signs and wonders were performed, and many "believed" in Jesus. When Peter and John heard this, they too came to Samaria and prayed for these people "that they might receive the Holy Spirit, for he had not yet fallen on any of them, but they had only been baptized in the name of the Lord Jesus" (vv. 15–16).

Acts 8:16 is surely one of the most extraordinary statements in the entire book: *it is, after all, the only record in the entire New Testament of people believing in Jesus Christ, being baptized in water, and not receiving the Holy Spirit.* Is the experience of the Samaritans normative for all other Christians in every other age? What is going on here?

The classical Pentecostal view is that the Samaritans experienced a "second" reception of the Holy Spirit, a work of grace that

---

[18] Grudem, *Systematic Theology*, 772–73 (emphasis his).

was obviously separate from and subsequent to the initial work by which they became believers in Jesus. They identified this second experience as the *baptism in the Holy Spirit*. But note that Luke says explicitly that the Holy Spirit had not fallen on them *at all* (see v. 16). He appears to say that what occurred in verses 16ff. was the first reception of the Spirit, not the second. In other words, for the Samaritans there had been no earlier or first coming of the Spirit to make this a subsequent or second coming.

According to one popular view, the Samaritans had already received the Holy Spirit, but they had not experienced his charismatic manifestations. In other words, it wasn't the Spirit *himself* they lacked; only *his supernatural gifts*. Advocates of this view point out that the words "Holy Spirit" in this narrative lack the definite article, thus pointing not to the person of the Spirit per se, but to the power or operations of the Spirit, that is, his gifts. However, it has been shown that no significant theological conclusions can be drawn from the presence or absence of the definite article.[19] Also, according to verses 15–19, it was the Holy Spirit, not his gifts, who came when the apostles laid on hands. Whereas the Spirit is certainly distinct from the gifts he imparts, when he comes it is always with his gifts.

Others suggest that this is an example of the principle that the Holy Spirit comes only through the laying on of hands. But if this were the case, how does one explain Acts 2:38, where no mention is made of "hands"? Also, if it were only a matter of laying on of hands, why didn't Philip simply do it? The apostle Paul received the Holy Spirit without the laying on of hands when he was converted (Acts 9). And when Philip led the Ethiopian eunuch to the Lord, he didn't lay hands on him (Acts 8:26–40). Finally, apart from Acts 19, nowhere else in Acts is the Holy Spirit connected to the laying on of hands. Not wanting to yield that easily, some say that "apostolic" hands were the key. But there is no record of the apostles traveling throughout the country in an attempt to keep pace

---

[19]See James D. G. Dunn, *Baptism in the Holy Spirit: A Re-examination of the New Testament Teaching on the Gift of the Spirit in Relation to Pentecostalism Today* (Philadelphia: Westminster, 1970), 68–70.

with the rapidly spreading gospel, as if the outpouring of the Spirit were in every instance suspended on the imposition of their hands.

Another view is that the Samaritans had not yet received the Holy Spirit because *they were not yet saved.* Their response was not one of saving faith, but one of mass emotion and mob hysteria. It was at best intellectual assent, not heartfelt commitment to Christ.

However, according to 8:14, they had "received the word of God," the same terminology used in 2:41 and 11:1, where genuine conversion is in view. Acts 8:12 is quite explicit about the nature and object of their faith: "they believed Philip as he preached good news about the kingdom of God and the name of Jesus Christ." The same terminology Luke uses here is found in Acts 16:34 and 18:8 to describe genuine faith in God. Furthermore, when Peter and John arrived, they didn't preach the gospel. They simply prayed for them to receive the Spirit. This is strange indeed if the Samaritans weren't saved in the first place. And if the Samaritans had in fact misunderstood Philip, shouldn't we expect the apostles to correct the problem through additional teaching (as Priscilla and Aquila did with Apollos in Acts 18:26)? Finally, they were baptized, literally, "*into* the name" of Jesus (8:16), a phrase common in commercial transactions when a property was transferred or paid "into the name" of someone else. Thus a person baptized "into the name of Jesus" was saying: "I have passed into *his* ownership; Jesus owns me lock, stock, and barrel. He is my Lord."

The most likely answer as to why God withheld the Holy Spirit from them and *them only* is found in the unique relationship between the Jews and Samaritans. An important fact to remember is that this was the first occasion on which the gospel was proclaimed not only outside Jerusalem but also *inside* Samaria. This is significant for several reasons.

It may be difficult for us today to grasp the depth of hatred between Jews and Samaritans. The Jews blamed the Samaritans for having destroyed the unity of God's people and the monarchy following the death of Solomon in 922. They were also regarded as half-breeds because they had intermarried with Gentiles. When the Jews returned to Jerusalem after the exile, the Samaritans hindered their efforts to rebuild the temple and constructed their own on Mount Gerizim. In AD 6, during the Passover, some Samaritans scattered the bones of a dead man in the court of the temple in Jerusalem, an act of defilement that enraged the Jews and only intensified their animosity. Indeed, the Jews publicly cursed Samaritans and prayed fervently that God would never save any of them. These are some of the reasons why the parable of the good Samaritan was so shocking to Jewish ears. As far as the Jews were concerned, the phrase *good Samaritan* was a contradiction in terms! Such animosity also explains why everyone was so surprised when Jesus dared engage a *Samaritan* woman in conversation at Jacob's well (John 4:9). In John 8:48 the Jewish leaders ask Jesus, "Are we not right in saying that you are a Samaritan and have a demon?" I suspect that if the Jews themselves had a choice between the two, they might prefer to be demonized rather than be a Samaritan!

One final observation will help. Geographically, Samaria was located between Galilee to the north and Judea to the south. The Jewish disgust for Samaria was so intense that when Jews had to travel from Galilee to Judea, or vice versa, they would first travel due east and then south, or north, in order to avoid even having to set foot on Samaritan soil!

All this compels us to ask what might have happened had the Samaritans received the gospel independent of the church in Jerusalem? Something needed to be done to insure unity, lest schism or division emerge. Frederick Bruner explains:

> The Samaritans were not left to become an isolated sect with no bonds of union with the apostolic church in Jerusalem. If a Samaritan church and a Jewish church had arisen independently, side by side, without the dramatic removal of the ancient and bitter barriers of prejudice between the two, particularly at the level of ultimate authority, the young church of God would have been in schism from the inception of its mission. The drama of the Samaritan affair in Acts 8 included among its purposes the vivid and visual dismantling of the wall of enmity between Jew

and Samaritan and the preservation of the precious unity of the church of God.[20]

Therefore, the unprecedented delay of the Holy Spirit was in order that the leaders of the church in Jerusalem, Peter and John, might vividly and personally place their imprimatur or stamp of approval on the movement of the gospel into Samaria (cf. Acts 1:8). In view of this historical background of racial and religious animosity, it was deemed prudent by God to take steps to prevent a disastrous split in the early church: hence the temporary and altogether unusual delay of the coming of the Spirit. An unprecedented situation demanded quite exceptional methods.

Having said all this, I have to be honest in admitting that this incident poses questions about the reception and experience of the Holy Spirit that may have to remain unanswered. For even the explanation that I have given as to why God suspended the gift of the Spirit in the case of the Samaritans does not explain theologically *how* they could have been regenerated, converted, and believing Christians, members of the body of Christ, without yet having received the Holy Spirit. Yet they did.

The second example cited from the book of Acts is that of *Cornelius and the Gentiles* (Acts 10:1–48; 11:12–18). Here is the second monumental extension of the gospel beyond the boundaries of Jewish exclusivism. The problem arises when it is argued that Cornelius was already saved when Peter arrived (10:2, 35). If he were, then his reception of the Holy Spirit in verses 44–48 would constitute a second blessing, or a postconversion "baptism in the Holy Spirit." But there are several reasons why we cannot regard Cornelius as having been saved prior to Peter's arrival.

Acts 11:14 identifies Peter's "message" as the way Cornelius "*will* be saved." The message or gospel is essential. The gospel alone is the power of God unto Cornelius's salvation (Rom. 1:16–17). Also, note that the tense of the verb is *future*. If he will believe Peter's gospel message, he *will be* saved (indicating that he is *not yet* saved).

---

[20] Frederick Dale Bruner, *A Theology of the Holy Spirit: The Pentecostal Experience and the New Testament Witness* (Grand Rapids: Eerdmans, 1970), 176.

If he rejects the message, he won't. Acts 10:43 says that the essence of salvation is the forgiveness of sins, a blessing that comes only through believing in the name of Christ. One cannot be saved until and unless he or she believes in the name of Christ. Elsewhere in Acts, even the most God-fearing and moral people (i.e., the Jews) are told they must repent and believe the gospel to be saved (cf. 2:5; 3:19). And Acts 11:18 indicates that Cornelius and the Gentiles received from God "repentance that leads to life" only when Peter preached the gospel and they turned to faith in Christ.[21]

In conclusion, then, Cornelius and the other Gentiles received the Holy Spirit when they were saved, and not at a time subsequent to their initial faith in Christ. Cornelius and the Gentiles were "baptized in the Spirit" at the moment of their conversion.

Finally, we come to the *Ephesian disciples* (Acts 19:1–10). The argument from this passage is that these were Christian men who had not yet received the Holy Spirit. It is only after Paul prayed for them (i.e., subsequent to their faith) that they were "baptized in the Spirit." I believe this interpretation is largely fueled by the erroneous translation of verse 2 in the KJV: "Have ye received the Holy Ghost *since* ye believed?" The correct translation is found in the ESV, NASB, and NIV: "Did you receive the Holy Spirit *when* you believed?" Paul's question in verse 2 is designed to uncover what kind of belief or faith they had experienced. If their belief was saving, Christian belief, then they would have received the Holy Spirit (Rom. 8:9). The fact that they had not received the Holy Spirit proved to Paul that their "belief" was not Christian belief. Says Dunn:

---

[21] If Cornelius was not truly converted until Peter preached the gospel to him, what does it mean to say that Cornelius was "welcome" or "acceptable" to God (Acts 10:35) prior to his hearing and responding to the gospel? John Piper's explanation is the best: "My suggestion is that Cornelius represents a kind of unsaved person among an unreached people group who is seeking God in an extraordinary way. And Peter is saying that God *accepts* this search as genuine (hence 'acceptable' in verse 35) and works wonders to bring that person the gospel of Jesus Christ the way he did through the visions of both Peter on the housetop and Cornelius in the hour of prayer. . . . So the fear of God that is acceptable to God in verse 35 is a true sense that there is a holy God, that we have to meet him some day as desperate sinners, that we cannot save ourselves and need to know God's way of salvation, and that we pray for it day and night and seek to act on the light we have. This is what Cornelius was doing. And God accepted his prayer and his groping for truth in his life (Acts 17:27), and worked wonders to bring the saving message of the Gospel to him. Cornelius would not have been saved if no one had taken him the gospel." *Let the Nations Be Glad: The Supremacy of God in Missions* (Grand Rapids: Baker, 1993), 146, 148.

It was inconceivable to him [Paul] that a Christian, one who had committed himself to Jesus as Lord in baptism in his name, could be yet without the Spirit. This is why the twelve had to go through the full initiation procedure. It was not that Paul accepted them as Christians with an incomplete experience; it is rather that they were not Christians at all. The absence of the Spirit indicated that they had not even begun the Christian life.[22]

Their response, "No, we have not even heard that there is a Holy Spirit" (Acts 19:2), does not mean they had never before so much as heard of the Spirit's existence. The Holy Spirit is frequently mentioned in the Old Testament, and John the Baptist's own words to his followers (among whom these people included themselves) were that the Messiah would baptize in "Spirit" and fire. The point is that although they had heard John's prophecy of Messianic "Spirit baptism," they were not aware of its fulfillment. In other words, *they were ignorant of Pentecost.*

But if these people were not Christian disciples, what kind of disciples were they? Beasley-Murray offers this explanation:

There is . . . nothing improbable in the existence of groups of people baptized by followers of John the Baptist and standing at varying degrees of distance from (or nearness to) the Christian Church. There must have been many baptized by John himself who had listened to the preaching of Jesus and his disciples, who had received the gospel with more or less intensity of conviction and faith and regarded themselves as His followers, yet who had no part in Pentecost or its developments. . . . In Paul's eyes these men were not Christians—no man who was without the Spirit of Jesus had any part in the Christ (Rom. 8:9). Probably Luke himself did not view them as Christians; his employment of the term . . . disciples, is a gesture in recognition that they were neither on a level with unbelieving Jews, nor classed with pagans. They were men who had paused on the way without completing the journey, half-Christians, occupying a zone of territory that could exist only at that period of history when the effects of John's labors overlapped with those of Jesus.[23]

---

[22] Dunn, *Baptism in the Holy Spirit*, 86.
[23] G. R. Beasley-Murray, *Baptism in the New Testament* (Grand Rapids: Eerdmans, 1974), 109–11.

Thus, when Paul discovered they had not received the Holy Spirit, he knew immediately they were not Christians. Upon realizing that they were but "disciples" of John, Paul proclaimed Jesus, in whom they believed, at which point they received the Holy Spirit.

Conclusion

In the final analysis, does it matter all that much whether we refer to a postconversion encounter with the Spirit as "baptism" or "filling"? Aside from the fact that we ought always to strive to be as biblically accurate as possible in our use and definition of terms, I think not. Perhaps an illustration will help in making my point.

Let us suppose that you reach into the cabinet for medication to relieve a persistent headache and take hold of what you believe is aspirin. Unfortunately, the label on the bottle has long since worn off. Nevertheless, the medicine works. Fifteen minutes after swallowing two tablets, your headache is completely gone. Your spouse then informs you that the medicine you took was, in fact, Tylenol. Does this news cause your headache to return? It shouldn't. The medicinal value of the Tylenol is not diminished simply because you mislabeled it. Calling it aspirin in no way altered the physical properties of what was, in fact, Tylenol.

My point is that the reality of postconversion experiences of the Holy Spirit is not undermined should it be discovered that we have mislabeled the event. The spiritual "medicine," so to speak, still works. The issue is whether or not the encounter was real, not what we call it. Whereas I prefer to reserve the terminology of Spirit baptism for what all experience at conversion, the fact that the Pentecostalist applies it to a subsequent and more restricted empowering does not in itself invalidate the latter phenomenon. The important issue is whether the New Testament endorses *both* the initial saving work of regeneration and incorporation into the body of Christ *and* the theologically distinct (though not always subsequent) work of anointing for witness, service, and charismatic gifting. I believe that it does.

So what happened to Paula? In my opinion, Paula was converted to saving faith in Christ at the age of eleven while at church camp. At that moment she was *baptized in the Holy Spirit*. The Holy Spirit also came to permanently indwell her. On that night nine years later Paula was *filled with the Holy Spirit* as she cried out to the Lord to renew her commitment and empower her for a life of service to his glory.

Recommended Reading

Brand, Chad Owen, ed. *Perspectives on Spirit Baptism: Five Views*. Nashville: B&H, 2004.

Bruner, Frederick Dale. *A Theology of the Holy Spirit: The Pentecostal Experience and the New Testament Witness*. Grand Rapids: Eerdmans, 1970.

Fee, Gordon. "Baptism in the Holy Spirit: The Issue of Separability and Subsequence." *Pneuma* 7, no. 2 (Fall 1985): 87–99.

Lederle, H. I. *Treasures Old and New: Interpretations of "Spirit-Baptism" in the Charismatic Renewal Movement*. Peabody, MA: Hendrickson, 1988.

Menzies, William W., and Robert P. Menzies. *Spirit and Power: Foundations of Pentecostal Experience*. Grand Rapids: Zondervan, 2000.

Stott, John R. W. *Baptism and Fullness: The Work of the Holy Spirit Today*. Downers Grove, IL: InterVarsity, 1976.

20

Should All Christians Speak in Tongues?

The short answer to the question raised in the title is no. But I assume you are hoping for a slightly more extensive reply, so let's explore this in a bit more detail.

An Ongoing Controversy

Many of you may have heard or read that the International Mission Board (known as the IMB) of the Southern Baptist Convention recently voted that they no longer will appoint Southern Baptist missionaries who employ a "private prayer language," their way of referring to the practice of praying in tongues.

According to an article in the online *Baptist Standard*, the Texas Baptist Newsjournal, "The Southern Baptist Convention agency already excludes people who speak in tongues in public worship from serving as missionaries. But the mission board's trustees voted Nov. 15 to amend its list of missionary qualifications to exclude those who use a 'prayer language' in private."[1] The article goes on to say

---

[1] "International Mission Board Seeks to Tie Tongues," posted December 2, 2005, www.baptist standard.com.

that "the restriction of 'prayer language'—a private version of the charismatic worship practice of tongues-speaking—was approved by a vote of 25–18. . . . Some trustees did not vote on the issue during their Huntsville, Ala., meeting, the agency reported."

I cite this example only to point out that the controversy over the spiritual gift of speaking in tongues shows no signs of going away. As long as there are Christians who believe the gift is valid today while others insist it is not, this issue will be discussed and debated. I have already addressed the question of whether God designed gifts such as speaking in tongues to function in the life of the church beyond the lifetime and ministry of the apostles. My answer to that question was unequivocally yes. So what follows in this chapter will simply assume that the gift of tongues is a valid expression of the Spirit's work in the church today. If you are among those who identify with cessationism and believe all alleged manifestations of tongues are spurious, you may wish to skip this chapter and move on to the next. But I would urge you to read on here, if for no other reason than to expand your understanding of this debate.

No one can deny that of the many spiritual gifts God has graciously imparted to the church, none has provoked as much controversy and confusion as has the gift of speaking in tongues. Yet, contrary to some distortions, the apostle Paul nowhere denigrates the gift of tongues. He wishes all Christians spoke in tongues (1 Cor. 14:5). He applauds the capacity of tongues to edify the believer (v. 4). He thanks God for tongues in his own prayer life (vv. 18–19) and explicitly warns against any temptation to forbid the exercise of this precious gift (v. 39).

But we're still left with the most controversial issue relating to tongues speech: Does Paul's statement in 1 Corinthians 14:5 mean that *all* Christians should or will speak in tongues? In that passage Paul states, "Now I want you all to speak in tongues, but even more to prophesy." The reason for Paul's preference of prophecy over tongues isn't that the latter is less spiritual or perhaps even dangerous. Rather, prophecy is to be preferred over uninterpreted tongues in the corporate gathering of the church because it is intelligible and thus can serve better than unintelligible tongues to build up, edify, and encourage the people of God. Paul is quick to qualify his elevation of prophecy over tongues by saying that this obtains only in the absence of an interpretation for the latter. If "someone interprets" (v. 5), then tongues can also serve to strengthen and instruct God's people. But let's not get derailed from our primary concern, which is whether Paul's declared "wish" in this text means that all believers ought to expect God to bestow this gift upon them.

Reasons to Answer No

Those who say no cite several important facts. First, they appeal to 1 Corinthians 7:7, where Paul uses identical language to what is found in 14:5. With regard to his own state of celibacy, Paul writes: "I wish that all were as I myself am. But each has his own gift from God, one of one kind and one of another." No one will argue that Paul intends for all Christians to remain single as he is. His "wish," therefore, should not be taken as the expression of an unqualified and universal desire. Surely, then, we should not expect all to speak in tongues either.

Second, according to 1 Corinthians 12:7–11, tongues, like the other gifts mentioned, is bestowed to individuals as the Holy Spirit wills. If Paul meant that "all" were to experience this gift, why did he employ the terminology of "to one is given . . . and to another . . . to another," and so forth? In other words, Paul seems to suggest that the Spirit sovereignly differentiates among Christians and distributes one or more gifts to this person, and yet another, different gift to that person, and still another gift to the next person, and so on.

The final and most oft-cited argument for this view is 1 Corinthians 12:28–30, where Paul quite explicitly states that "all do not speak with tongues," any more than all are apostles or all are teachers or all have gifts of healings and so on. His question is stated thus: "Are all apostles? Are all prophets? Are all teachers? Do all work miracles? Do all possess gifts of healing? Do all speak with tongues? Do all interpret? But earnestly desire the higher gifts. And I will show you a still more excellent way" (vv. 29–31). In English we have a particular way of asking a question for which we already know the answer. Think for a moment about the way you emphasize certain words, elevate your voice, and perhaps even utilize facial expressions when you intend for the person listening to know that the answer to your question is decidedly no.

But in Greek there is a specific grammatical structure designed to elicit a negative response to a question. Such is precisely what Paul employs here in 1 Corinthians 12. The translation provided by the NASB makes this slightly more explicit than does the ESV: "All are not apostles, are they? All are not prophets, are they? All are not teachers, are they? All are not workers of miracles, are they? All do not have gifts of healings, do they? All do not speak with tongues, do they? All do not interpret, do they?" You can clearly see from the way the questions are phrased that the author wants you to respond by saying, "No, of course not."

Counterarguments

Many think that this forever settles the argument. But the debate doesn't end there. Those answering yes to our main question begin by pointing out that 1 Corinthians 7:7 isn't the only place where Paul uses the "I want" or "I wish" terminology. One must also address passages such as these:

> For I do not want you to be unaware, brothers, that our fathers were all under the cloud, and all passed through the sea. (1 Cor. 10:1)

> But I want you to understand that the head of every man is Christ, the head of a wife is her husband, and the head of Christ is God. (1 Cor. 11:3)

> Now concerning spiritual gifts, brothers, I do not want you to be uninformed. (1 Cor. 12:1)

Each of these three texts uses the same Greek verb that we find in 1 Corinthians 14:5 ("I want" or "I wish"), and in all of them what the apostle wants applies equally and universally to every believer.

Furthermore, in 1 Corinthians 7 Paul goes on to tell us explicitly why his "wish" for universal celibacy cannot and should not be fulfilled. It is because "each has his own gift from God" (7:7). But in 1 Corinthians 14 no such contextual clues suggest that Paul's "wish" or "desire" for all to speak in tongues cannot be fulfilled.

Those who believe the answer to our question is yes also wonder why God would *not* want each believer to use this particular gift. In other words, why would God withhold from any of his children a gift that enables them to pray and to praise him so effectively, a gift that also functions to edify them in their faith?

An appeal is also often made to 1 Corinthians 14:23. There Paul says: "If, therefore, the whole church comes together and all speak in tongues, and outsiders or unbelievers enter, will they not say that you are out of your minds?" Paul envisions a scenario, perhaps not uncommon in Corinth in the first century, in which (nearly) everyone in the congregation speaks in uninterpreted tongues simultaneously, or at least consecutively. This is of no benefit to unbelievers who may be visiting because they have no idea what is being said. Their only conclusion will be that these people have lost their minds! This is why Paul later in the chapter insists that only two or three speak in tongues and that there always be an interpretation to follow. But aside from that issue, is it the case that Paul at least envisions the hypothetical possibility that every Christian in Corinth could speak in tongues, even if he advises against it in the corporate meeting of the church? Or could it simply be that he is speaking in deliberately exaggerated language when he says "all speak in tongues"?

Some also insist that 1 Corinthians 12:7–11 and 12:28–30 refer to the gift of tongues in *public ministry*, whereas 14:5 is describing the gift in *private devotion*. In 12:28 Paul specifically says that he is describing what happens "in the church" or "in the assembly" (cf. 11:18; 14:19, 23, 28, 33, 35). Not everyone is gifted by the Spirit to speak in tongues during the corporate gathering of the church. But the potential does exist for every believer to pray in tongues in private. These are not two different gifts, however, but two different contexts in which the one gift might be employed. A person who ministers to the entire church in tongues is someone who already uses tongues in his or her prayer life.

Well-known Pentecostal pastor Jack Hayford argues in much the same way, using different terms. He suggests that (1) the *gift* of tongues is limited in distribution (1 Cor. 12:11, 30), and (2) its public exercise is to be closely governed (1 Cor. 14:27–28), while the *grace* of tongues is so broadly available that Paul wishes that all enjoyed its blessing (1 Cor. 14:5a), which includes (1) distinctive communication with God (1 Cor. 14:2), (2) edifying of the believer's private life (1 Cor. 14:4), and (3) worship and thanksgiving with beauty and propriety (1 Cor. 14:15–17).[2] The difference between these operations of the Holy Spirit is that *not every* Christian has reason to expect he or she will necessarily exercise the public *gift*; but *any* Christian may expect and welcome the private *grace* of spiritual language in his or her personal time of prayer fellowship *with* God (1 Cor. 14:2), praiseful worship *before* God (1 Cor. 14:15–17), and intercessory prayer *to* God (Rom. 8:26–27).

Paul's point at the end of 1 Corinthians 12 is that not every believer will contribute to the body in precisely the same way. Not everyone will minister a prophetic word, not everyone will teach, and so on. But whether everyone might pray privately in tongues is another matter, and not in Paul's purview until chapter 14.

Consider what Paul says about prophecy. "All are not prophets, are they?" (1 Cor. 12:29, NASB). No, of course not. But Paul is quick to say that the potential exists for "all" to prophesy (14:1, 31). Why could not the same be true for tongues? Couldn't Paul be saying that whereas all do not speak in tongues as an expression of corporate, public ministry, it is possible that all may speak in tongues as an expression of private praise and prayer? Just as Paul's rhetorical question in 12:29 is not designed to rule out the possibility that all may utter a prophetic word, so also his rhetorical question in 12:30 is not designed to exclude anyone from exercising tongues in private devotional experience.

---

[2] Jack Hayford, *The Beauty of Spiritual Language* (Dallas: Word, 1992), 102–6.

Conclusion

As you can see, good arguments exist on both sides of the fence when it comes to answering this question. I must confess it seems unlikely that God would withhold the gift of tongues from one of his children who passionately and sincerely desires it. My suspicion is that, all things being equal, if you deeply desire this gift, it is probably (but not certainly) because the Holy Spirit has stirred your heart to seek it. And he has stirred your heart to seek it because it is his will to bestow it. So, if you long for the gift of tongues, persevere in your prayers. My sense (with no guarantee) is that God will answer you in his time with a satisfying yes.

On the other hand, it is important to remember that as far as we can tell, no other spiritual gift is ever described, defined, or portrayed in the New Testament as one that God bestows, or wants to bestow, on every single Christian. In other words, few if any would argue that God wants all to have the gift of teaching, or the gift of mercy, or the gift of leadership, or the gift of evangelism. Why, then, would tongues be unique, the only one among the many charismata that God intends for all believers to exercise?

In the final analysis, I must stand by my initial conclusion that the answer to our question, Should all Christians speak in tongues? is probably no. But I'm open to being persuaded otherwise![3]

Recommended Reading

Cartledge, Mark J. *Charismatic Glossolalia: An Empirical-Theological Study*. Burlington, VT: Ashgate, 2002.

Hayford, Jack. *The Beauty of Spiritual Language*. Dallas: Word, 1992.

Storms, Sam. *The Beginner's Guide to Spiritual Gifts*. 2nd ed. Ventura, CA: Gospel Light, 2013.

---

[3] For those who wish to go deeper, a recent scholarly and quite helpful discussion of this issue may be found in the *Asian Journal of Pentecostal Studies* (*AJPS*). See Max Turner, "Tongues: An Experience for All in the Pauline Churches?" *AJPS* 1, no. 2 (1998): 231–53; Simon K. H. Chan, "A Response to Max Turner," *AJPS* 2, no. 2 (1999): 279–81; Robert P. Menzies, "Paul and the Universality of Tongues: A Response to Max Turner," *AJPS* 2, no. 2 (1999): 283–95; and Max Turner, "A Response to the Responses of Menzies and Chan," *AJPS* 2, no. 2 (1999): 297–308.

21

What Was Paul's Thorn in the Flesh?

I've never experienced anything remotely similar to what Paul describes in the first few verses of 2 Corinthians 12:

> I know a man in Christ who fourteen years ago was caught up to the third heaven—whether in the body or out of the body I do not know, God knows. And I know that this man was caught up into paradise—whether in the body or out of the body I do not know, God knows—and he heard things that cannot be told, which man may not utter. (vv. 2–4)[1]

To be "caught up" (v. 2) into the third heaven and to hear "things that cannot be told, which man may not utter" (v. 4) is almost more than I can grasp. It's not that I would turn down the opportunity to make a similar journey into the celestial realm. Who would? But I suspect that what we think it might do for us is a bit overblown. After all, it seems reasonable, does it not, that an experience of the magnitude Paul describes (vv. 1–4) would

---

[1] Much of this chapter has been adapted from my book *A Sincere and Pure Devotion to Christ: 100 Daily Meditations on 2 Corinthians*, 2 vols. (Wheaton, IL: Crossway, 2010), 2:214–31.

serve to subdue and perhaps even eradicate sinful impulses from his soul. How could sin possibly continue to exert its influence in the heart of a person who saw and heard the things Paul did? Surely anyone who had been blessed with such a stunning privilege as was Paul's would forever cease to sin. Surely anyone who had heard such transcendently glorious things as fell on the ears of the apostle would be set free from sinful ambition and self-aggrandizement. Well, not exactly.

It's nothing short of shocking that rather than being wholly sanctified by his transport into paradise, Paul was immediately stirred to pride. As he reflected on his experience, it seemed only natural for him to conclude: "I must be special! No one else that I know of has entered the third heaven. There's obviously something unique about me that captured God's attention and warranted his favor." Well, not exactly.

The result of his "visions and revelations" wasn't humility but hubris, not gratitude but presumption, not holiness but arrogance. This isn't to say that revelatory experiences are sinful—only that Paul was.

Have you ever prayed like this? "Oh, Father in heaven, if only you would transport me into your glorious presence, I am convinced that I would be able to overcome this sinful addiction with which I daily struggle. If only you would disclose to me the marvelous revelatory truths that Paul saw and heard, I would have strength to resist all sin. If only you would grant me an experience like his, I'm sure that I would be humbled beyond words and filled with gratitude to such a degree that the mere mention of sin would turn me away in disgust." Have you prayed that prayer? I hope not. Here's why:

> So to keep me from becoming conceited because of the surpass-ing greatness of the revelations, a thorn was given me in the flesh, a messenger of Satan to harass me, to keep me from be-coming conceited. Three times I pleaded with the Lord about this, that it should leave me. But he said to me, "My grace is sufficient for you, for my power is made perfect in weakness." Therefore I will boast all the more gladly of my weaknesses,

so that the power of Christ may rest upon me. For the sake of Christ, then, I am content with weaknesses, insults, hardships, persecutions, and calamities. For when I am weak, then I am strong. (2 Cor. 12:7–10)

It was *in order to prevent Paul from falling into pride* that he was given what someone has called "a bridle that held him back from haughtiness." Whatever Paul's thorn may have been, there can be no mistake about its purpose: "to keep me from becoming conceited" (v. 7). The thorn was no accident. God's hand was evident at every turn. As Paul Barnett notes, "This verse [v. 7] is powerfully intentional; each of these elements is purposive: the 'thorn' was given to Paul *lest* he be 'over-uplifted,' *to* buffet him, *lest* he be 'over-lifted.' It was God's will for Paul."[2]

Let's begin with a number of questions and observations.

First, *where did the "thorn" come from?* What is its source? Observe that the subject is left unexpressed: there "was given me" (v. 7). Most commentators recognize this as an example of what is called "the divine passive," in which God is the unidentified cause or hidden agent that accounts for certain events in human experience. It is a conventional use of the passive voice to avoid mentioning the divine name.

Had Paul wanted to say that Satan was the ultimate source, he probably would not have used the Greek verb *didōmi*, the word typically employed to indicate that God has bestowed some favor (cf. Gal. 3:21; Eph. 3:8; 6:19; 1 Tim. 4:14). If Satan were the ultimate source of the thorn, more appropriate Greek words were available to express that thought (e.g., *epitithēmi*, "lay upon"— Luke 10:30, 23:26, Acts 16:23; *ballō*, "cast"—Rev. 2:24; or *epiballō*, "put on"—1 Cor. 7:35).[3]

That God is the ultimate source of the thorn is also evident from its purpose, namely, to prevent Paul from being puffed up in pride. Satan would have loved nothing more than for Paul to feel elated, elite, and arrogant as a result of his experience. Whatever

---

[2] Paul Barnett, *The Second Epistle to the Corinthians* (Grand Rapids: Eerdmans, 1997), 567.
[3] See Ralph Martin, *2 Corinthians*, Word Biblical Commentary (Waco, TX: Word, 1986), 412.

Satan's role in the thorn may have been, you can rest assured it wasn't his design that Paul be kept humble!

But if the thorn was from God, why does Paul say it was "a messenger [lit., "angel"] of Satan"? We must remember that God often uses the Devil to accomplish his purposes (cf. Job; 1 Cor. 5:5). Although Satan and God work at cross purposes, they can both desire the same event to occur while hoping to accomplish through it antithetical results. Satan wanted to see Jesus crucified, as did God the Father (Isa. 53:10; Acts 2:23; 4:27–28), but for a different reason. The same is true in the case of Job. What Satan had hoped would destroy Job (or at least provoke him to blasphemy), God used to strengthen him.

The same is true here. Although we can't be sure, it seems likely that the demon was not acting consciously in the service of God. Most likely by God's secret and sovereign providence this demonic spirit was dispatched to Paul intent on oppressing and thereby hindering (or even destroying) his ministry. The *divine design*, however, was to keep Paul from sinful pride and to utilize this affliction to accomplish a higher spiritual good (cf. 2 Cor. 12:9–10).

Our second concern is with the *nature* of the "thorn." What exactly was it? We begin by noting that the word translated "thorn" is found only here in the New Testament. In classical Greek it was used with reference to a pointed stake on which the head of an enemy was impaled after decapitation, or in reference to spikes used to impede a siege force. More commonly, though, it simply referred to a splinter or thorn stuck in the body. Paul apparently envisioned himself impaled by this affliction, pinned to the ground, as it were, and thus rendered helpless by it. This must have been an excruciating condition, whatever it was, for the man who willingly endured the sufferings and anguish and deprivations listed in 2 Corinthians 11 would not petition the Lord so strenuously for the removal of some minor irritation that could be easily endured.

Note also that the *purpose* of the thorn was "to harass me, to keep me from becoming conceited" (2 Cor. 12:7). The verb "harass," also translated "buffet," means "to beat or strike a blow with a fist" (cf. Matt. 26:67). The present tense of the verb may be Paul's way of telling us that the affliction recurred periodically throughout his life and was even at this time bearing down heavily and painfully on him. This is confirmed in verse 8, where Paul says he prayed three times that he might be delivered. Perhaps the affliction had flared up on three distinct occasions when its humiliating effect would have been most evident. Or again, the reference to his three-fold prayer may simply be Paul's way of likening his suffering to that of Christ in Gethsemane, who also petitioned God three times but was not delivered.

Others explain the "three times" differently. According to Barnett, "three times" may be "a conventional symbol for repeated prayer. . . . Threefold actions appear to have been customary in matters relating to piety (cf. John 21:17; Acts 10:16); prayer was offered three times a day (Ps. 55:16–17; Dan. 6:10, 13)."[4]

Of greater importance is that the thorn was "in the flesh" (2 Cor. 12:7). The Greek permits either of two translations, depending on how one interprets Paul's use of the word "flesh." If "flesh" is a reference to his physical body or his "mortal existence," *in* the flesh is the appropriate rendering. That is to say, the thorn was embedded in his body; some sort of physical malady or some experience battered his body in an extremely painful way. However, if "flesh" refers to his fallen nature, *for* the flesh or *with regard to* the flesh would be more accurate. If one adopts the second view, Paul is more likely describing a thorn that was relational in nature (see below). John Calvin contends for a slightly different nuance:

> I for my part think that this phrase is meant to sum up all the different kinds of trial with which Paul was exercised. For here in my view flesh does not mean body, but rather the part of the soul which is not regenerate, so that the meaning would be, "To me there has been given a goad to jab at my flesh for I am not yet so spiritual as to be exempt from temptations according to the flesh."[5]

---

[4] Barnett, *The Second Epistle to the Corinthians,* 571.
[5] John Calvin, *The Second Epistle of Paul the Apostle to the Corinthians,* trans. T. A. Smail (Grand Rapids: Eerdmans, 1973), 159.

Four Understandings of Paul's Thorn in the Flesh

We now come to the question everyone asks: What exactly was the thorn? There are four broad categories in which we may classify the many and varied interpretations.

The Thorn as Sexual Lust

Roman Catholic interpreters have largely based their view on the Vulgate (or Latin) translation *stimulus carnis*, a "stimulus" to the flesh. Thus they take it to be a reference to inordinate sexual desire or lust.

But would God have told Paul to cease praying for deliverance from sexual lust? I don't think so. Would Paul have boasted about sexual weakness (2 Cor. 12:9)? Again, no. Would Paul have gladly acquiesced to its power in his life (vv. 9–10)? Absolutely not. Furthermore, this view conflicts with 1 Corinthians 7:1–9, where Paul refers to his having received the gift of celibacy, which at minimum would have entailed a greatly reduced (or at least controllable) sexual drive.

The Thorn as an Emotional or Psychological Problem

A second option is that the "thorn" was an emotional or psychological problem from which Paul couldn't shake free, perhaps hysteria, periodic bouts with depression, or debilitating feelings of insecurity. Although Paul does refer to his depressed state prior to the coming of Titus (2 Cor. 7:6), there is no indication this was a recurring problem for him (see esp. 2 Cor. 4:8; 6:10).

The Thorn as Paul's Enemies

Many take the view of Chrysostom, a famous preacher of the fourth century. He was the first to suggest that "thorn" is simply a reference to all *the enemies of the gospel* who opposed and persecuted Paul during his evangelistic and theological labors. Alexander the coppersmith and Hymenaeus and Philetus are among the first who come to mind (see 2 Tim. 2:17; 4:14). Taking the term "Satan" in its Hebraic sense of "adversary," "thorn in the flesh" would be a collective and figurative expression for all of Paul's opponents: those who contended with him and fought against him, those who cast him into prison, those who beat him and led him away to death. In effect, the "thorn" is a collective reference to all those who were responsible for the sufferings he describes in 2 Corinthians 11:23–33. R. V. G. Tasker takes this view and explains:

> As there is nothing which tends to elate a Christian evangelist so much as the enjoyment of spiritual experience, and as there is nothing so calculated to deflate the spiritual pride which may follow them as the opposition he encounters while preaching the word, it is not unlikely that Chrysostom's interpretation is nearer the truth than any other.[6]

Appeal is often made to 2 Corinthians 11:14–15, where Paul's opponents are described as the "servants" (lit., "ministers") of Satan, who is himself "an angel of light" (but note that in 12:7 the word is "messenger," not "servant"). We are also reminded that in the LXX this word translated "thorn" is twice used metaphorically of one's enemies (Num. 33:55; Ezek. 28:24). Thus, on this view when Paul speaks of his "thorn," he means something similar to our modern idiom "a pain in the neck."

If this is the correct interpretation, the word "flesh" would then be a figurative expression referring neither primarily to his physical body nor to his fallen nature but simply to himself—to who he is and what he does as a minister of the gospel, to his whole earthly existence. Paul would be saying in effect, "These enemies are a constant source of pain and inconvenience to me; they are an irritating thorn in my side."

A related view is that of Barnett, who contends that the thorn refers not so much to Paul's enemies in general but to the Judaizing, anti-Paul movement, which was so obviously present and active in Corinth. Craig Keener also believes this view to be the likely one: "It is not difficult to envision 'an angel of Satan' stirring crowds to persecute Paul; it is also possible that the opposition

---

[6] R. V. G. Tasker, *The Second Epistle of Paul to the Corinthians* (Grand Rapids: Eerdmans, 1977), 176.

includes the agents of Satan against whom Paul has been railing ([2 Cor.] 11:13–15)."[7]

Others have rejected this suggestion (rightly so, in my opinion), contending that it is unlikely Paul would have said that God gave him something as evil as the Judaizing movement. Furthermore, it seems reasonable to conclude that the thorn was given to Paul immediately subsequent to the heavenly rapture. The latter occurred in AD 41–42, but Paul did not enter Corinth and encounter opposition there until some eight to nine years later.

There are other insurmountable problems with this interpretation.

1. The singular "a messenger of Satan" of verse 7 and the singular "it" or even "he" of verse 8 are hardly clear and unmistakable ways to refer to an entire group of people. If Paul had his opponents in mind, he chose an especially obscure way to make his point.

2. Paul has already said in 2 Corinthians 4:7–15; 6:9–10; and 11:23–28 that opposition and persecution are normal for *every* person in ministry. No servant of Christ is exempt from such resistance. Yet, Paul describes his thorn as something *uniquely* his, given to him for a particular reason subsequent to a truly *singular* event. Is it likely that Paul would have prayed to be delivered from an experience that was the common and expected lot of all who shared his faith? I don't think so.

3. Most decisive against this view is that Paul says he received the thorn "fourteen years ago" (12:2). Since we know that 2 Corinthians was written in either late AD 55 or early 56, Paul could have received his thorn no earlier than AD 41–42 (at which time he would have been in his native Syria-Cilicia—Acts 9:29–30; 11:25; Gal. 1:18, 21; 2:1), a full eight years after his conversion to Christ (assuming, as most scholars do, that Paul was converted in c. AD 33). Yet we know from Acts 9:23–30 and elsewhere that Paul encountered Satanically inspired opposition to his ministry from the moment of his conversion.

4. Finally, as Ralph Martin puts it, "would the apostle pray to be spared persecution? This is doubtful, since persecution was

---

[7] Craig S. Keener, *1–2 Corinthians* (Cambridge: Cambridge University Press, 2005), 240.

the fuel on which Paul seemed to thrive. The more he was perse-cuted, the more he seemed determined to press the claims of his apostolate."[8] And Paul knew better than anyone else (cf. 2 Cor. 2:12–17) that the success of the gospel was not in his power to control, but rested with the providential oversight of God.

On the other hand, Paul did solicit prayers for protection from those who were his enemies (see Rom. 15:30–31; 2 Thess. 3:1–2; cf. 2 Tim. 3:10–11; 4:16–18). Perhaps we should understand this to mean that whereas Paul anticipated persecution everywhere he went and knew that it was an inescapable part of his calling, he asked others to pray that this opposition not result in the silencing of his voice or perhaps the loss of life.

One more comment is in order. My sense is that the primary reason many have embraced this view is that they are uncomfort-able with the idea that God would afflict any of his children (and certainly not an obedient and faithful apostle like Paul) with a disease and then decline to answer their prayer for healing. They also struggle with the notion that disease or a lingering and painful physical malady of any sort can have a redemptive or sanctifying purpose in God's economy.

The Thorn as a Physical Affliction

But we must not allow a theological presupposition to dictate what the biblical text can or cannot mean. The data in the text itself must determine the most likely interpretation. And when all is said and done, I'm persuaded that the "thorn" is a reference to some form of physical affliction.

A few have argued that it was a speech impediment, possi-bly a severe stutter (2 Cor. 10:10; 11:6). But Paul readily denies dependence on rhetorical eloquence. Furthermore, if Paul stut-tered or had a more severe form of speech impediment, it was most likely something he had from childhood. Yet, he says here that the thorn came in response to his heavenly experience only fourteen years earlier.

---

[8] Martin, *2 Corinthians*, 415.

Other suggestions offered down through the centuries include epilepsy, malaria, gallstones, kidney stones, gout, deafness, dental infection, rheumatism, earaches, headaches, sciatica, arthritis, and leprosy (has anything been left out?).

Many have adopted the view that Paul suffered from a severe case of ophthalmia or conjunctivitis. In Galatians 4:13–15 he says:

> You know it was because of a bodily ailment that I preached the gospel to you at first, and though my condition was a trial to you, you did not scorn or despise me, but received me as an angel of God, as Christ Jesus. What then has become of the blessing you felt? For I testify to you that, if possible, you would have gouged out your eyes and given them to me.

Evidently Paul suffered from a painful eye affliction that was especially humiliating because loathsome and repulsive to others. Although the statement in verse 15 may only be figurative, emphasizing the sacrificial love the Galatians had for Paul, it is just as likely an indication that this distressing illness from which he suffered was related to his eyes. We should also note that Paul closes his letter to the Galatians by saying, "See with what large letters I am writing to you with my own hand" (6:11), a statement consistent with his suffering some sort of ophthalmic disorder.

Could it be that Paul contracted this eye affliction as a direct result of the visionary experience itself? Might the brightness of the experience, the impact of what he saw, have damaged his eyes? Some argue that he suffered from something similar to solar retinitis, an affliction caused by staring improperly at an eclipse.

Yet Another View

There is another interpretation of Paul's thorn that I mention here only to show the extremes to which some people will go in their attempt to make the text say what they *want* it so say. Charles Capps, for example, offers a totally fanciful interpretation of the purpose of the thorn.

According to Capps, when Paul says "to keep me from becoming conceited because of the surpassing greatness of the revelations," he is referring

> to the fact that if it had not been for the messenger of Satan as-signed against Paul to stir up trouble, to cause him problems everywhere he preached, Paul's revelations would have been ex-alted till they would have influenced the whole nation. But he was not able to preach them freely, for Satan hindered him on every hand.[9]

But note that it was *Paul* who was inclined to self-exaltation, not his "revelations." Perhaps what Capps means is that Paul would himself have been exalted above measure in the sense that every-one would have listened to his gospel and would have accepted it as true had not Satan prevented it from happening. But this is in conflict with the fact that this "revelation" Paul received was never intended to be proclaimed to others. He heard "things that cannot be told, which man may not utter" (2 Cor. 12:4).

It would seem that in his attempt to evade the force of this passage, Capps has turned it upside down. In other words, Capps argues that Paul's thorn in the flesh was not a good thing to keep him from doing a bad thing (namely, be puffed up in pride), but a bad thing to keep him from doing a good thing (namely, proclaim the "revelations" he received in paradise). Of course, in saying the thorn was a *good* thing I'm not suggesting it was inherently good, but only that it was designed by God to accomplish something ben-eficial in Paul's spiritual growth.

Conclusion

Many have noted (and I agree) that there was great pastoral wis-dom in Paul's decision not to identify the thorn in the flesh. If he had been any more specific as to its nature, those who themselves have never suffered from the same affliction could easily conclude that the passage has no bearing on their lives. But because he left the door open, so to speak, concerning the nature of the thorn, each

---

[9] Charles Capps, *Paul's Thorn in the Flesh* (Dallas: Word of Faith, 1983), 14.

of us is able to identify with Paul's struggle and to learn and grow from the way in which he yielded to the sovereignty and sufficiency of divine grace.

Recommended Reading

Schreiner, Thomas R. *Paul: Apostle of God's Glory in Christ, A Pauline Theology*. Downers Grove, IL: InterVarsity, 2001.

Storms, Sam. *A Sincere and Pure Devotion to Christ: 100 Daily Meditations on 2 Corinthians*. 2 vols. Wheaton, IL: Crossway, 2010.

Warrington, Keith. *Healing and Suffering: Biblical and Pastoral Reflections*. Waynesboro, GA: Paternoster, 2005.

22

Is There Healing in the Atonement?

One of the more divisive issues that I regularly confront in the body of Christ is whether it is always God's will to heal the sick. Some argue quite energetically that everything necessary for the healing of our bodies was achieved by Christ on the cross. To put it simply, God has already done everything he will ever do to make it possible for you to experience physical healing. If you are not healed, it isn't because God does not will it but because you do not believe it. Healing has been secured for us in the atonement of Jesus, and it is ours either to ignore or, in faith, lay hold of.

The Case from Isaiah 53:4–5

Perhaps the primary biblical passage cited in this regard is found in the prophecy of Isaiah, where he speaks of the suffering of the Messiah for his people:

> Surely he has borne our griefs
>   and carried our sorrows;
> yet we esteemed him stricken,
>   smitten by God, and afflicted.

But he was pierced for our transgressions;
  he was crushed for our iniquities;
upon him was the chastisement that brought us peace,
  and with his wounds we are healed. (Isa. 53:4–5)

It is not only those who identify with the Word of Faith and "health and wealth" wings of the Pentecostal-charismatic renewal who answer our question with a simple but very loud *yes!* Let's begin by noting what several say about this text. A. J. Gordon writes:

The yoke of his cross by which he lifted our iniquities took hold also of our diseases so that it is in some sense true that as God "made him to be sin for us who knew no sin," so *he made him to be sick for us* who knew no sickness. He who entered into mysterious sympathy with our pain which is the fruit of sin, also put himself underneath our pain which is the penalty of sin. In other words the passage seems to teach that *Christ endured vicariously our diseases as well as our iniquities.* If now it be true that our Redeemer and substitute bore our sicknesses, it would be natural to reason at once that he bore them that we might not bear them.[1]

Gloria Copeland agrees with Gordon. She says: "Jesus bore your sicknesses and carried your diseases at the same time and *in the same manner* that He bore your sins. You are just as free from sickness and disease as you are free from sin. You should be as quick to cease sickness and disease in your body as you are to cease sin."[2]

Colin Urquhart concurs:

When Jesus stood bearing the lashes from the Roman soldiers, all our physical pain and sicknesses were being heaped upon him. . . . It is as if one lash was for cancer, another for bone disease, another for heart disease, and so on. Everything that causes physical pain was laid on Jesus as the nails were driven into His hands and feet.[3]

---

[1] Quoted in Henry W. Frost, *Miraculous Healing* (Grand Rapids: Zondervan, 1972), 42 (emphasis mine).
[2] Gloria Copeland, *And Jesus Healed Them All* (Fort Worth: KCP, 1984), 2 (emphasis mine).
[3] Colin Urquhart, *Receive Your Healing* (London: Hodder and Stoughton, 1986), 38.

What is being said is that *Christ bore our sicknesses in the very same way that he bore our sins.* Just as God made Jesus to be sin for us, he also "made him to be sick for us." Supposedly, in a way rarely if ever explained, Jesus vicariously endured our diseases as well as our iniquities.

The Difference between Sin and Sickness

We know what the apostle Paul meant when he wrote in 2 Corinthians 5:21 that God "made him [Jesus] to be sin who knew no sin." He was declaring that the guilt of our sins was imputed to Christ and that it was because of that guilt that he was punished in our place. But what can it possibly mean to say that God made him "to be sick" on our behalf? Kenneth Hagin says that God "made him [Jesus] sick with your diseases that you might be perfectly well in Christ."[4]

But there is no guilt in disease or sickness. Having diabetes or a head cold is not sinful. The Bible tells us to pray, "forgive us our debts" and urges us "to confess our sins," but nowhere does it say that we should pray, "forgive us our arthritis," or, "Lord, I confess that I have the flu." *Sickness is not sin.* The Bible never issues the command "Thou shalt not commit cancer" or "Flee the flu." Nevertheless, many insist that Jesus bore the penalty for our sins and sicknesses. But if sickness is not a sin, how can it incur a penalty?

Of course, ultimately all sickness is a result of sin, in that Adam's fall introduced corruption and death into the human race. But that does not mean that every time we get sick, it is because of some specific sin we have committed. It does mean that had Adam not sinned, there would be no sickness. Sickness is the effect of sin (just like tornadoes, weeds, and sadness). But that is altogether different from saying that sickness *is* sin. We do not repent for having kidney stones, nor do we come under conviction for catching the measles. I didn't rebuke my daughter for coming down with the chicken pox, and I certainly didn't tell her younger sister to ask for forgiveness when she caught it from her. Jesus was not punished

---

[4] Kenneth E. Hagin, *Healing Belongs to Us* (Tulsa: Faith Library, 1969), 16.

for our diseases. Rather, he endured the wrath of God that was provoked by our willful disobedience of the truth.

Isaiah's Meaning

So what does it mean in Isaiah 53 when it says that he bore our sicknesses and carried our pains and that by his stripes we are healed? I believe we have in this passage a kind of figure of speech frequently found in Scripture and in everyday conversation. It is called a *metonomy*. For example, we read in Luke 16:29, "But Abraham said, 'They have Moses and the Prophets, let them hear them.'" What is meant is that they have the Scriptures written by Moses and the prophets. Moses and the prophets themselves, obviously, have long since died. The author has put the cause (Moses and the prophets) in place of the effect (the Scriptures), and this is called *a metonomy of cause for effect*. Had the figure of speech not been used, the passage would have read, "But Abraham said, 'They have the Old Testament Scriptures (of which Moses and the prophets are the cause or authors); let them hear them.'"

In 1 Peter 2:24 the apostle writes, "He himself bore our sins in his body on the tree." This is another example of metonomy, where the cause (our sin) is put in place of the effect (penal judgment). Christ "bore our sins" in the sense that he bore the wrath of God of which our sins were the cause. We use this figure of speech all the time without knowing it. Have you ever said to someone, "Don't give me any of your lip!"? What you really meant was, "Don't use your lip(s) (or mouth) to give me any back talk." Dozens of other examples from both Scripture and everyday speech could be cited (see esp. Col. 3:5; 1 Thess. 5:19).

Then there is the flip side, as it were, in which the effect is put in place of the cause. Having seen the baby Jesus, Simeon declared, "My eyes have seen your salvation" (Luke 2:30). That is, in seeing the cause of salvation (Jesus), Simeon saw the effect (salvation). Or again, Jesus said to Martha, "I am the resurrection and the life" (John 11:25). The effects (resurrection and life) are put in place of the cause (Jesus's work and ministry).

In the case of Isaiah 53 we have an example of this latter form of metonomy, in which the effect is put for the cause. Sin is the ultimate cause, of which illness is one among many effects. Jesus bore our sicknesses in the sense that he was punished for the sin that causes sickness. He carried our pains, not in the sense of personally experiencing stomach viruses and ulcers and earaches and gallstones as he hung on Calvary's tree, but by enduring the wrath of God against that willful human wickedness which is ultimately the reason there are such things as pain and infirmity. By his death at his first coming he has laid the foundation for the ultimate overthrow and annihilation of all physical disease, which will occur with the resurrection of the body at his second coming. Thus it is theologically misleading to say that Jesus bore our sicknesses in the same way he bore our sins. Rather he paid the price of the latter (sin) in order that one day, when he returns to glorify his people, he may wholly do away with the former (sickness).

The Atonement and Healing

May we conclude that there is healing in the atonement? Of course! Were it not for Jesus making atonement for sin, we would have no hope of healing in any form, either now or later. The redemptive suffering of Jesus at Calvary is the foundation and source of every blessing, whether spiritual or physical.

Perhaps it would be more accurate to say that there is healing *through* the atonement rather than *in* the atonement, insofar as the atoning death of Jesus is the *basis* for our healing. In this way we avoid suggesting that because of Jesus's death we are *guaranteed* healing *in this life*. Thus, to ask, Is there healing in the atonement? is like asking, Is there forgiveness of sins in the atonement? or, Is there fellowship with God in the atonement? There is even a sense in which we may say that the Holy Spirit is in the atonement! We are told in John 14:16–17, 26; 15:26; and especially 16:7–15, that the Holy Spirit's present ministry is a result of the death, resurrection, and exaltation of Jesus.

Everything we receive from God finds its ultimate source in what Christ did for us on the cross. Therefore, the question is not whether our bodies receive healing because of the atonement of Christ, but *when*. We are forgiven of our sins now because of Christ's atoning death, but we await the consummation of our deliverance from the presence of sin when Christ returns. We experience fellowship with God now because of Christ's atoning death, but we await the consummation of that blessed relationship when Christ returns. We profit immensely now from the Spirit's work in our hearts, but who would dare suggest that what the Holy Spirit is doing in this age is all he will ever do? There is a glorious harvest reserved in heaven for us of which the present ministry of the Holy Spirit is merely the firstfruits!

In other words, it is a serious mistake for us to think that every blessing Christ secured through his redemptive suffering will be ours now *in its consummate form*. All such blessings shall indeed be ours—let there be no mistake about that. But let us not expect, far less demand, that we experience *fully* those blessings now which God has clearly reserved for heaven in the age to come.

Life for the believer in this present age is a life of tension between the *already* and the *not yet*. We already have so very, very much. But we have not yet experienced it all. There is much yet to come. One "not yet" in Christian experience is the complete redemption and glorification of the body. "But our citizenship is in heaven," says Paul, "and from it we await a Savior, the Lord Jesus Christ, who will transform our lowly body to be like his glorious body, by the power that enables him even to subject all things to himself" (Phil. 3:20–21).

Paul tells us in Romans 8:18–25 that the consummation of our adoption as God's children, which he defines as the redemption of our bodies, is something we eagerly and anxiously await; it is a future experience for which we in the present "groan" (Rom. 8:23) in holy expectation. To insist that this physical blessing is future is not to detract from the efficacy or value of Christ's atoning work, nor to deny that God often heals (at times partially, at times wholly) now. It is simply to recognize, as Scripture does, that God's timing is often different from ours.

We must now take note of Matthew 8:16–17. We are told that Jesus "healed all who were sick" and that "this was to fulfill what was spoken by the prophet Isaiah: 'He took our illnesses and bore our diseases.'" Are these healings, performed by Jesus, *in the atonement*? Yes. To whatever degree we experience healing in this life, it is the fruit of Christ's atoning death. But it does not necessarily follow that where there is atonement there is *always* an immediate healing. This passage in Matthew affirms that whatever healing does occur comes as a result of Christ's redemptive work. But it does not necessarily mean that healing will always occur now as a result of that work.

In the case of 1 Peter 2:24 we have something different. As we saw earlier, frequently in Scripture the sinful condition of the soul is portrayed as analogous to a body suffering from various wounds. Forgiveness and restoration are therefore described in terms of a bodily healing. The apostle portrays us in our sin as if we were a wounded body in need of physical healing. By his atoning death the Great Physician has truly "healed" our hearts. We were continually straying like sheep, but by the redemptive grace of Jesus we have been enabled to return to the shepherd and guardian of our souls (1 Pet. 2:25). Thus the context of 1 Peter 2:24 clearly tells us that it is primarily spiritual healing from the disease of sin, not physical restoration of the body, that the apostle has in mind. The sickness or affliction is that of our having strayed from God. The disease or illness is that of our having departed from him. The healing provided by Christ, therefore, is his bringing us back to God and restoring our relationship with him.[5]

Conclusion

We must never cease to pray for the sick to be healed. We must continually give thanks that there is bodily healing for us in the atonement of Jesus Christ. We must forever acknowledge that whatever healing and health we experience now is a blessing that flows from Calvary's tree. But let us also remember that there are certain blessings that God intends to bestow in their consummate

---

[5] This is clearly the case in our passage when we take note of the word "for" with which v. 25 begins. The word "for" or "because" indicates that the "healing" in v. 24 is from the punishment we deserved for the wandering in v. 25.

fullness only when the Lord Jesus returns. Until then we weep, suffer, and die. On that glorious day when the Savior appears, then shall come to pass the words of Revelation 21:3–4:

> And I heard a loud voice from the throne saying, "Behold, the dwelling place of God is with man. He will dwell with them, and they will be his people, and God himself will be with them as their God. He will wipe away every tear from their eyes, and death shall be no more, neither shall there be mourning, nor crying, nor pain anymore, for the former things have passed away."

Recommended Reading

Brown, Michael L. *Israel's Divine Healer*. Grand Rapids: Zondervan, 1995.

Carson, D. A. *How Long, O Lord? Reflections on Suffering and Evil*. Grand Rapids: Baker, 2006.

Wimber, John, with Kevin Springer. *Power Healing*. San Francisco: Harper & Row, 1987.

23

Why Doesn't God Always Heal the Sick?

God loved the apostle Paul. Yet God sovereignly orchestrated Paul's painful thorn in the flesh and then declined to remove it, notwithstanding Paul's passionate prayer that he be healed. We are not apostles. Yet, God loves us as his children, no less than he loved Paul. We don't know the nature of Paul's thorn (although see chap. 21 for an attempt to identify it), but each of us has undoubtedly suffered in a similar way, and some considerably worse. We, like Paul, have prayed incessantly to be healed. Or perhaps knowing of a loved one's "thorn," we have prayed for him or her. And again, as with Paul, God declined to remove it. Why?

It's hard to imagine a more difficult, confusing, and controversial topic than why God chooses not to heal in response to the intercessory pleas of his people. I don't profess to have all the answers, but I think I've got a few. I'm sure that this chapter will provoke many to anger and frustration, while others, I pray, will find a measure of comfort.

In the final analysis, virtually everything about healing remains a mystery. I don't mind saying that I'm weary of those who claim to reduce healing to a formula or a manageable cause-and-effect phenomenon in which we can know with certainty why some are healed and why others are not. I labor in this chapter to avoid falling into that trap. That said, I would like to suggest that the reason why many are not healed may *possibly* be answered in any of seven ways.

Seven Possible Answers

1. Although we must not give more weight to the role of faith than does the New Testament itself, we must be willing to acknowledge that occasionally healing does not occur because of the absence of that sort of faith that God delights to honor. This does *not* mean that every time a person isn't healed, it is because of a defective faith, as if healing inevitably follows a robust and doubt-free faith. But it does mean that faith is very important. How can we conclude otherwise in view of the many texts that closely link healing to someone's faith? I hope you'll take the time to pause and read these passages: Matthew 9:22, 28–29; 15:28; Mark 2:5, 11; 5:34; 9:17–24; Mark 10:52; Luke 17:19; Acts 3:16; 14:8–10; James 5:14–16.

In my book on spiritual gifts,[1] I ask, "Why did Jesus emphasize faith?" Neither he nor his Father needs it. They could have orchestrated life such that something other than faith would be the condition on which they would heal. They are not hampered by the faithlessness or prayerlessness of the sick person or those who pray for his or her healing. The reason Jesus emphasized is this: *faith glorifies God.* Faith points us away from ourselves to him. Faith turns us away from our own power and resources to his. Faith says: "Lord, I am nothing and you are everything. I entrust myself to your care. I cling to you alone. My confidence is in your word and character no matter what happens."

Faith is not a weapon by which we demand things from God or put him in subjection to us. Faith is an act of self-denial. Faith is a renunciation of one's ability to do anything and a confession that God can do everything. Faith derives its power *not from the spiri-*

---

[1] Sam Storms, *The Beginner's Guide to Spiritual Gifts*, 2nd ed. (Ventura, CA: Gospel Light, 2013).

tual energy of the person who believes, but from the supernatural efficacy of the person who is believed: God! It is not faith's *act* but its *object* that accounts for the miraculous.

2. Sometimes healing does not occur because of the presence of sin for which there has been no confession or repentance. James 5:15–16 clearly instructs us to confess our sins to one another and pray for one another that we may be healed. Again, please do not conclude from this that each time a person isn't healed it is because he or she has committed but not repented of some specific sin. But in *some* cases (not necessarily all) this is undoubtedly true. We have to reckon with the possibility that lingering bitterness, anger, resentment, envy, or unforgiveness in our hearts is the reason why God withholds physical healing from our bodies.

3. Odd as it may sound to hear it, healing may not happen because the sick don't want it to happen. Jesus asked the paralyzed man in John 5:6, "Do you want to be healed?" What on the surface may appear to be a ridiculous question is, on further examination, found to be profoundly insightful.

Some people who suffer from a chronic affliction become accustomed to their illness and to the pattern of life it requires. Their identity is to a large extent wrapped up in their physical disability. I realize that sounds strange to those of us who enjoy robust health. Why would anyone prefer to stay sick? Who wouldn't jump at the opportunity to be healed? But I've actually known a handful of folk who in a very real sense enjoy their dependence on others and the special attention it brings them. They are convinced that the only reason people take note of them and show them kindness and compassion is their affliction. They fear that if they were healed, they would lose the love on which they've come to depend. To them, remaining sick is a small price to pay to retain the kindness and involvement of those who otherwise would simply ignore them.

Then, of course, in some instances people don't want the responsibilities that would come with being healthy. To their way of thinking, it's easier (and perhaps even more profitable) to remain the object of others' beneficence and good will than it would be to be healthy and thus expected to get a job and show up nine to five on a daily basis. This is not a common phenomenon, but it does happen in a few cases.

4. We must also consider the principle articulated in James 4:2, where we are told that "you do not have, because you do not ask." The simple fact is that some are not healed because they do not pray. Perhaps they pray once or twice, and then allow discouragement to paralyze their petitions. Prayer for healing often must be prolonged, sustained, persevering, and combined with fasting.

5. Some are not healed because the demonic cause of the affliction has not been addressed. Please do not jump to unwarranted conclusions. I am *not* suggesting that all physical disease is demonically induced. Of course, it is interesting, is it not, that in Paul's case God used "a messenger of Satan" to inflict the thorn? There is also the case of the woman in Luke 13, who had "a disabling spirit [or, a spirit of infirmity] for eighteen years. She was bent over and could not fully straighten herself" (Luke 13:11). According to Jesus, "Satan" had "bound" her (Luke 13:16; see also Acts 10:38). It takes considerable discernment, time, and patience to determine whether an illness has a demonic cause, together with even greater commitment to praying for the individual in question and leading him or her to address the reasons for such spiritual oppression. When these factors are ignored, healing may not be forthcoming.

6. We must also consider the mystery of divine providence. There are undoubtedly times and seasons in the purposes of God during which his healing power is withdrawn or at least largely diminished. God may have any number of reasons for this to which we are not privy, whether to discipline a wayward and rebellious church or to create a greater desperation for his power or to wean us off excessive dependence on physical comfort and convenience or any number of other possibilities. If this leaves you confused, that's why it's called a mystery!

But what must we say when the problem isn't the absence of faith or the presence of a demon or the refusal to repent or the failure to pray or a lack of desire? How then do we account for ongoing physical affliction, as in Paul's case? I strongly urge you to read the next point carefully.

7. Oftentimes there are dimensions of spiritual growth and moral development and increase in the knowledge of God in us that he desires *more* than our physical health, experiences that in his wisdom God has determined can *only* be attained by means or in the midst of or in response to less-than-perfect physical health. In other words, healing the sick *is* a *good* thing (and we should never cease to pray for it), but often there is a *better* thing that can be attained only by means of physical weakness.

More important to God than our physical health is our spiritual holiness. This isn't to say that the body is unimportant. God isn't a gnostic! He values and has redeemed our bodies and now dwells within them as his eternal temple. But while we live in this corrupt and decaying world, inner and spiritual conformity to the image of Christ often comes only at the expense of or at least simultaneous with physical deterioration and suffering (see 2 Cor. 4:16–18).

Let me personalize this principle. If I believe Romans 8:28, that God sovereignly orchestrates all events in my life for my ultimate spiritual good (and preeminently for his ultimate glory), I can only conclude that, all things being equal, if I'm not healed *it is because God values something in me greater than my physical comfort and health* that he, in his infinite wisdom and kindness, knows can be attained only by means of my physical affliction and the lessons of submission, dependency, and trust in God that I learn from it.

Conclusion

In the final analysis, we may never know why a person isn't healed. What, then, ought to be our response? In the first place, don't stop praying! Some people find this difficult to swallow. Many times I've been asked, Why should Paul bother to pray for release from something that God wills to inflict? The answer is that *Paul didn't know* what God's will was in this particular case until such time as God chose to make it known. And neither do you or I with regard to any particular illness we may suffer.

If the Lord had never said in response to Paul's prayer, "No, it isn't my will that you be relieved of this thorn," Paul would have been justified, indeed *required*, to continue to pray for his healing. I once heard my friend Jack Taylor put it this way: "Never cease praying for healing until you are shown otherwise either by divine revelation or by death!" If, like Paul, you are able to discern, through some prophetic disclosure or other legitimate biblical means, that it is not God's will now or ever to heal you, you may cease asking him to do so. Otherwise, short of death itself, you must persevere in prayer. You never know but that God's long-term will for you is complete healing after he has for a season accomplished his short-term sanctifying purpose.

In Paul's case, the only reason he ceased asking for deliverance was that God, in effect, told him to shut up! "No, Paul. I'm not going to heal you. It isn't my will in this instance that you be set free from this affliction. Rather, I have a higher purpose in view: your humility and my Son's glory manifest in the context of your ongoing weakness." And Paul in effect replied: "Okay, Lord, I'll shut up and submit to your merciful purpose in my life. I know you love me and desire what is ultimately of greatest good for my spiritual growth. Therefore, my prayer now is that you maximize in me the beneficial effects of this pain. Don't let me miss out on any spiritual good that might come my way from this malady. Teach me everything I need to know, and sustain me that I might be a platform for the glory of Christ and a source of comfort to other suffering saints."

I'm sure there are other ways to account for why God chooses not to heal, but I trust that these have proved helpful. There is much I do not know about this matter, but of this I'm quite certain: God's grace is sufficient in all circumstances so that we, "for the sake of Christ" (2 Cor. 12:10), might learn that in our weakness his power is made perfect!

Recommended Reading

Lawrence, Peter. *The Spirit Who Heals*. Eastbourne, UK: Kingsway, 2006.

Storms, Sam. *The Beginner's Guide to Spiritual Gifts*. 2nd ed. Ventura, CA: Gospel Light, 2013.

Tada, Joni Eareckson. *A Step Further*. Grand Rapids: Zondervan, 1978.

24

What Is Legalism?

The word *freedom* has a variety of meanings for a variety of people. To a man imprisoned for armed robbery, it means early release from prison. To a small businessman, it may be defined in purely economic terms. To someone in a formerly communist-bloc country, it may mean the absence of social and political oppression. But what does freedom mean to the Christian? What does it mean to you?

In Galatians 5:13 Paul says, "For you were called to freedom, brothers. Only do not use your freedom as an opportunity for the flesh, but through love serve one another." Why did God the Father set his saving love on you? Why did God the Son die for you? Why did God the Holy Spirit call you to faith in that sacrifice? Freedom!

For the Christian, freedom means one of three things. There is, first of all, *freedom from the condemnation of God's wrath*. This is what Paul has in mind in Romans 8:1 when he declares, "There is therefore now no condemnation for those who are in Christ Jesus." Second, there is *freedom from the compulsion of sin*. Romans 6:14 assures us that "sin will have no dominion" over us since we "are not under law but under grace." Then, third, there is *freedom from the conscience of other people*, which is the primary theme of the fourteenth chapter of Romans. It is on the third of these manifestations of Christian freedom that I want to concentrate.

The Threat of Legalism

There are people, professing Christian people, who are determined to bring you under their religious thumb. They are bent on making you a slave of their conscience. They have built a tidy religious box, without biblical justification, and strive to stuff you inside and make you conform to its dimensions. They are legalists, and their tools are guilt, fear, intimidation, and self-righteousness. They proclaim God's unconditional love for you, but insist on certain conditions before including you among the accepted, approved elite of God's favored few.

I'm not talking about people who insist that you obey certain laws or moral rules in order to be saved. Such people aren't legalists. They are lost! They are easily identified and rebuffed. I'm talking about Christian legalists whose goal is to enforce conformity among other Christians in accordance with their personal preferences. These are *lifestyle legalists*. They threaten to rob you of joy and to squeeze the intimacy out of your relationship with Jesus. They may even lead you to doubt your salvation. They heap condemnation and contempt on your head so that your life is controlled and energized by fear rather than freedom and joy and delight in God.

Rarely would these folk ever admit to any of this. They don't perceive or portray themselves as legalists. If they are reading this, they are probably convinced I'm talking about someone else. They'd never introduce themselves: "Hi! My name is Joe. I'm a legalist and my goal is to steal your joy and keep you in bondage to my religious prejudices. Would you like to go to lunch after church today and let me tell you all the things you're doing wrong?"

I suspect that some of you are either legalists or, more likely, the victims of legalism. You live in fear of doing something that another Christian considers unholy, even though the Bible is silent on the subject. You are terrified of incurring others' disapproval, disdain, and ultimate rejection. Worse still, you fear God's rejection for your violating religious traditions or cultural norms that have no basis in Scripture but are prized by the legalist. You have been duped into believing that the slightest misstep or mistake will bring down God's disapproval and disgust.

When you are around other Christians, whether in church or a home group or just hanging out, do you feel free? Does your spirit feel relaxed or oppressed? Do you sense their acceptance or condemnation? Do you feel judged, inadequate, inferior, guilty, immature, all because of your perceived failure to conform to what someone else regards as "holy"? Jesus wants to set you free from such bondage! As Paul said, "you were called to freedom"!

Defining Legalism

Legalism has been defined in a number of ways, but here is my attempt: *Legalism is the tendency to regard as divine law things that God has neither required nor forbidden in Scripture, and the corresponding inclination to look with suspicion on others for their failure or refusal to conform.* One might also call this a religious spirit insofar as man-made religion and legalism go hand in hand. It all comes down to this: I create rules and expectations not found in the Bible and then feel good about myself and my relationship with God for having obeyed them, all the while I judge others for having failed to live up to this artificial standard of godliness.

So, how do I know whether I'm a legalist? Here is a simple test consisting of five questions.

1. *Do you place a higher value on church customs than on biblical principles?* Many of our so-called rights and wrongs in church life are products not of the Bible, but of family background, culture, social and economic factors, geographical locale, and a long-standing institutional commitment to doing things the way they've always been done. Once again, as long as the Bible doesn't prohibit such practices, you may well be free to pursue them. But you are not free to insist that others do so as well.

2. *Do you elevate to the status of moral law something the Bible does not require?* Let me mention just a few examples.

Whereas the Bible explicitly forbids drunkenness, it nowhere requires total abstinence. Make no mistake: total abstinence from alcohol is great. As a Christian you are certainly free to adopt that as a lifestyle. But you are not free to condemn those who choose to drink in moderation. You may discuss with them the wisdom of such a choice and the practical consequences of it, but you must not condemn them as sub-spiritual or as falling short of God's best.

The Bible encourages modesty in dress. Both men and women are to be careful not to dress in a way that flaunts their sexuality or is unnecessarily ostentatious and seductive. But we have no right to condemn others for their wearing of colorful clothing or the use of makeup or a particular hairstyle.

The Bible condemns lust in no uncertain terms. But the legalist uses this to condemn as unholy everything from television to the Internet to movies (even PG) to mixed swimming. Make no mistake: you may be significantly better off by severely curtailing your use of TV and the Internet, and I strongly advise that you be more discerning than ever when it comes to trash from Hollywood that often passes for "art." But these forms of media can also be powerful tools for the expression of kingdom truths when wisely utilized.

Parents are to raise their kids in the nurture and admonition of the Lord. About that there is no mistake. As a parent, you may believe that all public schools are tools of the Devil and cesspools of secular humanism. It is certainly your right to hold that opinion and make your decisions concerning your child's education accordingly. But you have no biblical right to question the spirituality of Christian parents who hold a different view. Whether you educate your children at home or send them to a private school or public school is a matter on which Scripture is silent. Hold your conviction with passion and zeal, but do not seek to enslave the consciences of others who may disagree with you.

The Bible commands weekly gatherings for prayer, Bible study, worship, and celebration of the sacraments. But the legalist condemns as carnal anyone who ever, for any reason, misses a Sunday service or dares to watch a football game in the afternoon or chooses to mow the lawn after church. If you prefer not to work on Sunday or watch athletic events or perform household chores, that's wonderful. But don't condemn others who differ. Why? Because God doesn't condemn them.

Let's take a moment and explore this Sabbath issue in a bit more detail. Do you recall the incident when Jesus and his disciples were walking through the grain fields on a Sabbath day (Mark 2:23–28) and "began to pluck heads of grain" (v. 23)? The Pharisees went ballistic: "Look, why are they doing what is not lawful on the Sabbath?" (v. 24).

The Old Testament Sabbath law wasn't all that complicated. Six days were to be set aside for work, but on the seventh day, the Sabbath, no work was to be done. The people of Israel were to rest. The Old Testament, however, gave very few details as to what actually constituted the kind of "work" that was forbidden on the Sabbath. So the Jewish rabbis over the years took it upon themselves to supply what the biblical text left open-ended. They identified thirty-nine different expressions of what they called work prohibited on the Sabbath day.

As time passed, the various schools of Jewish rabbis added regulation after regulation, law upon law to the original commandment, going far beyond the requirement of Scripture and making the Sabbath and its observance a horrible burden to the people of Israel. God had meant for the Sabbath to be a day of rest. It was the day on which God wanted his people to be relieved from their burdens and to celebrate his goodness and provision for them. But the religious leaders of Israel had turned it into a day of incredible stress, anguish, and one heavy burden after another. In the years following the life of Jesus, literally hundreds of man-made restrictions were added to the original command. So many extra rules and regulations were heaped upon the original commandment that *it actually became harder to rest on the Sabbath than on the other six days of the week!*

Sabbath regulations increased exponentially. One law specified that a Jew could not carry a load heavier than a dried fig; but if an object weighed half that amount, you could carry it twice! If the Sabbath began as you were reaching for some food, the food had to be dropped before you drew your arm back, lest you be guilty of *carrying a burden!* Nothing could be bought or sold, and clothing could not be washed. Baths could not be taken for fear that water might spill onto the floor and "wash" it, something forbidden by these rules. A chair couldn't be moved, lest by dragging it you make a furrow in the ground. A woman could not look in a mirror, lest she see a grey hair and be tempted to pluck it out!

Though not as bad during Jesus's time on earth as later on, Sabbath regulations imposed a heavy religious burden on the Jewish people that God never intended. This, then, is the backdrop when Jesus and his disciples engaged in a gentle stroll through the grain fields one Sabbath day. Picking the heads of grain and eating was not itself a violation of the law (Deut. 23:25). But the Pharisees argued that it constituted "reaping," one of the thirty-nine types of so-called work they determined to be in violation of Jewish tradition.

We see almost the same scenario played out in Mark 3:1–6. Once again it was the Sabbath day and Jesus dared to heal a man with a withered hand. And once again the Pharisees were up in arms that Jesus broke their cherished traditions. We'll come back in a moment to how Jesus responded to their accusations. But notice for now the spirit of legalism that energized these men.

One unmistakable sign of a legalistic spirit is the tendency always to be looking for what's *wrong* in other people's lives in order to *judge* them, instead of looking for what's *right* in order to *encourage* them. None of us does everything right. We all fall short in many ways. It may be how we respond to the poor or our style of worship or the way we preach or how we try to share Christ with non-Christians. But we never do it perfectly.

By way of illustration, suppose an especially godly believer is doing things well 95 percent of the time. If you are a religious legalist, you will look right past the 95 percent that she does well and hone in on the 5 percent that she does poorly. Since legalists love picking away at how others fall short, you will highlight how she fails to live up to your expectations of perfection. Her 5 percent failure rate undermines the 95 percent she does well. Any good that she does suddenly counts for nothing. You are blinded to the fruit it produces and incapable of understanding her best motives.

Legalists feel good when they can identify another person's errors. It reinforces their feelings of superiority. They actually think themselves more spiritual, more godly, and more favored and loved by God.

There's a flip side to the legalistic spirit. In addition to being quick and dogmatic in identifying the small and rare failures of others, *the legalist never acknowledges his own faults and failures.* To admit and confess to sin or misjudgment is to run the risk of losing power, losing face, or losing prestige.

What drives this spirit? It is the belief that one's own efforts and achievements merit acceptance with God and approval from men. Instead of resting in Christ's achievements, confident of what he has done for us, legalists redouble their own works and take pride in what they do in view of what others don't.

Look again at Mark 2:24: "And the Pharisees were saying to him, '*Look*, why are they doing what is not lawful on the Sabbath?'" Or again, Mark 3:2: "they *watched* him closely" (NIV). That's the legalists' spirit: always on the lookout for someone else's sin; always scanning the horizon for someone's failure to measure up to their rules, rules that aren't in the Bible; always spying on the behavior and beliefs of the other person to root out the slightest deviation from their traditions. They nitpick and judge, nitpick and judge, nitpick and judge!

"Ah! You actually drink alcohol! You attend movies! You mow your lawn on Sunday! You don't wear a coat and tie to church on Sunday! I've got my eye on you. I noticed that you read a different version of the Bible rather than the one we approve! You don't believe everything I do? Oh, my! You have a tattoo! I also noticed that you don't always close your eyes when you pray! You tithe out of your net income rather than your gross. Ah! God'll get you for that! And you call yourself a Christian!" Such is the energy that drives the spirit of legalism and man-made religion.

3. *Do you tend to look down your spiritual nose at those who don't follow God's will for your life?* I remember hearing Chuck

Swindoll tell the story of a missionary family that served in a place where peanut butter was hard to obtain. This family arranged for friends in the United States to send them peanut butter so they could enjoy it with their meals. They soon discovered that other missionaries in the same country considered it a mark of spirituality to abstain from peanut butter. It was their "cross to bear"! This family didn't flaunt their enjoyment of peanut butter, but they did continue to thank God for it and enjoyed it in the privacy of their own home. But the pressure and condemnation from their fellow missionaries intensified to such a degree that the family eventually returned home, disillusioned and cynical.

Someone might argue that the couple should have yielded and agreed not to eat peanut butter out of deference to the beliefs of their associates and for the sake of the gospel in that country. Perhaps. But to do so would also serve only to reinforce what was likely a larger pattern of error in the minds of the legalists. You are not doing anyone a favor by behaving in a way that encourages or emboldens such legalistic views.

Part of being a Christian is the freedom not to eat peanut butter. But it is not part of being a Christian that you condemn others if they do. *You are free to exercise your freedom, but you are not free to insist that others not exercise theirs!*

4. *Are you uncomfortable that the Bible does not explicitly address every ethical decision or answer every theological question?* Legalists tend to fear ambiguity. Their favorite colors are black and white. They are uncomfortable with biblical silence and insist on speaking when the Word of God does not. They feel something of a calling to fill in the gaps left by scriptural silence or to make specific and often detailed applications that God, in the Bible, chose not to make.

5. *Are you more comfortable with rules than with relationships?* I'm not talking about explicit biblical rules. In Psalm 119 we see the proper Christian response to biblical laws and commandments and precepts and rules. We are to rejoice in and celebrate the laws of God and to obey them joyfully. But do your interactions with people center on rules of your own making, rules you feel are the

only legitimate applications of what the Bible does say? God-given rules are good and righteous, but they are designed to enhance and develop Christian relationships, not stifle, crush, and kill them.

Why Would Anyone Want to Be a Legalist?

What is the appeal of legalism? Let me mention five things that draw people to embrace legalism.

First, legalism provides us with a sense of security in that it enables us always to know precisely what to do in every conceivable moral dilemma. There is a sort of psychological safety in being stiff morally.

Second, legalism nurtures pride. "Look at what I'm willing to forgo! Others may indulge themselves, but I have discipline and a moral standard they lack. I possess a willpower that really loves God. Therefore, God really loves me" (with the implication that God doesn't really love those who choose another path, or at least doesn't love them as much as he loves me!).

Third, it provides an excuse to maintain control. One need never fear the unknown because there is always a rule or law (of my own making, of course) to govern every situation. After all, without rules things will get out control (or so legalists think).

Fourth, there is comfort in conformity. It is always reassuring when other people live as we do, even if there is no explicit biblical warrant for it.

Fifth, some embrace legalism out of a genuine, heartfelt concern for other believers. They are actually motivated by love and compassion, worried that the spiritual welfare of others is at risk. They fear that others will assuredly fall if they walk down a certain path, even though that path is nowhere prescribed in Scripture (see esp. Rom. 14:4).

Concluding Words on Christian Freedom

Inasmuch as the antidote to legalism is Christian freedom, let me conclude with three brief comments about genuine Christian freedom.

First, the Christian is not free to do what the Bible forbids. Christian freedom does not entail the right to fornicate or to steal or to lie or to persist in an unforgiving attitude or to do anything else that Scripture explicitly prohibits. And a person who lovingly points this out to you is not a legalist for having done so!

Second, God does not want your Christian life to be characterized or dominated by fear and guilt and intimidation. He wants you to experience optimum joy, freedom, intimacy, and delight in him. He wants you to enjoy your freedom and to use it in the service of love for others. This leads directly to the final comment.

Third, there is something more important than the mere exercise of freedom, namely, *love*. Read Galatians 5:13 again and Paul's exhortation: "through love serve one another." No one's freedom is more important than the spiritual welfare of a weaker and less knowledgeable brother or sister. By all means celebrate your freedom, but do not become enslaved to it!

Recommended Reading

Bolton, Samuel. *The True Bounds of Christian Freedom*. Carlisle, PA: Banner of Truth, 1978.

Mahaney, C. J., ed. *Worldliness: Resisting the Seduction of a Fallen World*. Wheaton, IL: Crossway, 2008.

Swindoll, Charles. *The Grace Awakening*. Nashville: Nelson, 2010.

25

Are Christians
Obligated to Tithe?

I should let you in on the fact that I was raised a Southern Baptist and that in my church experience while I grew up, tithing was viewed as an essential element in Christian living.[1] Not that giving 10 percent of one's income was regarded as necessary for salvation. But no one questioned the basics of tithing, nor was it ever debated in the open whether all Christians were biblically obligated to give in this way. It was simply assumed, and I never questioned the practice until years after I left Southern Baptist life. But before we go any further, let's be sure we know what the debate is and what it is not.

The question before us is not whether Christians are responsible to be generous with their wealth in giving back a portion of it to support the work of the ministry. Second Corinthians 8–9 and other texts make it quite clear that we are. The question, rather, is whether *new covenant* Christians are biblically and morally ob-

---

[1] Most of this chapter has been adapted from my book *A Sincere and Pure Devotion to Christ: 100 Daily Meditations on 2 Corinthians*, 2 vols. (Wheaton, IL: Crossway, 2010), 2:33–38, and is used here with permission of Crossway. I also highly recommend the chapter by David A. Croteau, "The Post-Tithing View," in *Perspectives on Tithing: 4 Views*, ed. David A. Croteau (Nashville: B&H Academic, 2011), 57–83.

ligated to give according to *old covenant* laws. The question is not whether Christians are *free* to tithe of their income. Certainly, they are. The question is whether Christians are *obligated* to tithe of their income. Does the Bible legislate to believers under the new covenant a specific percentage of their income that they are to give?

The Secular, Extrabiblical Tithe

In ancient times tithing was not restricted to religious people, such as the nation Israel. Giving a portion of one's income either to a pagan deity or to the governing authority was a widespread custom. One need only read Genesis 47:24, where the Egyptians were required to pay 20 percent of their harvest to Pharaoh. Other extrabiblical documents indicate that tithing was commonly practiced throughout the ancient world among such people as the Syrians, Lydians, and Babylonians.[2]

Was tithing a mandatory or even common practice among God's people prior to the giving of the Mosaic law? There are two examples of pre-Mosaic tithing.

We read in Genesis 14:18–20 that *Abraham* gave "a tenth of everything" to Melchizedek. Personally, I am reluctant to appeal to the example of Abraham to justify contemporary tithing, for the following reasons.

First, we don't know whether Abraham tithed because of some divine mandate that was binding on all God's people at that time or because he was following a common ancient Near Eastern custom. Nothing in the Old Testament indicates that Abraham ever received divine or revelatory instructions concerning tithing. There is no command associated with this incident or any other evidence indicating that what Abraham did on this one occasion is binding for all believers in every age.

Furthermore, observe that Abraham tithed out of the spoils or booty of *war* (see the preceding context in Gen. 14:13–16; cf. also Heb. 7:4). Nothing is said about his tithing from his yearly income. We should also note that *he didn't tithe to God but to a*

---

[2] See the discussion of this in the article "Tithe," in *The Zondervan Pictorial Encyclopedia of the Bible*, ed. Merrill C. Tenney, 5 vols. (Grand Rapids: Zondervan, 1976), 5:756.

man, Melchizedek. And as far as I can tell, there's no evidence that Abraham ever tithed to anyone again. He may have, but we have no record of such activity and thus no way of knowing if this was a singular event or one example of a common practice.

Finally, the only other reference to this incident is in Hebrews 7. There the author is determined to prove the superiority of the new covenant priesthood of Jesus Christ to the old covenant priesthood. He does this by proving the superiority of Melchizedek to Abraham. Remember, it was Abraham who paid a tithe to Melchizedek, not the other way around. It was Melchizedek who blessed Abraham, not the other way around. And as Hebrews 7:7 states, "the inferior [or "lesser"] is blessed by the superior [or "greater"]."

Our author then says that, in a certain sense, Levi also paid a tithe to Melchizedek because he was in the loins of his great-grandfather Abraham when the incident recorded in Genesis 14 occurred. The point he is making, notes F. F. Bruce, is this: "Abraham was a great man . . . but in the account of his interview with Melchizedek, it is Melchizedek who appears as the greater of the two. And if Melchizedek was greater than Abraham, his priesthood must be greater than a priesthood which traces its descent from Abraham."[3] Therefore, Jesus, who is our High Priest "after the order of Melchizedek" (Heb. 6:20), is greater than any and all priests of the order of Aaron and Levi. It is exegetically tenuous, then, to appeal to this text in defense of contemporary tithing.

The other example of pre-Mosaic tithing is found in Genesis 28:22, where it is said that Jacob promised to give a tenth of all he had to God. Is this a solid biblical reason why we should do the same?

First, note well that this is a *vow* made upon the *condition* that God would bless Jacob. This isn't the case of someone saying, "Tithe to God and God will bless you," but rather, "God, you first bless me and then I will tithe to you."

Second, do we have good reason to believe that Jacob's act is *normative* for all believers in every age? I might be willing to grant that we should follow Jacob's example if the rest of Scripture were

---

[3] F. F. Bruce, *The Epistle to the Hebrews* (Grand Rapids: Eerdmans, 1973), 139–40.

silent on the subject of financial stewardship. In other words, if all we had on the subject of giving were the story of Jacob, perhaps then it would be wisdom to pattern our giving after his. But the New Testament is anything but silent on this subject, as our study of 2 Corinthians 8–9 below will reveal.

Tithing in the Mosaic Covenant

A brief word is in order about how tithing was practiced under the Mosaic or old covenant. Some believe the Israelites paid nearly 22 percent of their income to the Lord every year!

According to Leviticus 27:30–33, 10 percent of all grain, cattle, fruit, and so forth was to be set aside as a tithe to the Lord. This tithe, in turn, was to be given to the Levites for the work they did while serving at the tent of meeting. The Levites constituted the tribe of Israel from which the priests were taken. We read in Numbers 18:20–32 that they received this tithe because they were not given an inheritance in the land.

Thus, it would appear that the first 10 percent of the Israelites' income was to be given to the Levites, who in turned tithed from that 10 percent, giving the resulting 1 percent to the high priest (Num. 18:26–29). Clearly, the Levites, or those who ministered in the tabernacle and temple, were supposed to live off the tithes of the other eleven tribes.

In 1 Corinthians 9:13, Paul reminds the church that in the Old Testament economy the Levites who worked in the temple lived off the tithes brought there: "Do you not know that those who are employed in the temple service get their food from the temple, and those who serve at the altar share in the sacrificial offerings?" He then says in verse 14, "In the same way, the Lord commanded that those who proclaim the gospel should get their living by the gospel."

Paul's argument is that those who spend their lives ministering the Word of God should be supported by other Christians. To make his point, he draws attention to the way it was done in the Old Testament. At minimum, Paul is saying that other believers are to financially support those in so-called full-time ministry. Whether he is saying that they should do it by giving precisely 10 percent is less certain.

On the basis of Deuteronomy 14:22–27, some argue that a second tithe (or 10 percent of the remaining 90 percent, hence 9 percent) was to be taken once a year to Jerusalem and there consumed by a man and his family in a sacred feast or meal. If a person lived too far away to transport his tithe to Jerusalem, he was permitted to exchange his goods for silver. When he arrived in Jerusalem, he was to convert his cash back into cattle, sheep, wine, and so forth (vv. 24–26). If this is the correct interpretation, we now have Israelites paying 19 percent of their income in tithes. But there is more to come.

According to verses 28–29, what was perhaps an additional tithe of 10 percent was to be paid every third year. This tithe was to be given to the Levites, the aliens, the fatherless, and the widows. In other words, every third year the Israelite was to take an additional 10 percent from the remaining 81 percent. If my math is correct, this means that every year the Israelite was required to pay approximately 21.7 percent of his income in tithes to the Lord!

Others have objected to this interpretation, arguing that these passages in the Old Testament all refer to the same tithe. It is only one tithe, 10 percent, to be used in different ways. In other words, 10 percent of one's yearly produce or income (Leviticus 27) was to be taken to Jerusalem and consumed there (Deut. 14:22–27). Whatever was left over was to be given to the Levites (Num. 18:20–32). Every third year, however, the entire 10 percent was to be given to the Levites, the aliens, and the orphans and widows. On this interpretation, the Israelite was required to pay only 10 percent a year.

Regardless of which view one takes, the important point to note is that the Israelite was *required* to *pay* his tithe. It was tantamount to a national income tax. That is why Malachi 3:6–12 speaks of those who did not pay their tithes as "robbing" God. In Israel, under the Mosaic covenant, there was no such thing as separation of church and state. One's tithe was a religious tax designed to sustain the theocratic state of God's chosen people.

The New Testament twice (Matt. 23:23 [Luke 11:42]; Luke 18:12) refers to people tithing *who were still living under and therefore morally obligated to obey the dictates of the old, Mosaic covenant.* But these people were required to pay their tithes for the same reason they were required to bring a lamb for sacrifice, and required to observe the civil code of Leviticus, and required not to touch a dead body, and required to obey all the legislation instituted by God in the covenant with Israel. On what grounds, then, do we say that the Old Testament law concerning tithing is still binding on the conscience of new covenant believers, but its laws concerning other matters are not?

Is it *permissible* for a new covenant Christian to tithe, that is, to give 10 percent of his or her income to the work of the church? Not only is it permissible, but I would strongly recommend and urge you to do so. In choosing to give 10 percent of our income to the Lord, we are honoring a God-given, Old Testament principle. In the absence of a prescribed percentage for giving in the New Testament, why not adopt the Old Testament pattern?

However, this does not mean you are sinning if you don't. To give only 8 percent or to give 15 percent is equally permissible. Not to give at all, or to give disproportionately to your income (which is the case with most Christians today), or to give grudgingly is indeed sin. Let us be joyful and generous in our giving. After all, everything we own belongs to God anyway!

New Testament Teaching on Financial Stewardship

Just as the New Testament knows nothing of an unbaptized Christian or a churchless Christian, so also the New Testament knows nothing of a Christian who does not give faithfully and generously to the work of God. Faithful, generous stewardship of one's financial resources to support the life and ministry of the local church is as much a mark of a true Christian as is love for one's neighbor and sharing the gospel with an unbeliever. Giving in support of the local church isn't optional. It is no more optional for the Christian than sexual purity or telling the truth or sharing your faith. Can you imagine a professing Christian saying, "Well, I love and follow

Jesus but I've decided that sexual purity and faithfulness to my spouse just isn't for me"? Or "I've decided that lying and stealing are the best way to get along in the world"? It is no less a contradiction of our Christian faith to say: "I'm not going to utilize my resources to support the work of the local church. That's just not who I am or where I think God is leading me."

God should always receive the firstfruits of our labor, not the leftovers. My wife and I have made a commitment to this in that the first thing we do is set aside our giving to the local church, and only then do we pay our bills or purchase something we want. I fear most professing Christians spend and save and use their money for any number of purposes and then, if there is anything left over, they give to God.

It almost seems that people in ministry today either rarely talk about money or rarely talk about anything else! The former are afraid of sounding greedy and manipulative, while the latter consider wealth a spiritual birthright of all Christians. For the one, money is an enemy; for the other, an entitlement.

The apostle Paul would take issue with both groups. He is unashamed to issue what amounts to a passionate and persistent appeal to the Corinthians that they contribute generously to the impoverished church in Jerusalem. In doing so, he provides us with profound insight into the nature of God's grace, the principles that should govern our giving, and the joy that is found in the convergence of the two in the life of the church.

Space does not permit an extensive examination of 2 Corinthians 8–9, so I have decided to summarize Paul's instruction in a series of eight principles.

1. Giving that magnifies the glory of God is always the fruit of the grace of God (2 Cor. 8:1–5).

From a strictly human point of view, the odds were stacked against the Macedonians from the start. Common sense would tell us that such folk were hardly the sort who could be expected to alleviate anyone's suffering. Their own "severe test of affliction" and "extreme poverty" (v. 2) would appear to excuse them from participation in any fund-raising venture, except perhaps one that would serve to improve their own pitiful condition.

This grace had been "given" or bestowed or poured out on the churches of Macedonia, and ultimately that alone accounts for their remarkable generosity toward their brethren in Jerusalem. Yes, Paul appeals to what believers in Macedonia had done. But he is quick to acknowledge that their serving their brethren was the fruit of what God had done in serving them! If the Macedonians "gave themselves first to the Lord" in this ministry (v. 5), it was because *God* had first "given" his grace (v. 1) to them. Whatever achievement on their part is praised, whatever example they may have set for others to follow, it is ultimately attributed to the antecedent activity of divine grace (this is the principle Paul articulates in Phil. 2:12–13).

I need to say something about the use of the word *charis,* "grace," throughout this section of 2 Corinthians. It is used in 8:1, 4, 6, 7, 9, 16, 19 and 9:8, 14, 15 with a wide range of meaning, from divine enablement to human privilege to a monetary gift to a word of gratitude to divine favor. This should remind us that grace is more than an attitude or disposition in the divine nature. It is surely that, but if thought of *only* as an abstract and static principle, it is deprived of its deeper implications.

Grace, however, is not only the divine act by which God initiates our spiritual life, but also the very power that sustains, nourishes, and moves us through that life. The energizing and sanctifying work of the indwelling Spirit *is* the grace of God. Therefore, grace is not something in which we merely believe; it is something we experience as well. Grace is a dynamic and experiential reality that empowers the human heart to look beyond its limitations and accomplish things that defy rational explanation. Grace is the power that enables impoverished and suffering saints to give when, by all accounts, they should be the ones to get. Such was the operation of grace in the giving of these Macedonian believers. And such ought to be its operation in us as well.

I once heard John Piper sum up the spiritual dynamics of this text by saying that *grace comes down, joy rises up, and generosity flows out.* The sequence is crucial. Grace must initiate all giving that glorifies God; otherwise we would take pride and praise for our support of others. This grace alone accounts for genuine joy; otherwise joy is misplaced and degenerates when circumstances turn bad. Finally, grace-given joy is always other-oriented. Having germinated in the soil of grace, it blooms in generous bounty to those in need. Such is the nature of true love.

2. Giving that magnifies the glory of God often flourishes in the midst of poverty and affliction (2 Cor. 8:1–5).

I know it sounds ridiculous to say that giving flourishes in poverty, but how else do we make sense of verses 1–5? I confess that when I read those verses, I shake my head, less with disbelief and more with disgust at my own selfish and shortsighted perspective on life here and hereafter. Please don't console me with the assurance that I'm being excessively hard on my own soul. I *need* Scripture to do this to me, for in being rebuked and reproved by what I see in the example of the Macedonians, I'm awakened to the unending pleasure and effusive joy that are available through God's grace as I am taught and trained to rest in the all-sufficiency of who he is for me in Christ Jesus. I've never known poverty, and my exposure to affliction, at least when compared to what the majority of Christians in the world have endured, has been minimal. Yet, the way I respond to financial stress and other such trials is embarrassing—especially in the way it affects my relationship toward others.

I confess to having used affliction and hardship as an excuse *not* to give to those in need. Suffering seems like the perfect reason why people should be generous to me, but hardly an occasion for me to be generous to them. Financial stress, in particular, all too often breeds self-pity. It turns our attention inward to self and an obsessive concern for our own welfare. And it doesn't stop there, but typically leads to envy of those whose troubles are significantly less than ours and bitterness toward God for not alleviating our pain.

The sort of troubles that plagued the Macedonians can also produce in us a sense of *entitlement* as we wonder why others are not taking notice of our plight and offering us what we are persuaded is our *right* as the children of God.

Are you beginning to see why this passage has the effect on me that it does? Paul describes their "severe test of affliction" and "extreme poverty" and yet points us to their "wealth of generosity" toward the saints in Jerusalem. The very people who, at least to my way of self-indulgent and sinful thinking, ought themselves to have been the *recipients* of generosity are here described as the *donors*! When I'm in need, I presumptuously expect others to jump to my aid. But the Macedonians were different. That's what makes Paul's citing of them so profoundly painful, yet powerful in challenging how I think and life-changing in what I value most.

Something had happened in the hearts of these people that runs counter to all common sense and cross-grain to every fleshly impulse of self-preservation. It is as if the fast-flowing current in their souls had not simply been diverted but *reversed*. Something suprahuman had inverted their values, turning their thinking on its head and their behavior topsy-turvy. There's no escaping the fact that their joy in God undercut and severed their joy in money. God wants us to know that the same grace given in Macedonia and available in Corinth is still operative and available to *us* today.

Okay, so the grace of God awakened and sustained a *joy* in them that liberated their hearts from selfish dependence on what they had formerly believed only money and physical comfort could achieve. But joy in what? In whom? Perhaps God had struck a secret deal with the Macedonians, making a behind-the-scenes promise that if they would provide other Christians with this stunning example of generosity, he would deliver them from their affliction and bless them with riches untold. Only the most cynical or uninformed would offer such a ridiculous and unbiblical theory. The whole point of the passage is not that financial blessing had resulted in their joy but that their joy in something other than money had issued in a financial blessing—for others!

So what accounts for this joy? I can only surmise from the rest of God's Word that grace had drawn them to the well of eternal life to drink of the ever-refreshing, soul-satisfying water that is Jesus Christ. To use the words of the psalmist,

> You have put more joy in my heart
> than they have when their grain and wine abound. (Ps. 4:7)

Money had made its promises to the Macedonians, and it all seemed so reasonable, so right. It had assured them that if they would give their hearts to what it could provide and consider all the discomfort and inconvenience and anxiety from which it could protect them, unbroken happiness would inevitably follow. That's the principle that drives our society and undergirds every commercial advertisement.

But they said *no*. This wasn't because of some inherent virtue in poverty or, worse still, a perverted attraction to pain and distress. It was because grace had opened their eyes to the splendor of Jesus! Grace had imparted a taste for the sweetness of the Son of God! The alluring aroma of money and safety was replaced by the superior fragrance of knowing Christ Jesus as Lord! Grace made known the incomparable beauty of seeing God in Christ, and the grip of greed was broken.

But wait. How can poor people be generous? Is Paul merely playing with words when he speaks of a "wealth of generosity" flowing out from the Macedonians to the poverty-stricken church in Jerusalem? What are we to make of this? Needless to say, if the monetary gift of the Macedonians were measured strictly in quantitative terms, it would fall far short of what other churches, including the one in Corinth, might provide. A hundred dollars will always be *more*, mathematically speaking, than ten dollars, and Paul is not so dull as to deny this obvious truth. What made the Macedonian gift so generous, such that it could rightly be called "wealth," was that it came from people who themselves were in the very depths of poverty. When measured *proportionately*—that is to say, in the light of how much was available to them—it far exceeded what anyone might have expected.

A further word of explanation is in order here, for Paul's language is nothing short of outrageously provocative. The word translated "poverty" in 2 Corinthians 8:2 is *ptōcheia* and of itself signifies extreme destitution. Yet Paul doesn't stop there, but adds the stunning qualification *kata bathos*, which means "down to the depth" and therefore "ever-deeper poverty" or "rock-bottom poverty."[4] The "severe test of affliction," most likely a reference to persecution, had undoubtedly contributed greatly to their extreme financial plight. This oppressive suffering, far from crushing their hearts or creating despair or cultivating bitterness, became the occasion for not simply "joy" but "abundance" of joy. When they chose to participate in this ministry of mercy, it was no grudging concession to a moral obligation but a spontaneous eruption of delight. When Paul says that "they gave according to their means, as I can testify, and beyond their means" (v. 3), he is telling us that they looked at their ability to give, took into consideration both their present situation and their future needs and obligations, and then showed total disregard for both!

This is not because they were foolish. Undoubtedly they knew the consequences for themselves and willingly embraced them. In all likelihood, they first determined what they could reasonably give and then went above and beyond that amount. They were able to take this approach because *grace* was operative in their hearts. Whatever financial lack their giving might have induced would be more than compensated by an abundance of grace and spiritual joy. And if you are tempted to dismiss this as so much religious hyperbole that ignores the harsh realities of physical deprivation, I can only say that you have not yet seen the eternal beauty or tasted of the sweetness of the Savior as the Macedonians obviously had.

And again, attributing this marvelous act of beneficence to divine grace in no way diminishes the moral value of what was done, for Paul insists that they gave not because they felt compelled or coerced but "of their own accord" (v. 3), that is to say, voluntarily and without any coercion from Paul or the people in Jerusalem. They didn't contribute out of *greed*, as do so many in our own day, having been assured by some unscrupulous evangelist that giving

---

[4]C. K. Barrett, *A Commentary on the Second Epistle to the Corinthians* (New York: Harper & Row, 1973), 216.

guarantees a multiplied return. It wasn't a *guilty conscience* that drove them, as if great monetary sacrifice might somehow make up for sins previously committed. And it certainly wasn't because Paul *intimidated* them or employed manipulative tactics of pressure and fear. In fact, to make this point with crystal clarity, Paul tells us that he refused to ask them for money for the collection, knowing full well their financial condition. He would never have dreamed of taking up an offering.

Permit me to speculate, but I can imagine Paul on the verge of closing the meeting with prayer, and loud shouts of urgent and insistent protest coming from these Christians: "No, Paul, you can't stop now. You have to pass the plate! Please, we beg you; don't deprive us of the inestimable favor and joy of giving to our hurting brethren." "Paul, how dare you not take up an offering and give us the unparalleled privilege of demonstrating the sufficiency of God's grace and his provision!" Amazing! Most people beg to get money; the Macedonians begged to give money! Grace giving, indeed!

3. Giving that magnifies the glory of God is always rooted in the gospel of God (2 Cor. 8:9).

"Greed is good," declared corporate executive Gordon Gekko (played by Michael Douglas) in the movie *Wall Street.* "Greed works." It was a shock when I first heard those chilling words spoken with such forthright and unashamed simplicity. To this day it's hard to shake free of them. Hollywood is well known for its determination to mock, deny, or otherwise undermine Christian values, and these stunning words are a vivid case in point.

So how does one deal with greed? What is the most effective counterattack to this insidious force? The truth of verse 9 is the key. There Paul directs our attention to the one truth that has the power to liberate our hearts from the grip of greed and release in us the joy of generous giving: "For you know the grace of our Lord Jesus Christ, that though he was rich, yet for your sake he became poor, so that you by his poverty might become rich" (v. 9). Three questions need to be answered.

First, in what sense was Christ "rich"? The first thing that comes to mind is the incalculable wealth of his eternal glory. The sacrifice of the Son will have its sanctifying effect on us only to the extent that we are in touch with the immeasurable splendor and limitless majesty of his preexistent glory in fellowship with God the Father and the Holy Spirit (see Isa. 6:1–4). This is but one portrait of what Jesus had in mind when he spoke to his Father of "the glory that I had with you before the world existed" (John 17:5). Paul described it as being "in the form of God" and experiencing eternal "equality with God" (Phil. 2:6). But it was more than splendor, more than radiant beauty, more than the unending adoration of angelic hosts. It was joy! The "riches" of Christ that he so lovingly forsook entailed the mutual and immeasurable delight of the Father in the Son and the Son in the Father and the Spirit in the Father and the Father in the Spirit and the Son in the Spirit and the Spirit in the Son. Each beholding the beauty of the other. Each exulting in the excellence of the other. Their eternal and energetic love for one another is beyond our capacity to grasp.

So, second, in what sense did Christ become "poor"? Perhaps we should again let Isaiah make the point. Hear him prophesy of the humiliation of holiness:

> He had no form or majesty that we should look at him,
>   and no beauty that we should desire him.
> He was despised and rejected by men;
>   a man of sorrows, and acquainted with grief;
> and as one from whom men hide their faces
>   he was despised, and we esteemed him not. (Isa. 53:2–3)

"Surely there's been a mistake," you may be wondering. Is Paul suggesting that the one on whom the seraphim dared not look (Isa. 6:2), whose glory filled the earth (6:3), is also the one who "has borne our griefs / and carried our sorrows," a man "stricken, / smitten by God, and afflicted" (53:4)? Is Paul suggesting that the one who sat enthroned in power and glory (6:1–2) was somehow "pierced for our transgressions" and "crushed for our iniquities" (53:5)? How can it be that "the King, the LORD of hosts" (6:5) "was oppressed" and "afflicted" like "a lamb that is led to the slaughter / and like a sheep that before its shearers is silent" (53:7)?

"Rich"? This is our third question: In what sense have we become wealthy through his poverty? Here we must refuse to tolerate the spiritually sick and perverted claims of the prosperity "gospel" that would find here a reference to material gain. Our riches and wealth are the sort that cannot be earned by effort or secured at a sale. They are the gift of sovereign grace. Where does one begin to enumerate them? Election before the foundation of the world? Yes! Forgiveness of sins? Yes! Adoption into the family of God? Yes! Justification by faith alone? Yes! Union with Christ? Yes! The permanent indwelling presence of the Holy Spirit? Yes! Did not Paul assure the Ephesians that God has "blessed us in Christ with every spiritual blessing in the heavenly places" (Eph. 1:3)? Yes! And above all else, the richest and most precious blessing of all is God himself! He is our inestimable treasure. Beholding his beauty is our inheritance. Enjoying his excellency is our wealth.

But to what end does Paul speak in this way? For what purpose? To stir up lethargic and presumptuous souls to give with exceeding generosity! Greed is *not* good. Greed does *not* work. It cripples and paralyzes and anesthetizes our souls to the needs of others. Worse yet, it ignores the magnanimous mercy and grace of Christ and the sacrifice he made so that we, through his poverty, might become truly rich.

4. Giving that magnifies the glory of God is not percentage giving but proportionate giving (2 Cor. 8:12).

Paul reminds the Corinthians that all giving is to be *proportionate* to wealth. He says, in verse 12, that "if the readiness is there, it is acceptable according to what a person has, not according to what he does not have" (cf. also v. 11, where giving is "out of what you have"). God does not ask us to give beyond our means, but it is certainly permissible if we do (as in the case of the Macedonians; see v. 3). The apostle wrote much the same thing in 1 Corinthians 16:2, saying that each "is to put something aside and store it up, *as he may prosper*." Paul's words in 2 Corinthians 8:12 indicate that he is *not* suggesting that the Corinthians (or anyone else, for that matter) borrow money in order to give. He assumes that they have "disposable income" from which they might draw to provide the needed help. At minimum, we should be extremely cautious about going into debt to make financial contributions.

5. Giving that glorifies God must be voluntary, not coerced or forced (2 Cor. 9:1–5).

As for the Corinthians and their earlier commitment to join in this endeavor to alleviate the poverty of the church in Jerusalem, Paul's initial excitement has been somewhat tempered. Titus has come from Corinth with the discouraging report that the collection was put on hold. Paul's point in verses 3–5 is that his previous boasting about them could now be a cause of some embarrassment to both him and them.

Whereas some think that verse 5 is describing two attitudes toward giving, either generosity or stinginess, I'm inclined to see here two ways that Paul envisioned securing their participation in the offering: either voluntarily or by pressure. On the one hand, Paul does not want them to give simply because he's an apostle and they are bowing to his authority (although there's nothing inherently wrong with that). Giving motivated by fear of him or guilt over sins or pride and a competitive drive to exceed the Macedonians would not constitute the kind of giving that he later says results in God's bountiful supply. "I want it to spring spontaneously and joyfully from your heart," Paul says in effect. "I want it to be primarily your idea, not mine. You've already shown a willingness in this regard that even stirred the Macedonians. So now bring it to fruition. Don't humiliate yourselves by a failure to follow through on your promise, and don't put me in the position of having to exercise an authority to exact from you a grudging and unwilling gift."

6. Giving that glorifies God must be bountiful, so as to ensure a bountiful return (2 Cor. 9:6).

Here's what you must keep in mind, says Paul: "whoever sows sparingly will also reap sparingly, and whoever sows bountifully will also reap bountifully" (v. 6). But doesn't this play directly into the hands of the proponents of prosperity? There it is: give a lot so you can get a lot. Well, not exactly. Yes, on the one hand, bountiful giving does result in bountiful getting. But bountiful getting, as he will make clear in the verses that follow, isn't for hoarding or padding one's retirement account or moving up in scale from a Buick to a Bentley. It's for more, greater, effusive, bountiful giving. But I'm getting ahead of myself.

Let's be sure we understand Paul's point in verse 6. In farming, what may initially appear to be a loss (sowing) is in fact a gain (reaping). As one sows, so one reaps. But what determines whether a gift is "sparing" or "bountiful"? We have already seen from the example of the Macedonians in 2 Corinthians 8:1–2 that it is not the quantity of the gift considered in the abstract. A gift may be comparatively small and yet spiritually large. Rather, whether a gift is sparing or bountiful depends on two factors: First, one must take account of the *means* of the giver. Giving that is bountiful is in *proportion* to one's wealth (cf. 8:3, 11–12; 1 Cor. 16:2). I've already discussed this and need say no more. Second, and perhaps even more important, bountiful giving is determined by the *mind* of the giver. This means that it is possible to give much but to sow sparingly. So what kind of mind or heart or spirit or attitude does Paul have in view, the sort that turns even a quantitatively small gift into a bountiful and generous sowing of seed? The answer comes, at least in part, in 2 Corinthians 9:7 and leads to our next principle.

7. Giving that glorifies God must be glad-hearted and free (2 Cor. 9:7).

What thoughts fill your mind as you sign a check made payable to your local congregation? Do you give *grudgingly* ("I'm getting tired of them asking me for money; they must think I'm a millionaire"), from *guilt* ("The last time I said no and used the money on a new car"), or *gladly* ("Praise God for this opportunity to participate in the spread of the gospel")?

When you hear of massive needs in Haiti, for example, is your heart paralyzed with fear that excessive giving might cast you into the throes of poverty? Can you think only of that new computer that will be out of your financial reach or that family vacation that will have to be postponed?

These are uncomfortable but unavoidable questions. There's no escaping the fact that when it comes to money, motivation matters. Paul's statement in 2 Corinthians 9:7 may well be the most famous of all biblical texts on the subject of giving and Christian steward-ship. If so, it is certainly deserving of this honor. "Each one must give as he has decided in his heart," writes the apostle, "not reluc-tantly or under compulsion, for God loves a cheerful giver" (v. 7).

But first we must take note of two preliminary points. Observe that giving is a universal responsibility. "Each one," says Paul, which is to say *everyone*, should be energetically engaged in this act of stewardship (see also 1 Cor. 16:2). No one is exempt. Indeed, why would anyone want to be? Second, the phrase "as he has decided in his heart" employs a verb found only here in the New Testament. Its focus is on personal deliberation and freedom of choice. Giving is never to be impulsive or careless or lacking in preparation and planning. *Think about what you are doing.* More importantly, think about *why* you are doing it. Pray about it. Plan it. Pursue it in a calculated and intentional way.

We now come to the three critical elements in all Christian giving, the first two of which are negative in force while the third is more positive.

First, sowing a bountiful seed, the sort that reaps a correspond-ing bountiful harvest, must be devoid of *reluctance*. Some offer the translation "with regret" or "grudgingly" or "out of sorrow." Paul's point is that our giving must never be accompanied by a sense of loss or by the sorrow that comes from thinking about what we otherwise might have done with the money. If your giving is char-acterized by grief over what you might have gotten had you kept the money for yourself, God is not pleased. If your giving is ac-companied by fantasies of the physical and material comforts that might otherwise have been obtained, God is not pleased.

Second, neither is God pleased when we give under the gun, or to use Paul's phrase, "under compulsion." Are we concerned about what the church treasurer will think when he issues our end-of-year giving statement? Do we give to impress pastoral leaders and others in the church with our generosity? Do we give in the same way we pay our income tax, from a sense of legal obligation or even fear of criminal prosecution? Do we give because everyone else does? Paul doesn't want the awkwardness or pressure of the moment to influence the Corinthians' decision. He doesn't want the weight of his apostolic authority to exert undue influence on their choice.

But does the intent of the heart really affect the moral value of the act? The only way to answer that question is by looking at the third characteristic of Christian giving. We must be diligent to avoid monetary regret when we give and we must never contribute under compulsion "for God loves a *cheerful* giver"! The word translated "cheerful" has been the basis for countless sermons and extravagant illustrations. Yes, as you have no doubt heard, it is the Greek word *hilaron*, from which is derived the term *hilarious*. No, you cannot use the meaning of our English word *hilarious* to interpret Paul's statement in 2 Corinthians 9:7. You can't define the Greek *hilaron* in light of an English word derived from it. This would be to commit a fallacy known as *semantic anachronism*, which occurs when a late use of a word is read back into earlier literature. Interpreting the meaning of Paul's first-century Greek word by appealing to the meaning of the twenty-first-century English derivative, as understood by you and me, would be semantic anachronism.[5]

Needless to say, if God *loves* a cheerful giver, he is *displeased* when people give but don't do it gladly, even if their giving is generous in terms of quantity. "When people don't find pleasure (Paul's word is 'cheer'!) in their acts of service, God doesn't find pleasure in them," Piper reminds us.[6] Does that mean if we don't have joy we shouldn't give at all? If I'm grumpy next Sunday or depressed or feeling especially guilty for sins committed, do I have a legitimate

---

[5] Unfortunately, preachers also make this mistake with the Greek word for power, *dynamis*, from which is derived the English term *dynamite*. No, you can't appeal to what *dynamite* means or how it is used in our language to provide insight into what Paul meant.

[6] John Piper, *Desiring God: Meditations of a Christian Hedonist* (Sisters, OR: Multnomah, 1996), 104.

excuse not to give? After all, I don't want to incur God's displeasure! No. Whereas joyless giving is certainly less than ideal, it is better than not giving at all.

"Cheerful" giving is neither frivolous nor foolish and does not require that one laugh hilariously as the plate passes by. The "cheerful" giver is the one whose heart is rapturously filled with the knowledge of the goodness and greatness of God, whose mind is captivated by the beauty of Christ, whose soul is satisfied with all that we have in him, and who, in spite of all adversity and in defiance of every circumstance, rejoices with joy inexpressible and full of glory (1 Pet. 1:8). Such a giver God loves!

8. Giving that glorifies God is giving that
gets in order to give (2 Cor. 9:8–11).

"But Sam, what will become of me if I sow bountifully? Will there be enough for my needs? Will I be able to provide for my family? What about the next offering? Will there be anything left for me to contribute to what may prove to be an even greater cause than the former one? Worse still, what's to prevent my generosity from creating a financial crisis of my own? After all, an unexpected downturn in the market could put me in the position of being the next person who's dependent on the church for survival." Ah, the fears that grip the human heart when it comes to giving. But oh, the grace that triumphs over all!

Paul addressed this fear in verse 6, declaring that "whoever sows sparingly will also reap sparingly, and whoever sows bountifully will also reap bountifully." Most folk believe the opposite: if you want more, give less. But Paul says, if you want more, give more. How can this be? The answer is provided in yet more detail in verses 8–11.

Clearly, God promises to supply abundantly to those who give generously. Paul wants the Corinthians to be free from the fear that generous giving will leave them impoverished. His language is effusive and unmistakable: "God is able to make all grace abound to you." God "will supply and multiply your seed," and "you will be enriched in every way." So, does that mean the prosperity people are right after all? Well, not exactly. One must never claim a promise without noting its purpose. In other words, we must ask, to what end or for what purpose or with what goal in mind does God cause the generous Christian steward to abound? Simply put, why does God promise financial abundance to those who cheerfully and freely give to others?

Paul leaves no room for argument. His words are unequivocal and to the point. So that there might be no confusion or discord, he says it three times over:

> And God is able to make all grace abound to you, so that having all sufficiency in all things at all times, *you may abound in every good work*. (v. 8)[7]

> He who supplies seed to the sower and bread for food will supply and multiply your seed *for sowing* and increase the harvest of your righteousness. (v. 10)

> You will be enriched in every way *to be generous in every way*, which through us will produce thanksgiving to God. (v. 11)

This is breathtaking language, not unlike what Paul wrote to the Philippians: "And my God will supply every need of yours according to his riches in glory in Christ Jesus" (4:19; see also Ps. 84:11; Matt. 6:33). Once again, this is not a guarantee that our circumstances will improve or that we will be insulated against suffering and hardship. Don't forget his earlier description of the Macedonians, who were recipients of this marvelous and effusive grace and yet were not spared from "a severe test of affliction," nor delivered from "extreme poverty" (2 Cor. 8:2).

Rather, *God's promise is that he will never stir your heart to give and then fail to supply you with resources to do so.* But the idea that we should give so that God will enrich us personally with a view to increasing our comfort and convenience and purchasing power is foreign to Paul's teaching. Personal wealth is here viewed

---

[7] Observe how Paul strings together a series of universals to make his point clear: "And God is able to make *all* grace abound to you, so that having *all* sufficiency in *all* things at *all* times, you may abound in *every* good work" (v. 8).

not as an end in itself, but as a means to a yet higher goal: continued generosity to those in need. The principle at work in this divine scenario is that if you give generously now, you will discover that God not only sustains your desire to give but also will greatly increase your resources for yet more joyful and even more glorious giving in the future. The point is that we receive in order to give, not in order to hoard.

Conclusion

I can hardly think of a more unbiblical and damaging perspective on money than that found among many in the so-called Word of Faith or "prosperity gospel" movements, according to which God wills that all be wealthy based on some alleged promise of Scripture that if we will but give more, we will get more. Give, we must. Get, we will. But what we get, by the grace of God, should in turn become the source for even greater and more sacrificial giving. We must see ourselves never as the reservoir of God's beneficence (as if it were ultimately intended for us), but as its conduit (that we might be a blessing to others).

Recommended Reading

Croteau, David A., ed. *Perspectives on Tithing: 4 Views*. Nashville: B&H Academic, 2011.

Schreiner, Thomas R. *40 Questions about Christians and Biblical Law*. Grand Rapids: Kregel, 2010.

General Index

Scripture Index

RE:LIT

Resurgence Literature (Re:Lit) is a ministry of the Resurgence. At theResurgence.com you will find free theological resources in blog, audio, video, and print forms, along with information on forthcoming conferences, to help Christians contend for and contextualize Jesus's gospel. At ReLit.org you will also find the full lineup of Resurgence books for sale. The elders of Mars Hill Church have generously agreed to support Resurgence and the Acts 29 Church Planting Network in an effort to serve the entire church.

FOR MORE RESOURCES

Re:Lit – relit.org
Resurgence – theResurgence.com
Re:Train – retrain.org
Mars Hill Church – marshill.org
Acts 29 – acts29network.org

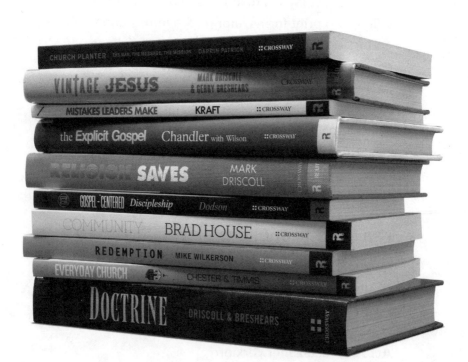